What peopl

High Heels

A fascinating look into life in Britain on the brink of the 'Swinging' Sixties. Well-bred, conventional young ladies still wore gloves and hats, while among them a rare few, more adventurous, rejected the stereotypical careers expected of them and chose a life in the armed forces, with all its considerable challenges.

In this coming-of-age story written from the heart, the author relates her life, loves, heartbreaking loss, and her military career. I found it an engrossing read and valuable social history record that took me back on a wave to nostalgia to a bygone era. **Susie Kelly**, author of *I Wish I Could Say I was Sorry*, and *Safari Ants, Baggy Pants & Elephants*

A moving tale of ambition, love and loss set in post-WWII Britain and featuring Jackie, whose life changes when she joins the Women's Royal Army Corps. The touching story is enhanced by the details of life as a woman in the army, which come from the author's own experience.

Harriet Springbett, author of *Tree Magic*

High Heels
& Beetle Crushers

The Life, Losses and Loves
of an Officer and Lady

High Heels
& Beetle Crushers

The Life, Losses and Loves
of an Officer and Lady

Jackie Skingley

Winchester, UK
Washington, USA

JOHN HUNT PUBLISHING

First published by Chronos Books, 2019
Chronos Books is an imprint of John Hunt Publishing Ltd., No. 3 East St., Alresford,
Hampshire SO24 9EE, UK
office@jhpbooks.com
www.johnhuntpublishing.com
www.chronosbooks.com

For distributor details and how to order please visit the 'Ordering' section on our website.

ISBN: 978 1 78904 290 0
978 1 78904 291 7 (e-book)
Library of Congress Control Number: 2018961971

A CIP catalogue record for this book is available from the British Library.

Design: Stuart Davies

UK: Printed and bound by CPI Group (UK) Ltd, Croydon, CR0 4YY
US: Printed and bound by Thomson-Shore, 7300 West Joy Road, Dexter, MI 48130

We operate a distinctive and ethical publishing philosophy in
all areas of our business, from our global network of authors to
production and worldwide distribution.

Contents

The Women's Royal Army Corps was formed on 1 February 1949 and disbanded on 6 April 1992.
To mark the 70th anniversary, I would like to dedicate this memoir to those who served in the Corps, with special mention to my sisters in arms:
Elaine, Wendy, Lesley and Florian

Acknowledgements

I wish to thank my friends who inspired, supported and urged me write this story:

Carol Hilton	Chief instigator
Melanie More	English teacher extraordinaire
Peta Woolley	Fellow adventuress
Nikki Emmerton	Beta reader and talented cook
Susie Kelly	Author and mentor

The wonderful members of Charente Creative Writers Club:
Kate, Teresa, Sally, Gill, Tina and Mel, who gave me critiques, encouragement and laughter.

Chronos Books for offering the opportunity to publish.

I salute you all.

Author's Note

All of the characters who appear in these pages are real, however, I have changed some of their names where I have thought appropriate or where I have been asked to do so in order to maintain their anonymity. The events are based upon my memories as I recall them and are honestly retold. With the exception of very few people mentioned, I continue to respect and hold dear all those friends and individuals referred to in this memoir

Author at 18 years old.

Follow me down the halls of time
Secret places where memories hide.
They whisper, jostle, march in line,
Senses explode, colours collide.

And did we love in slow time?
And did we dance to ragtime?
And did we speak in real time?
Recaptured memories.

REIGATE, SURREY, JANUARY 1944

That night, as the north wind buffeted our home, enemy planes crossed the English Channel, flying another sortie to London along Bomb Alley. Inside, cold draughts blew under doors and around window frames. To compensate for the drop in temperature, a coal fire burned and spluttered in the living room. My mother and grandmother, Nanny Rose, sat in deep armchairs on either side of the Victorian fireplace, ears straining for familiar and fearful sounds. First came the undulating high-pitched whine of an air raid siren, followed by the drone of approaching enemy aircraft.

'They're early tonight,' remarked Nan, as she carried on knitting a baby's matinee coat.

Thud! Thud! beat out the rhythm of falling missiles on the edge of town. *Fee, Fi, Fo, Fum,* they whistled through the air, shaking the earth on impact like an ogre's footsteps. The explosions came closer, rattling buildings and causing the houses in the street to tremble. I remember Mummy throwing down the *Rupert Bear* annual she'd been reading to me, my favourite bedtime story. I knew all the words and, if she made a mistake, I would tell her no short cuts or Rupert Bear, Bill Badger and Algy Pug wouldn't play their part. I absorbed the coloured cartoon strips while Mummy turned the pages and the world of Nutwood seeped into my memory, a place of magic and adventure. The story abruptly ended, the book flying out of her hands onto the hearthrug, as she hugged me close. Rupert and Bill hadn't even finished their journey to the bottom of the sea.

'Quick, Mum, we must go down to the shelter!' Mummy urged Nan.

I started to cry, cross with Mummy and scared by the

screaming sirens. The frequency pierced my brain and induced a fear I'd learnt from grownups; a fear I didn't understand, the fear of death and dying.

'Come on, darling,' coaxed Mummy, lifting me off her lap. She eased forward, her round tummy heavy with the new baby.

I didn't want to go down into that dark place. I put my hands over my ears and howled. Climbing down the stairs to the Morrison shelter I felt claustrophobic fingers ready to wrap themselves around my throat. One feeble low watt electric bulb lit the cellar. The room had a musty smell mixed with a faint fragrance of dried fruit, and mice would often scamper into Nanny Rose's stock for her grocery shop. We'd hear the resounding snap of a trap as we lay there in the dark, huddled together, announcing one less rodent to nibble into the currants and raisins.

Too late! The bomb blast shook the house to its foundations, blowing in the taped-over windowpanes behind the blackout curtains. Mummy pushed me under the square dining table and fell on top of me, the unborn baby kicking in protest, nudging me.

'Mum, come under here!' she called to Nanny Rose.

'I'm not moving for blooming old Hitler!' Nan shouted above the din. Purl one, knit one, clack went her needles in defiance.

The lights failed, the room plunged into darkness. Nan reached for the spill jar, taking out a taper and holding it to the dying embers. She stood up with the burning paper and lit two candles on the mantelpiece. The flames guttered in a sudden breeze, making strange jagged shadows on the wall. Unperturbed by the intrusion, she took up her knitting again. I stopped crying, fascinated by the flickering lights and the waving fringe on the crimson velour tablecloth. Bobbles danced around its edge and swung to and fro like cherries on a tree. I wanted to be under the red tent, an oasis, snuggled up, a place to hide from bad things, rather than in the black shelter, but there wasn't much room because of Mummy's tummy.

To me, there was no significance in the fading roar of the Luftwaffe Bombers' engines. But for my mother and grandmother, time hung, suspended between each breath until they heard the continuous tone of the All Clear. I understood that sound, the sound of relief.

'Thank goodness it's over,' exclaimed Mummy. The frown on her forehead softened, her shoulders relaxed and she hugged me. Her dress shook as the baby's tiny feet drummed against her womb, sharing the surge of release. We were all safe. Mummy crawled out from under the table, hauling herself up.

'Let's have a nice cuppa to settle our nerves before we see to the window,' she said to Nan, carrying a candle into the kitchen to light the hurricane lamp. I scrambled after her, not wanting to be left alone. Nan laid out teacups and poured water into my beaker over concentrated orange, a health benefit issued to babies and children under five years old during the war. Mummy picked up the caddy Daddy had given her for Christmas and lifted the lid. The calming aroma of tea floated out.

That Christmas, Grandma Skingley had travelled down from Bedford to join us. The minute she saw me, she gathered me up to her ample bosom and covered me with kisses.

'Pretty dear,' she had said, inspecting me with violet blue eyes. Daddy was her only child and Grandpa had died prematurely, a result of his wounds from the First World War. Nanny Rose and Grandma had been friends; both widows and women of strong character. They reminisced about the 'old days' as they busied themselves in the kitchen, creating recipes out of our food allowance. Grandma had saved up all her ration book coupons to make a Christmas cake, which she had brought with her. There was no spare sugar or egg whites to make royal icing, so she'd cut out a white card cover and stuck a piece of holly on the top. This frivolous gesture in the face of austerity reflected my Grandma's personality and resilience. I admired her spirit and sense of fun, and I strove to be like her as I grew up, to make the most of difficult situations.

She and Nan were preparing carrot pudding for lunch. I sat watching them from the floor, playing with my building bricks and Mummy washing up when Daddy walked in through the back door. She flew past me and flung herself into his arms, the drips from her wet hands falling onto his uniform. Grandma and Nan came to kiss him with surprised exclamations at his unexpected homecoming.

'Where's my little girl gone?' he called out, pretending he couldn't see me.

'Daddy, Daddy,' I screeched and jumped up, throwing chubby arms in the air as I ran towards him. His strong hands scooped me up and held me high so I could touch the ceiling. He smelt different to Mummy, of smoke and spicy oil from his hair. His blue eyes twinkled as he laughed and gave me a prickly kiss.

What excitement when he brought in the fir tree on Christmas Eve. The room filled with a new odour, fresh like wet grass, damp and pungent. Daddy placed the slim trunk into a bucket of earth against a corner of the sitting room. I helped him decorate the tree with wads of cotton wool and scraps of coloured knitting wool left over from Nanny Rose's workbasket. I tried to wind them up like him but my small hands weren't big enough. He made balls with loops and hoisted me up to hang them on the spiky branches. All the colours I knew, red and yellow and green and blue. Mummy showed me the pretty angel she had created from pipe cleaners and bits of lace, which Daddy perched on the top branch. When the tree was dressed, Grandma and Nanny came to admire our handiwork with a tray of biscuits, cups of tea, my juice and a glass of beer for Daddy.

Father Christmas left me a big present on Christmas morning wrapped up in crinkly paper and string. My tiny excited fingers pulled and ripped until a push along toy dog on a red walking frame appeared, shiny metal carrying a smiling terrier, which I hugged and called Teddy. I must have been a good girl that year. But Daddy went away the next day to return to what Mummy called the war, so perhaps I wasn't especially good after all.

* * *

That evening, whilst my mother secured me in her arms under the dining table, Lancaster Bomber JB731F waited for clearance to takeoff at RAF Bourne, Lincolnshire.

Flight Lieutenant Jack Skingley RAFVR and the aircrew were tense, silent, deep in their own thoughts after the banter and joking earlier in the Mess. Jack's concerns were with Marjorie and their second child, due in two weeks. He hoped it was a boy. The Skingleys needed an heir. A green light flashed from the control tower. The seven airmen focussed on their roles. The pilot advanced the throttles and the heavily laden aircraft lumbered forward. The fuselage shook, the wings waggled as the big bird gathered speed along the runway and rose up into the Lincolnshire night sky. Twenty other Lancasters followed from 97 Pathfinder Squadron RAF. In formation they headed out over the North Sea: destination Brunswick, Germany.

55,573 Aircrew from Bomber Command were killed. My father, Jack, was one of them.

CHAPTER 1

SUSSEX, 1948

'What do you think you're doing?' a gruff voice boomed.

We shielded our eyes from the August sun and looked up at the big man wearing a policeman's uniform. His domed helmet shaded an unfriendly face.

'Wait 'til your parents hear about this. You both deserve a good hiding for damaging the harvest. Now give me your names.'

Our small bodies trembled, fearful of him and the threatened punishment.

'Jackie,' I quavered as my little brother cried. 'He's Ross,' I added as we clung to each other.

The giant took out his notebook.

'Ah yes, I know you, you're Mrs. Skingley's children. I'll be having a word with her. Now be off with you, no more playing in the wheat field.'

We ran across the road through the gate into our driveway. Ross's sobs stopped when we reached the safety of the open backdoor and saw Mummy in the kitchen, ladling warm plum jam into glass jars. The smell of sweetness filled our nostrils, carrying the promise of homemade sticky tarts. A knotted scarf covered her bobbed black hair, her cheeks flushed from the heat of the stove.

'What have you been up to?' she asked, looking up from the copper pan to see our dirty clothes, grubby socks and scuffed sandals.

'Nothing,' I replied and hung my head.

'She made me,' said Ross lifting up his tearstained face.

'Made you do what?' She put down the ladle and bent over to speak to him.

'Play hide and seek with her in the field and – and – and then he came along and frightened me.'

Ross's tears began to fall down his freckled cheeks.

'Who frightened you?' she asked, holding his shoulders.

'The policeman,' I admitted.

She was the best Mummy in the whole world, even when she was cross. She frowned, stood up and let out a long sigh. Nanny Rose appeared in her floral pinny at the doorway, carrying a tin of pilchards she'd taken from the pantry for tea.

'They're both in trouble, Mum. They've been over the road,' said Mummy. 'I told them to play in the garden and not go outside the gate.'

'You should know better, Jackie, you'll be seven soon,' Nanny said, her dark, reproachful eyes giving me one of her 'I know best' looks over her spectacles.

'He's coming to give us a hiding. What does that mean?' I let out a squeal. This was the first time in my young life I feared punishment by a man, the consequence of my disobedience.

'Who is?' she asked.

'The horrid policeman,' I gasped.

'Now, Jackie, you know policemen aren't horrid. Your Daddy wasn't, he was kind.'

I threw myself against her.

'Don't let him hiding us,' I begged.

'It's all right, darling, nobody is going to hurt you. But you must remember to do what you're told. Do you understand? We'll tell him that you and Ross won't do it again.'

I nodded. Ross grabbed Mummy's hand and I buried my face in Nan's apron.

* * *

Three years before, Mummy, Nan, Ross and I had moved to the village from Reigate. We were little then – Ross was a year old, and I was nearly four. Uncle Harry and Auntie Bessie lived up the road and they would tell us about our father, said he was a war hero. Mummy went to see the King at Buckingham Palace who gave her a medal with Daddy's name on it. A silver cross with a white and purple striped ribbon. I couldn't remember him very well, but I always smiled at his photo in Mummy's bedroom and he smiled back.

My great Uncle Harry was Nan's brother. His old hands were engrained with dirt from working in the garden. I loved his wife, Auntie Bessie, who felt like a big cushion when she cuddled me. They had no children but did have lots of chickens and Uncle Harry had a big greenhouse where he grew strange plants. One year he grew loofahs but Mummy didn't like using them to scrub her skin in the bath, they were too scratchy.

Nan took us on Saturday afternoons to collect eggs at Ryefield. We lifted lids on nesting boxes, ready to discover the weekly treasure, sliding our hands into prickly straw to pick up the smooth ovals, speckled brown or white. The hen coops smelt of dusty feathers and chicken feed, mashed up cooked potato peelings. This particular smell still takes me straight back to my childhood remembering Auntie Bessie in one of the outhouses, seated on a chair plucking a chicken, its lifeless head dangling over her lap, a cloud of down floating around her while the potato peelings boiled in an old bucket on a gas ring. This image of the past was a time of contentment when I felt safe and secure.

We searched for eggs and, afterwards, Uncle Harry would show us a new batch of chicks, yellow balls of fluffs that chirped like crickets and ran around in golden circles under a heat lamp. Nan and Auntie Bessie gossiped in the kitchen while we hunted outside. They laid the table and put on the kettle. Uncle Harry carried the egg basket to them and we counted our clutch. His gnarled fingers felt like sandpaper when he pressed two bronze coins into Ross's and my hands, our weekly pocket money. Auntie Bessie then gave us tea, a slice of Victoria sponge on square painted china plates. We sank our teeth into the yellow cake to taste her strawberry jam, red and juicy. How I loved those Clarice Cliff cream plates with green edges and swirly trees sheltering a small house with a red roof; a magic place where a little girl could have an adventure.

Back then, we had no men in our lives other than Uncle Harry. That was all to change when Mummy invited Mr. Pearce over for tea.

He read Ross and me stories and played magic tricks, producing pennies from behind our ears. We'd never seen such things before and jumped up and down with excitement. Full of wonder, we fell under his spell. Mummy did too. She changed her hairstyle, put on her best dress, seamed stockings and high heels. Her face lit up when he came to the front door to take her out for the evening. Nan didn't look too pleased and didn't read our bedtime story like Mummy, her face closed tight like a drawer of secrets, except for when she kissed us goodnight. Mummy showed us, one morning at breakfast, the sparkly ring on her finger and announced that we were going to have 'a new daddy'.

They married in October 1949. I shivered with cold during the wedding ceremony in a thin blue satin bridesmaid's dress. Nanny Rose and Grandma weren't smiling when the photographer took the family wedding picture outside the church. In the village hall, they whispered together looking serious and grim. I rushed over to tell them that Ross had made himself sick. The grownups were too busy drinking punch and eating sausage rolls to notice a small boy hiding under the table with a jar of pickled onions. When I found him he was crying to go home. It would not be the last time that I tried to help him.

Reginald Pearce came from a good family and had the airs and graces of a middle-class man. He resembled the actor, Paul Newman, with his waved hair, blue eyes and chiselled features, but the likeness ended there. He told Mummy he had been a

Squadron Leader in the Royal Air Force. It wasn't until she had married him and lost her war widow's pension, that my mother realised her marriage was built on lies. He had not received a commission in the RAF, like my father, but had been a leading aircraftsman. This alone would not have bothered her. But he had become stern and controlling. Mummy may well have considered leaving him once she discovered his real character. However, in those days, divorce carried a social stigma, a disgrace. She learnt to accept her lot like many other women in a similar position.

Nan decided to leave after the marriage and returned to Reigate. Ross and I were inconsolable. Nan, loving and generous, had been with us since we were born, soothed us when we were ill, took us to Bognor for days out, helped Mummy with the cooking, knitted our winter scarves, and didn't smack us.

Our new 'daddy' gradually became dictatorial and abusive. We were soon to learn the reality of 'hidings,' rather than the policeman's empty threats, and of being sent to bed without tea. There were few treats and I no longer had dresses from Marshall and Snelgrove in London. Our clothes were patched, mended or let down and Mummy cooked sparse meals. Uncle Harry occasionally bought a rabbit, shot by one of the farmers, to supplement our larder. We didn't know our new 'daddy' didn't earn much money. We only knew that Mummy didn't laugh as she used to, before he came to live with us. Ross and I looked forward to our infrequent visits to Ryefield after Nan left. The eggs, pocket money, cake and cuddles brought us fleeting happiness.

However, I must thank my stepfather for his intervention when I was eight. The local boys in the class above, chased me one day from the village school and I arrived home breathless. Alarmed by the state of my appearance, Mummy put her arm around me.

'Whatever's the matter, darling?' she asked.

'I was running away from the big boys because they wanted to shag me,' I gasped. I didn't know what it meant but something warned me to escape. That did it. Reg encouraged Mummy to write to the RAF Benevolent Fund to apply for an educational grant on my behalf. No doubt he wanted the recognition of having a 'daughter' attending private school. My father's sacrifice had made it possible, which I was never to forget.

Travelling six miles on the green and cream Southdown bus to the Villa Maria Convent in Bognor Regis was an adventure. I wore my season ticket in a little leather holder on a strap around my neck and was joined by other girls en route, recognisable by our royal blue uniform. The Bognor bus station in the high street was the last stop. At eight years, and on my own, I navigated main roads until I reached the convent on Campbell Road; sometimes I tagged on behind bigger girls, wanting to be like them, clever and grown up.

The school didn't provide lunch, so at a quarter to one we walked in crocodile to the Commercial Café on London Road. Food was still rationed and meals consisted of restricted menus – tinned corned beef fritters, tasteless butter beans and plain boiled potatoes. After lessons we streamed out of school and I made my way back up the high street to the bus station, passing a baker's shop on the way. The feast of éclairs and scones displayed in the window increased my hunger and I hoped there were cakes at home for tea. We had them every day when Nan stayed with us, but things had changed. Mummy only baked when she had eggs and margarine to spare.

* * *

One day in September the following year, she wasn't at home to greet me. She had confided in me, as her tummy grew fatter, about my new baby brother or sister. As I came through the front door I saw Aunt Edna, standing in the kitchen fidgeting with a handkerchief, her face like a boiled crab. On the table lay an open bag with some of my clothes.

'Where's Mummy and Ross?' I asked.

'Well, dear, you're coming home with me because your Mummy is in the maternity home.'

'Is she having the baby?'

'Your Daddy will tell you all about it this evening when he comes back,' she replied. 'Ross is staying with your Aunt Bessie.'

Why couldn't I go there too? I didn't like Aunt Edna, my stepfather's sister, and she didn't have Victoria sponge for tea. I was excited about a new baby brother or sister, imagining different Christian names for it. Sadness engulfed me when my stepfather explained the baby had died before it was born. There would be no chance to push its pram, dress it in all the little clothes Nan and Mummy had made, give it cuddles and teach it all the nursery rhymes I knew.

Mummy had to stay in the maternity home at Bognor for ten days to recover. I wanted to see her; the loss of the baby and being parted from her felt like a penance for a sin I'd committed. The nuns had been teaching us about sin and punishment. It must have been all those naughty thoughts I had about 'daddy', how I could banish him from our lives, wave a magic wand and turn him into a toad so we could have our Nan back again. At nine years old, I had already decided to be a nun and was studying my catechism with great diligence. The notion of leading a religious life to follow their example only lasted a term, much to the amusement of my mother, but the concept of sin had a much longer impact. Sister Bernadine smiled at my serious expression as I recounted my fears. She said no, it wasn't my fault and I wouldn't go to hell or purgatory. What a relief to my young mind. I still had a chance to go to heaven. Her old face, encased in the white coif and long black veil, radiated serenity and I found the courage to ask her how to find the maternity home. It wasn't too difficult and I marched up to the big oak door and pressed a brass button. The door opened and a nurse in a crisp uniform looked surprised to see me on the doorstep.

'No visiting for children,' she said.

She must have taken pity on my crestfallen face and bent down.

'What's your name?' she whispered.

'Jackie,' I whispered back. 'My Mummy is Mrs. Pearce.'

'Wait over there on the lawn, dear,' she said and gave me a wink. 'I'll go and see if your mummy can come to her window.'

After a while, Mummy appeared in her nightdress at an open sash window on the first floor. She waved, blew a kiss and threw down an apple. I missed her comforting arms and the gentle tones of her soothing voice. I waved back, blew a kiss in return, tears streaming down my face.

During this traumatic time, my stepfather worked away during the week, living in digs. I stayed with Aunt Edna and Uncle Peter. At night he would come upstairs and turn off the light in my bedroom, which I had deliberately chosen to leave on. I was terrified of the dark and monsters that lived under the bed. The black room reminded me of the cellar and fears that haunted me from the air raids.

The baby had been a girl and the reason, some years later, why my mother asked me if I would change my name to Pearce. I was adamant.

'No!' I said to her. 'Never!'

She then suggested I keep my name Skingley and add Pearce to it. Eventually I agreed, not wanting to upset her, but I was never comfortable with the double-barrelled name. What was worse, it often was abbreviated to Pearce. I wanted to be my father's daughter not Reg's.

Reg, despite everything, was a clever man and became a Civil Servant. Promoted several times, he was given a good position at the Royal Aircraft Establishment at Farnborough. As a result, we moved to Deramore Cottage in Camberley when I was thirteen.

Straightaway I loved the house, which sat high on Camberley Hill in mature gardens, the view from my bedroom window stretched across tree tops to distant hills. I had been allowed to choose the soft furnishings and to have such a private and harmonious room of my own was a dream.

We arrived in July. I sat the entrance exam for the Convent at Farnborough and Ross passed his interview for the Silesian College. We started a new chapter in our lives, made new friends and built a stronger bond against Reg. His good fortune had bought him a Daimler and handmade Church's shoes from Regent's Street. Mummy, however, didn't have enough money in her purse to buy a new lipstick.

There were no more hidings from Reg, instead a new episode surfaced. I was growing fast and almost twelve when I first experienced his 'special' attention, when he started to sexually molest me. On the last occasion he did so, I found my voice. The light switch in the hall had become loose and the electrical contact broken, making the steps down to the cloakroom area difficult to negotiate in the dark. I had just come out of the lavatory after supper one evening and found him waiting in the shadows. He was silent, a strange look on his face, one I had learned to recognise. He blocked my ascent, instead placing his hands under my armpits, picking me up like a doll and kissing me hard on the lips, his tongue forcing them open. I froze, alarmed by his actions, and held my breath until he let me go, sliding my body against his. I wanted to cry out when his hands reached inside my dress but scared that if Mummy came to see what had happened, I'd be in trouble. I wanted to stop him but lacked the necessary strength. His heavy breathing filled the black space and my skin prickled with fear; at last my strangled voice rose in protest.

'Stop it!' I gasped and pushed against him.

'Don't tell your mother,' he said, finally letting me go.

'You leave me alone or I will,' I hissed back.

I became wary and avoided being on my own in a room with him. My new bedroom had a lock and key, providing a sense of safety and protection. Ross wasn't so lucky; he was in line for a clip around the ear at the slightest disagreement.

We both had reasons to dislike our stepfather. He repulsed me with his mask of respectability, his bullying and selfishness. As I grew up, I found myself attracted to men who were courteous, amusing and generous, the polar opposite to Reg.

CHAPTER 2

FIRST DANCE

'If you kiss a boy for longer than three seconds,' said Mother Mostyn. 'It's a mortal sin.'

'I wonder what happens then,' I whispered to my best friend, Frances, and giggled. Frances nudged me, trying hard not to explode with laughter. We were in fourth form at Farnborough Hill Convent for girls. The nuns decided we needed to learn how to sleep in our beds, our arms crossed over our chests. We thought it was in case we died in the night. Kissing was the next topic and Mother Mostyn was doing her best to save us from damnation.

At school we had no sex education except for the biological facts of reproduction; the male contribution was briefly glossed over, homosexuality unheard of, and we hadn't a clue about 'French letters'. My mother warned me about periods when I was eleven and didn't elaborate on the subject, and now Frances and I were about to discover the alien world of boys. I had long since buried the memory of abuse from my stepfather, lying dormant beneath layers of self-protection.

Frances's father Freddie was in the Royal Engineers, and now we were nearly sixteen, her mother 'Bubbles' arranged for us to go to a chaperoned teenage dance at the Officers' Club in Aldershot. I'd been invited to stay over at 'The White House' in Heath End, a palatial residence with tennis courts and walled gardens, 'quarters' which went with 'Uncle' Freddie's post as Brigade Commander. Here, I had a chance to be with a loving family. No harsh words were spoken and amusing banter was encouraged at the dining table; quite the opposite to my home where silence and obedience were expected.

I whirled in front of the long mirror in Frances's bedroom,

admiring the way my dress swung. Mummy had sewn it especially for the occasion, calf length, turquoise taffeta with a full skirt and silky to touch. My long legs were encased in seamed stockings and I wore white winkle-picker shoes, my first high heels. The girl in the looking glass with the powdered face and chestnut hair reflected my happiness.

'Do you remember the dance steps Daddy taught you?' Frances asked. 'I'm scared I've forgotten mine.'

We'd been practising to Victor Sylvester's long-playing vinyl record, *The Best of All Quicksteps*. Frances and I danced together and, the same height, took turns at leading. Uncle Freddie had shown us the extra moves, the heel pivot and the fishtail, in preparation for our first dance.

'We'll be ok, it's the boys I worry about,' I replied, fingering the turquoise and pearl necklace at my neck, a gift from Nan. 'Will they know what to do?'

'Mummy has found some partners for us, sons of members of the Club. I'll need your moral support when we meet them.'

I wasn't going to be much help. I didn't know how to speak to boys, discounting my younger brother, and I'd be embarrassed too. Reg didn't like me speaking to boys. Were they some kind of threat? I was soon to find out.

Frances applied candy pink lipstick, contrasting with the satin green dress and the pearls her mother, my 'Aunt' Bubbles, had lent her. Curlers couldn't tame Frances's blonde curls, and they struggled free to form a halo around her head.

'Want to try some?' she asked, handing the lipstick case over. I nodded, pulled off the silver top to expose the little stick of magic and glided the colour over my pouting lips, feeling so grown up.

There was a knock at the door, and statuesque Aunt Bubbles came in wearing an elegant maroon dress and long matching gloves. A lady always wore gloves when dressed for town, church, luncheon or dinner engagements – strict etiquette in the

1950s.

'Girls, are you ready? The driver is waiting for us,' she said. 'You both look very pretty. Come on or we'll be late.'

We simpered at her compliment and, gathering up our beaded evening bags, eagerly followed her downstairs.

The Aldershot Officers' Club on Farnborough Road looked impressive from the outside. A large single storey brick building set in spacious grounds, a flight of wide steps led up to double glass doors. We climbed them, full of excitement and anticipation, looking forward to our first dance. Aunt Bubbles led the way with confidence and dignity. A Mess steward smartly opened the door and we found ourselves in a large foyer. A group of teenagers milled about, dressed in party clothes, accompanied by glamorous ladies, their chaperones. Aunt Bubbles shepherded us towards them and introduced us. The 'how do you dos' and firm handshakes were formal and stiff. Frances and I fidgeted, the boys hung back.

'Anthony, don't forget your manners,' I heard one large lady say to a spotty boy.

I can remember the sinking feeling. I hoped all the boys weren't like him, gauche and covered in acne. I'd expected a handsome partner, like Rhett Butler in *Gone With The Wind*. I didn't want to dance with any of them. What was I going to say when they asked me? Snatches of music reached the foyer as we followed Aunt Bubbles into the ballroom. The live band was playing 'You Make Me Feel So Young', a Frank Sinatra number. Under watchful eyes, the boys pulled out chairs for girls to sit down at reserved tables on the edge of the dance floor. A steward arrived with a jug of non-alcoholic punch, the chaperones retired to a table at the back of the room, and the evening was set for us 'young things' to improve our dance repertoire and social skills. I caught Frances's eye and she raised her eyebrows.

The bandleader stepped forward to the microphone.

'Everyone on the floor for the Paul Jones! Girls make a circle in the middle and boys one on the outside.'

This was it; we all stood up to obey his command. I dreaded making a fool of myself but I'd no time to be self-conscious. Someone grabbed my hand and I was on the dance floor. The music played an upbeat tune as I was pulled around in the ring of girls one way and the boys dragged each other in the opposite direction. I began to feel giddy when suddenly the music stopped. There in front of me stood my partner, the shortest and ugliest boy in the room. He grinned and clutched my waist with one hand and clenched my right one in the other, his face pressed on my budding bosom. Help! I didn't like the way he touched me and he was counting to himself, *one-two-three*. I suppose it gave me a clue what to do with my feet. Frances staggered past with a tall thin boy intent on crushing her toes. She made a face at me like she had swallowed a fly. When the ordeal was over, we both rushed off to the ladies, ostensibly to powder our shiny noses but naturally, we were dying to gossip about the experience of our first dance.

'Did you see that drip?' she asked, dabbing her face with a powder puff. 'He couldn't dance for toffee.'

'And what about that boy I ended up with? I could see right over his head, he only came up to my armpit,' I moaned as I combed my hair.

'Have you seen the young men on the table by the bandstand?' she continued. 'They look a lot more interesting, especially the one with the blonde hair.'

'I'll have a peek,' I winked at her, sharing the secret.

Thank goodness the boring youths were dancing with the other girls on our table when we returned. We were alone and I checked out Frances's dreamboat. He did seem quite handsome, but I preferred the dark-haired chap talking to him. Frances and I were mesmerised.

'Frances, they're coming over,' I whispered. 'I think they're going to ask us to dance.'

They skirted around the dance floor, edging towards us. I kicked Frances under the table. Please God let it be the dark one who asks me, the taller one wearing a gorgeous dinner jacket lined with red silk. A red flash caught my eye when he stood up.

'May I have the pleasure of this dance?' he asked – looking at me, not Frances.

'I'd love to,' I replied as Scarlett O'Hara, looking at Rhett Butler.

He offered his hand and I took it.

'Alan,' he said. 'And you?'

The music changed and the band played Benny Goodman's 'Sing, Sing, Sing,' He led me onto the floor and began to jive, spinning me round like a top. My heart pounded with excitement, my feet tripped to the rhythm and he pulled me towards him with strong arms. He held me close, our thighs pressed against each other. I tingled all over and a blush crept up from the neckline of my dress. By the end of the dance I was glowing.

'Come outside in the garden,' he said, his hand in mine.

He guided me to the open door and into the cool air scented with roses. The teenagers continued their gyrations in the ballroom and we were alone in the darkness. Alan seized me and planted a brief kiss on my lips. He pushed me against a hedge, his hands on my shoulders and then over my breasts. I was confused. Was this the mortal sin? I wasn't ready for hell, and he was rough. I panicked, broke away and ran back into the ballroom, straight into Aunt Bubbles.

'Everything all right, Jackie?' she enquired with a frown.

'Yes, I'm fine,' I panted.

'Are you sure dear? You look flustered.'

I nodded and took a deep breath. My partner came rushing into the room looking for me but, on seeing Aunt Bubbles, he stopped abruptly, seemed to change his mind and strode back towards his table.

'Were you with him?' she asked, her concern apparent by the

deepening lines on her forehead.

'Not for long, I didn't like him,' I replied.

'Ah, I see,' she commented, watching his back view disappearing among the dancers. She searched my face for more information, which was not forthcoming. Ashamed of the incident, I blamed myself for being so easily led. I shouldn't have allowed myself to be taken in by his charm, like my poor mother had been with Reg.

'Have you seen Frances?' Bubbles asked.

'I think she went to the Ladies,' I answered, in case my friend needed an alibi.

My heart began to slow and my breathing felt easier.

'Ah, there she is now,' she said, swivelling her eyes to observe the blonde boy with her. 'I don't know that young man, do you, Jackie?'

'No, Aunt Bubbles, I don't,' I pretended.

She strode off to discover his pedigree and I followed. Frances looked mortified as her mother quizzed her partner. I recognised a couple of girls from Elmhurst Ballet School on the next table, reminding me of home as I passed the school grounds every day to catch the bus to Farnborough Hill. I'd been so excited about my first dance and now I simply wanted to leave, to be alone in my bedroom, shut in and safe. Disappointment and regret had replaced my anticipation of a romantic evening. That is, until Richard on our table got up and held out his hand.

'Like to dance?' he asked nonchalantly.

What joy! Taller than me, *and* he knew how to quickstep. The only problem was that he had a rolled up handkerchief in his pocket, which pressed into my leg and groin. It was strange; I thought that I must ask Frances if she had the same experience with her partners.

Uncle Freddie heard about my adventure in the rose garden from Aunt Bubbles. He laughed. Next time they'd put taillights on me so I could be seen outside in the dark. I blushed, embarrassed, making a mental note never to find myself in such a situation again.

The following year, Uncle Freddie retired from the army and became a gentleman farmer, and so the family moved to Devon. I was very sad to see them go. Frances and I had been inseparable for three years at Farnborough Hill. Both daygirls, I had spent many weekends at their imposing Heath End house. Aunt Bubbles gave wonderful lunch and dinner parties, where I met interesting people and learnt the art of social etiquette and repartee. It was fun to dress up on these occasions. Frances and I would swap clothes and experiment with make-up and had enjoyed many happy times together.

The summer after Uncle Freddie bought the farm, Reg paid for my train fare to Paignton. He approved of my friendship with Frances, he had met her father, a Brigadier, and what kudos that had given him. Packed in my suitcase were two of Mummy's creations, a polka dot sundress with a bolero and a pink cotton sleeveless frock. Frances tried the second one on the moment she saw me unpacking and wore it throughout the holiday. That's the kind of friendship we had; we shared her bedroom, played Peggy Lee records and talked long into the night of her new school and our old friends.

Clear skies, sea air and the company of my adopted family were ingredients for happiness. I learnt to milk cows, pluck chickens and help to harvest vegetables from the kitchen garden with Frances, reminiscent of Ryefield and my childhood in Sussex before Reg. Aunt Bubbles served up delicious meals with the produce for an army of guests who came and went throughout the long summer days. The house was filled with laughter from two of Frances's younger siblings, Patrick and Lizzie, who played their pranks and games. Tom, her other younger brother joined in but preferred to read his *Eagle* comics and make up jokes. He was fourteen and attended a boarding school in Cheltenham, following in his father's footsteps.

We picnicked on Slapton Sands, swam in the sea and helped Patrick and Lizzie build sand castles. Uncle Freddie taught us to sail his sloop *Tempest*, moored in Paignton harbour. He enjoyed taking Frances and me out to cruise around Torbay. He'd count how many hellos and wolf whistles we received from passing boats. We pretended to be embarrassed but secretly we enjoyed the attention from the opposite sex. Freddie was a father figure, my male role model - kind, positive and amusing. I admired and trusted him. There must be younger men like him out there, so perhaps I would meet my Rhett Butler one day.

In direct contrast to Uncle Freddie, my stepfather continued to exert his control over me by vetting all potential boyfriends and making the decisions about what parties I attended.

I used to meet up with a group of teenagers in Tekels Park during the school holidays. Hilary, Heather, Anthony and Mark were boarders at a 'progressive' boarding school near Petersfield, where no harsh rules and regulations were practiced. I envied their freedom. We went out as a gang and enjoyed each other's company without any complications. Anthony, the proud owner of an Austin 7, allowed us to take turns in driving. When it was my go I grabbed hold of the steering wheel, rammed the gear into first and drove erratically around the rhododendron-lined paths to the accompanying chorus of screams and laughter. I loved the excitement and sense of adventure, but it was a miracle I didn't kill anybody. We shared records, playing them on Heather's turntable and boogied to the new rock 'n' roll songs by Elvis Presley. We rode an old knackered horse belonging to Hilary and, occasionally, they came around to my house for lemonade and biscuits. I always hoped Reg wouldn't be around to ingratiate himself with the girls. Mark did kiss me once but it wasn't anything special, all teeth and awkwardness. He wasn't quite the Rhett I had in mind.

Within a year I was invited to balls at Sandhurst. The family home was in Camberley, so I was bound to meet up with officer cadets at some point. The Royal Military Academy was set back from the London Road, and the impressive buildings and grounds of this establishment gave testament to its importance. There were three different Colleges, New, Old and Victory for more than eight hundred Officer Cadets.

I met Charles at a party in February 1959. He was very attentive and, at the end of the evening, asked if I would like to go out with him. Aged nineteen, he was in his second term at the Academy. He was about an inch taller than me, fit and athletic. His green eyes fixed me in their sights. I was hooked by his impeccable manners and kind voice. Finally, here was a man who attracted me. I accepted his invitation to see *South Pacific* showing at the Odeon cinema and he arranged to collect me from my house.

I plucked up courage to ask Mummy if she'd speak to Reg about my date, telling her he'd come about teatime on Saturday. She made scones, laid the table with the best china and the silver teapot, in which to serve the Darjeeling tea. She was curious to meet this boy. Reg had asked searching questions about Charles, impossible questions, but the fact that he was a Sandhurst cadet was already a point in his favour.

The wide gate to our driveway swung open and there he was, heading up the path to the front door. My heart pounded to the crunch of gravel. The sharp knock at the front door made me start. Reg pushed past to open it. *Oh, please don't let him say anything to embarrass me in front of Charles,* a small voice in my head repeated over and over.

'Right, young man,' he said once the customary greetings were over. 'You'd better come in.'

Reg eyed Charles up and down, his clothes immediately giving him a passport to enter our domain. Then came questions about his family and, on learning that Charles's father was a colonel, Reg, snob that he was, had no more doubts. Charles had passed muster. He made polite conversation with my mother and ate her scones with relish. He promised Reg to bring me straight home after the film and, with this assurance, I was allowed to accompany him.

The darkness in the cinema cocooned us and he searched for my hand. The musical *South Pacific* burst onto the screen with colour and light. I was transported to a tropical island where Joe, a young American Lieutenant, met a beautiful Tonkinese girl, Liat. It was romantic, filled with stirring songs and I cried at the end when the hero was killed. To comfort me, Charles put his arm around my shoulder and kissed me. I was doomed to hell. I had committed the mortal sin of kissing a boy for longer than three seconds, the lingering of his lips having sent shivers up my spine. Later, when he said goodbye, I discovered that he too kept something hard in his trouser pocket.

* * *

'When am I going to meet this Charles of yours?' asked my vivacious Australian girlfriend, Lynette, who lived on the next road from us in Camberley. Lynette, a student at the Kingston Art College, was a pretty, dark-haired girl with vivid blue eyes. I envied her being a year older than me and no longer a schoolgirl. I was preparing for my advanced level Art exam and loved seeing her portfolio of work with innovative use of different media and her sketches of nude studies. There was definitely no opportunity to draw those at the convent! Lynette's father, a pilot with Qantas, the number one Australian airline, had been posted to London. She had two younger brothers, one of whom had fallen out of a window when he was little and sadly became disabled. It was only later in life that I learnt Lynette had suffered at the hands of her father, far more than I had with Reg. Her immersion in art was her way to cope with the abuse and emotional pain of her experiences.

'Oh, I don't know, he can't get out much and, apart from the course, he's training for the fencing team, which takes up more time,' I replied.

'Why don't you ask him if he'd like to come over here next Saturday and bring a friend from Sandhurst? That would be good for me too, and we can listen to my records. I've got Harry Belafonte's new one. Mum and Dad are going out for the evening and taking the boys, so it'll be just us. I'll ask Mum if it's ok.'

A chance to be on our own, unrestricted, away from adults; I was thrilled to bits with her suggestion. Luckily Charles was free on Saturday and found someone to bring from his college.

'Mike's a good chap, plays rugby and boxes for the Academy,' Charles spoke of his friend.

Late afternoon on Saturday, I told my mother that I was going to visit Lynette. I hurried down to her house keen to meet Charles and maybe have a bit of privacy to practise sinning. There was always that nagging worry of how far I should go. Mother Mostyn's warnings rang in my head, despite the mortal sin I had already committed with the longer-than-three-second kiss – and tongues! But I was still determined not to lose my virginity for years.

Charles arrived just after me at around half past five. Mike was playing in a rugby match and would be along later. I introduced Lynette. We went into the sitting room and sat together on the sofa chatting whilst Lynette went to find some beer. Charles was in his element, running his hands up my thighs while I purred like a cat. We pulled apart when Lynette came back with three bottles of beer and glasses.

'I forgot to bring the opener,' she confessed.

'Ok, I'll go,' I offered, a little flustered, smoothing down my skirt and heading for the kitchen. I had just reached the hallway when the doorbell rang. Lynette's record was playing the upbeat calypso rhythm of 'The Banana Boat Song'. 'Day-O!' sang out Harry Belafonte, his voice reverberating throughout the house. I was closest to the door and opened it. There on the doorstep was a tall, handsome young man, quite a hunk. He had a mop of blonde hair, the bluest eyes and wore a brown tweed suit, a mustard-coloured waistcoat, checked shirt, and a red, gold and blue striped Sandhurst tie.

'Hello,' he said. 'Are you Lynette?'

'No, I'm Jackie,' I answered; registering how lucky Lynette was to have him as a date.

'What a pity!' he remarked.

I thought so too; he had such an air of confidence and vitality. I liked the way he looked at me, his eyes conveying his regret.

'You must be Mike,' I said with a smile.

The next opportunity to meet was at an officer cadet party held in April at The Cambridge Hotel in Camberley. For the occasion, my mother had made me a cocktail bell-shaped dress of black and peacock-blue shot taffeta. We had chosen the fabric and the Vogue pattern together, the newest fashion to hit the catwalks, chic and seductive. I wanted to look like the model on the cover and couldn't wait to wear such a desirable creation. Nan had sent some money to pay for my treat. It wasn't until Mummy started cutting out the material that she discovered how much work was involved. Undeterred by the extra hours, she stitched and machined until the finished dress, shimmering and silky, hung on a hanger.

'Cinderella shall go to the ball,' Mummy announced, showing me the result of her commitment. Overcome with happiness, I kissed and thanked her. She always wanted to give me the best, perhaps to compensate for Reg, her way of encouraging me to enjoy life, as she had done when she had gone dancing with my father. I stood in my underwear, lifted the masterpiece off the hanger and slipped it over my head. The skirt rustled, the fabric flashed like butterfly wings, iridescent and magical. I smiled and twirled, sensing its transforming power.

'You look beautiful,' she declared with a wistful countenance, and I blushed with pride at her compliment.

Charles too was impressed when he collected me. He grinned when I emerged in my taffeta frock with poise and confidence, his partner for the evening. The event was for Gaza Company in New College, to which Charles and Mike belonged. I bubbled with happiness to be invited to such an exclusive party.

On our arrival at the Cambridge Hotel, Mike was lounging with a group of cadets drinking beer at the bar. I received admiring glances from the men. Filled with delight I knew that my dress was a success. On a crowded dance floor, couples danced to 'Venus' sung by Frankie Avalon, and the room buzzed with energy and laughter. Charles ordered a round of drinks and, while he was occupied with the barman, Mike asked me to dance. It was customary, and part of their social etiquette, for the cadets to request a dance from other girls at parties. Mike was no longer going out with Lynette, having only taken her on one date, and she was disappointed not to have been included that night. I was flattered and, because I liked Mike, I accepted. He led me to the knot of dancers and we swayed to the music. He knew how to dance and I willingly followed his lead. Taller than Charles, my head came to the top of his shoulder and he smelt of Old Spice. At first, he held me loosely in his arms, but as the music gathered tempo he pulled me closer, until I could feel the rise and fall of his chest. An attraction fought its way between us, my heart raced and fine hairs on my neck stood up, acknowledging his charisma. The music stopped, he bent down and kissed me then, abruptly, pushed me away.

'You're my friend's girl, so forget what just happened,' he said.

I was too taken aback to reply. What would Charles say if he'd seen Mike breaking their code of honour? I was Charles's girlfriend and 'off limits'. I looked round for him. He was still at the bar chatting with the other cadets. He would have been furious and might have thought that I'd deliberately provoked his best friend by flirting with him, which was not the case. But

I remembered Mike's stolen kiss for a long time. I didn't see him after that evening until the end of term.

Not long after the dance, Charles took me to his parents' house in Farnham for lunch. I can remember the apprehension of meeting them, an elderly couple with Edwardian values. Charles formally introduced me and I felt like a new recruit, not quite announcing my name, rank, and number, but close. We sat in the drawing room sipping dry sherry on the Ercol furniture, making polite conversation until his mother announced lunch was served. We followed her, and the aroma of roast lamb, into the dining room. The table was set with porcelain china, silver cutlery and white damask napkins. I was convinced that this was in my honour and therefore demanded my best behaviour and table manners. His father carved and served the joint while his mother uncovered the vegetable bowls to expose the roast potatoes and green peas. I watched the gravy congealing on my Spode plate, waiting for my hostess to pick up her knife and fork, a sign we could begin the meal. Charles's father, a gallant old gentleman, did his best to make me feel at home. On the other hand, I didn't feel the same about his mother. I caught her scrutinising me, weighing me up to determine if I was a suitable girlfriend for her only child. Outwardly she was considerate, but she had a certain reserve, a cool demeanour, contenting herself by engaging in a private conversation with her son. Inwardly we were like feral cats on the prowl, wary of each other.

* * *

At the beginning of the summer term, Mother Hogan, the headmistress of the convent, spoke to Reg about my career prospects. I've no idea why I wasn't invited to participate in my assessment. No doubt Reg preened himself before the appointment, put on his polished Church's shoes, tailor-made suit and parked his Daimler outside the front doors of the convent building, originally the home of Princess Eugenie, widow of Napoleon III. The grand entrance was Reg's style and I'm sure he thought the nuns considered him a refined gentleman. Mummy told me he liked going to the convent, where he would receive the respect befitting his status as head of our family. He never received any such respect from Ross and me – we knew he was a sham.

I could visualise him arriving at the convent and being ushered into the inner sanctum, the Music Room off a long corridor, reserved for guests. His day would have been completed by one of the pupils curtseying to him as she walked to the library, passing the open doors of the Music room. New pupils were taught to curtsey, which caused a great deal of giggling and falling over until we had mastered this strict etiquette and could bob down on the move when encountering guests. It was good practice for the few girls in the sixth form, daughters of well-connected rich families, preparing to be presented to HM the Queen, at the Queen Charlotte Ball in May. The 'Coming Out' Ball, announcing the start of 'The London Season', the social round of tea parties, racing at Ascot and more Balls. These events were considered venues to find suitable husbands, the candidates known as 'Deb's Delights'.

After school, Reg waited for me in his car. I cringed at the thought of his company, preferring to ride home on the bus, but I wanted to know the outcome of Mother Hogan's evaluation of my future employment prospects. I climbed in beside him and hugged my satchel, waiting for the verdict.

'It has been agreed that you would be well suited to working in a hotel as a receptionist or a clerk,' he said with a sneer. As long as I could get away from him as soon as possible, I didn't care what I did.

Once home, I began to list the hotels in the area and composed a draft letter, an application for employment. Mummy approved the final copies, written in my best handwriting. I was delighted to receive a reply a few weeks later, inviting me for an interview as a trainee receptionist at Great Fosters in Virginia Water, the most prestigious hotel in the county. At last, if successful, I had the means of escape, a chance to meet new and exciting people, to have a life of my own. I had a goal and studied hard to pass my exams.

I didn't see Charles during this period, but the promise of the June Ball compensated for his absence. This was the social event of the year at The Royal Military Academy. My school friends were envious. Reg gave me permission to attend and, yet again, Mummy made me a beautiful ball gown, one of green taffeta, overlaid with white organza with embroidered green sprigs in the style of Scarlet O'Hara's dress. I was thrilled. Was that really me in the mirror? I hardly recognised myself. My dress was a dream, my carefully made up face smiling back as I thought of the good time ahead, dancing in my high heels and partying at Sandhurst to celebrate the end of my schooldays.

Charles arrived looking handsome in his dinner jacket, my Rhett Butler. His glances were admiring, both of my dress and me.

'Make sure she comes home at a reasonable time,' my stepfather insisted.

'Of course, Sir,' replied Charles, catching my eye behind Reg's back, both of us knowing that I would be late home.

I climbed into his borrowed Austin A30, and in no time we were through Old College Gates into the grounds of the RMA. By the lake, three large marquees had been erected and music filled the air. The scene was like a film set with glamorous couples strolling in the grounds carrying champagne glasses. My role awaited me. Lights! Camera! Action! Rhett opened the passenger door and out stepped Scarlett. My dress rustled, the taffeta smooth and cool against my bare legs as I took hold of his arm. I felt as light as air beside him, floating across the grass in my dancing shoes. Charles led me into one of the large tents to his friends and reserved seats at their table. Mike was there with his new girlfriend, Diane, a pretty, slim girl in a peach-coloured gown. I avoided making eye contact with him, still feeling awkward after his stolen kiss. Cocktails arrived, wine flowed and Charles and I danced to the live bands, each one with its own beat in the different marquees. Skiffle, jazz and big band sounds pumped out all night. Flushed from jiving, we made our way back to the table to join our party. Mike didn't ask me to dance, he was too occupied with the lovely Diane.

A magician from The Magic Circle entertained us during dinner, playing tricks and mind reading. I felt glad that he didn't read mine! After the delicious meal, we wandered outside to watch boats filled with riotous young people making their way across the lake to howls of laughter and the slap of oars. Charles and I sat in the back of his car romancing under the light of the June moon, sipping champagne from crystal glasses.

The day I arrived at Great Fosters to embark on my adult life, filled with anticipation and hope for the future and ready for adventure, I was naïve and a virgin. The nun's influence had continued, even though I'd crossed the line with the three-minute kiss and 'petting'. But Mother Mostyn's warning had stopped me going further, much to the chagrin of Charles.

CHAPTER 3

GREAT FOSTERS, 12th JULY 1959

Mummy stood in the doorway of my bedroom, watching as I fastened my case. Dark brown eyes gazed out from her oval face, eyes that danced when she laughed. They weren't dancing now, but immobile with concentrated stillness. On this day of my departure, perhaps she was thinking of my father. The fifteenth anniversary of his death was coming up in a few days. Would he have been proud of me, his tall daughter with his high cheekbones? I wished I could remember him.

'Have you packed your warm jacket, raincoat and enough underwear?' she asked, fussing. She was about to let me go, to step into a new world. Did she see my vulnerability, despite the outward confidence? I gave her a bright reassuring smile and turned to look through the window one last time. Fifteen miles away, lay the uninterrupted view to the Hogs Back Ridge. Below in the garden, rhododendrons and azaleas had just finished blooming, their leathery leaves shining in the sunlight.

Mummy went downstairs and asked Reg to collect my luggage, who arrived and muttered about the amount I was taking. He puffed with the effort of carrying the case to show the inconvenience imposed upon him. I grabbed a bag containing my last things and left the bedroom I'd called my own for four years. Here I'd studied for exams, written my first love letters and slept in my single bed dreaming of new adventures. I skipped down the stairs, tapping out light beats with my high heels on the treads, a dance to freedom. Outside, Ross hung about waiting to speak to me.

'Bye Sis, wish it were me leaving,' he whispered. 'I'll miss you.'

I swallowed hard, unable to speak. Escaping to the wood

store, he wheeled out his bike ready to pedal away the minute we left. We were allies against Reg. Ross's summer holidays would be spent avoiding him, his sarcasm and the hidings. Reg had replaced the ogre of the village policeman. He had laid down his rules and his mantra, 'What will people say?' Yes, what would they say if they knew about him? I loathed everything about Reginald Pearce.

'Be back in time for tea,' Mummy called out to Ross.

She climbed into the passenger seat beside Reg, who looked his usual snobbish self, hoping to impress someone with his shiny Daimler. I waved at my brother through the rear window as his figure disappeared to a dot, the car gathering speed onwards to Virginia Water.

Independence was minutes away and I was eager to start my new life. Reg slowed the car as we arrived at the hotel's impressive wrought iron gates. Adrenalin raced through my blood, pumping out fear and flight mode to a hymn of liberty. The long sweeping driveway led to a large Tudor house, its roofs covered in tall chimneys and finials. We turned right onto a gravelled road towards the staff flats in the converted coach house. I was to live here with Miss Violet, the accountant on one side, and Mrs. Ghost, the head receptionist, on the other.

Reg parked the car and collected my case from the boot. Mummy and I followed him up the stairs with the rest of my things, every step bringing me closer to emancipation. The door to my room was unlocked. It had looked warm and cosy when I'd been shown the accommodation at my interview in May. Was it the same two months later? Nobody was about but I heard raised voices coming from one of the other rooms, a crescendo of cheering. It had to be a wireless, a comforting sound, although there was no one to personally greet me.

I clutched a bag with some books and a rug making kit, a pastime to keep me occupied when not on duty. Mummy opened the door and we crowded into the 'bedsit'. My new home was a small rectangular room with a single bed against the far wall. An upholstered armchair represented the 'sit' part. A wardrobe, a chest of drawers and a bedside table completed the furnishings. We piled my belongings on the bed.

'I'll sort all this out after you've left,' I said, trying to avoid a lingering farewell.

'You'll be ok then?' Mummy asked. 'You'll come home and see us often, won't you, darling?'

'Of course I will. You mustn't worry about me.'

I was more concerned for her. Reg would belittle and criticise her and I wouldn't be there to tell him to 'drop dead'. He gave me a perfunctory peck on the cheek. My hand itched to wipe off all trace of him. Mummy gave me a hug, squeezed my hand and kissed me, her eyes moist with tears. Mine threatened to spill down my cheeks, but I held them back and bit my lip. The hardest part was saying goodbye to her.

Miss Violet's door opened, the full blast of loud music assaulting us, a big band number. Dressed like my grandma in a 1940's style floral dress, I could see the bones of a corset through the material. Her old face beamed at me.

'Ah, there you are, Jackie,' she exclaimed. 'We've been expecting you.' She introduced herself and reassured my mother that she would keep an eye on me. Mummy's sad face brightened at this promise, eliciting a parting smile as she followed Reg downstairs.

Then the full impact of their departure hit me. I was delighted at the prospect of living by myself, earning a salary and standing on my own two feet. At the same time, the confidence of youth struggled against the nagging self-doubt of my abilities to hold down the position of trainee receptionist and fit into the demands of hotel life. Alone in my new surroundings, I unpacked and stowed everything away.

Excitement prevented sleep at the end of such a significant day, my mind preoccupied with thoughts of new responsibilities, new people, new situations. Charles would also be there to share my experiences when he came to take me out. Different sounds filled my head as I lay in my strange bed; the creak of floorboards in the corridor, a car's wheels driving over gravel, the hoot of an owl. Everything felt right. The room put its arms around me and finally I closed my eyes.

The month I joined the staff, the Cold War was in its twelfth year. Military and political tensions between the Western and Eastern Bloc countries continued to mount. At the American National Exhibition in Sokolniki Park, Moscow, Richard Nixon, Vice-President of the United States of America met Nikita Khrushchev, the Soviet premier. The two politicians squared up beside a display of a modern American kitchen, the discussion becoming known as The Kitchen Debate. Through interpreters, they argued over the merits of capitalism and communism, a million miles away from my new world.

In the kitchen of Great Fosters, there was no debate that chef was king. I was introduced to him on my first day. Not long after my arrival, one of the waiters, Frank, collided with me coming through the same side of the kitchen swing doors. He was carrying a jug of boiling water, which accidentally spilt over my right arm.

'Look where you are going! You're on the wrong side of the passage,' he shouted, furious.

I had so much to grasp in that alien environment. The Portuguese couple on duty in the Still Room poured cold water over the burn and covered the area with mixture of egg white and olive oil, followed by a bandage. Thanks to their kindness and prompt action I was not left with a scar. Other employees also played an important role in expanding my experience, as I learnt how to interact with them and deal with the clientele. I discovered a world beyond home and the convent. I learned to fit in, grateful to most of them for their company.

My first weeks at the hotel were a source of wonder and

discovery. Great Fosters, the hunting lodge of Henry VIII, had retained its architectural façade. The interior, furnished with tapestries and old oak furniture, smelled of beeswax and antiquity. The ambiance and opulence of the hotel attracted famous actors who stayed there during their latest productions at Shepperton and Pinewood studios. Hidden between the tooled leather covers of the visitors' book, a long list of glamorous people's names awaited to impress me.

Mrs. Ghost, Miss Cox and I staffed reception. Mrs. Ghost's name fitted into the history of the house as a benign phantom was said to have haunted the property for a hundred years. The present Mrs. Ghost, the head receptionist, was a middle-aged woman with wispy hair who enjoyed being in charge. She had an odd habit of talking to people without making eye contact, her sight always trained about six inches to her left, which I found disconcerting.

Miss Cox lived on the top floor at the hotel and suffered from arthritis. Her gnarled hands had long red painted nails that clattered on the typewriter. She seemed ancient to me, and chain-smoked Players cigarettes, filling the office with pungent smoke.

I had been working for about a week, coming to grips with the flashing switchboard and typing menus, when I noticed an old man with a white beard in the gardens outside the reception office. He came up to the open window, peered in and saw me.

'Ah, so you're the new girl. Put £50 on my bill for the staff, Mrs. Ghost,' he instructed.

'Thank you, Mr. de Vere,' she replied with that special smile she reserved for important guests, looking six inches to her left.

'M' dear,' he addressed me, 'I need you to find my shoes. I think I left them at the Ritz in Paris last week. Get on to them and find out, will you?'

This delightful, eccentric man was a multimillionaire but dressed like a tramp. It was his plimsolls that he had mislaid and here I was, phoning the Ritz hotel in my best O Level French, trying to locate them. My oral exam syllabus at the convent had not covered this particular lesson. My encounter with Mr. de Vere taught me not to judge people by their appearance. In this grown up world I had much to learn. I had swopped the restrictions of home and school for the disciplines required of a trainee receptionist and had to succeed. There was no going back.

Miss Violet handed me my first wage packet, three crisp green pound notes nestled together inside the envelope. But then adult responsibility weighed in when Miss Violet suggested that perhaps I would like to open a savings account. Adulthood came with its downsides and, reluctantly, I agreed to put away seven shillings and sixpence a week. I wanted immediately to rush out and blow the rest of my wages on something frivolous, but the opportunity didn't arise for weeks because of my working hours and limited transport. At times the hotel seemed like an island, inhabited by strange people, claustrophobic and cut off from the outside world. It became essential that I made sorties to the mainland of reality, enabling me to appreciate the insular but stimulating life the hotel offered.

Finally, one Thursday, I was able to take the bus to Staines. High Street window displays beckoned, encouraging me to part with the notes in my wallet, but I resisted until in a dress shop, where I saw the fashion statement of that year: a bright orange duster coat. The temptation was irresistible. What a pleasure to twirl in front of the shop mirror, feeling that I looked 'cool', although the coat cost three pounds ten shillings – a fortune. I didn't care and handed over my hard-earned cash. I couldn't wait to show Mummy, hoping she would approve of my spontaneity and not reprimand me for squandering my wages.

The following Friday I travelled home for the weekend on the late afternoon train, needing to reassure myself that Mummy was coping without me. Opposite me in the carriage was a man who, I imagined from the cut of his expensive suit, worked in the City. He had been glancing my way since I boarded the train at Egham. I avoided his gaze, mindful of not talking to strangers. Just before Bagshot station he stood up, took his briefcase from the rack above, and said in a clipped, posh voice, 'Thank you for brightening up my evening.'

I blushed, my red cheeks clashing with my orange coat.

My first visit home made me realise how my perception of Reg had changed. Now independent and away from his scrutiny, I saw him for what he was, a pathetic man. There must have been less conflict in the house after I left home, although my brother still had problems. He was playing truant from school, a sure sign of unhappiness, which he bottled up. Only later would his emotions explode after a life-changing event.

Mummy had found solace in dressmaking and growing her roses. She was delighted to see me, to hear my news and smiled when she saw my orange acquisition. I returned to work thinking about her. She hadn't seemed her usual bright self. I didn't know when next I would see her, my visits infrequent because I had no transport. The bus journey to Egham, train to Camberley, and walk up the hill took precious free time. I wrote to her and Charles drove me to see her whenever he could borrow the family car and his busy schedule at Sandhurst allowed.

On other occasions Charles would take me out for a drink and pork pie at the Foresters Arms in Bagshot. A meeting place for his fellow cadets, it was a lively pub that I always enjoyed visiting. The walls were decorated with a curious necktie collection, all bearing different logos and patterns. The last six inches were cut off and pinned up as trophies. The star attraction for the cadets was the publican's wife, a pretty French woman, who loved the attention of young men, expertly whisking up soufflé omelettes to order, to help satisfy their hunger.

Charles also took me to the newly opened Wimpy bar in Staines, an innovative introduction to fast food. The plastic interior did not offer the cosiness of the pub but was something to discover, a different experience. Little did I realise that this was the beginning of a fast food revolution that would expand throughout my lifetime. Afterwards, replete on American-style burger and chips, and having a limited budget, we returned to my room. My resistance to his advances was getting low; especially now we had a place to be alone.

I wouldn't recommend losing your virginity in an Austin A30, unless you are a contortionist or a dwarf. Charles had taken me out for a drink to celebrate my eighteenth birthday and, on the way back to the hotel, he parked in a little lane and switched off the engine. It was a dark night. Nobody was about. Foreplay had been practised for months and Charles skilfully knew his way around my anatomy. The receptors in my brain would light up like an exploding star and my body responded to his touch. But Mother Mostyn and the threatened consequences of mortal sins had kept me fearful, never mind the thought of getting pregnant and the disgrace. In 1959, the pill had not arrived on the scene and family planning, as such, was only available to married women.

'What are you worried about?' he asked, holding me in his arms. 'I am prepared, look I'll show you.'

He disentangled himself, took out his wallet and produced a packet of Durex. It could have been more romantic but, alone in his car and urged on by a mutual desire, I knew it had to be then. To make things worse I got cramp in my leg at the critical moment of passion, just as a couple walked by the car with a dog. It was, literally, a case of *coitus interruptus.*

From then on, Charles began to stay the night whenever he could. He had to return to Sandhurst before first parade and sneak in the back way of the College to avoid being discovered AWOL (absent without leave), which would have resulted in loss of privileges, a fine, or even dismissal. To leave my room in the coach house undetected was difficult due to the creaking main door, and he would creep down the stairs in his socks. Once in the moonlight, he would replace his shoes and tiptoe to his parked car. There was no chance of disguising the noise of the engine starting up. Although I felt grown up with this new physical relationship, which was fun and filled a need in both of us, Charles had not completely bowled me over and I secretly yearned for a man who would. Charles was attentive and caring but conservative in his dress and manner, and he expected me to share his ideals. My rebellious spirit craved something more, but he represented my escape route from the hotel.

The equilibrium of my life had been established: I was working in a prestigious hotel where I enjoyed meeting film stars and, after hours, I would go out with Charles. I have since learnt that everything is impermanent, never more so than in the spring of 1960 when my mother became seriously ill. I knew she hadn't been feeling well, but when Reg blurted out that she had cancer and only six months to live, the news came as a great shock. His lack of compassion and coldness made me depend more on Charles for support. He took me to St Luke's Hospital in Guildford where I found her lying, gaunt and pale, in bed. Cut adrift from us, she was isolated in a world of suffering. The cloying smell of disinfectant permeated the ward. She opened her eyes as if she knew I was there and smiled. Pain flitted across her gentle face and she shifted a little between the sheets, trying to find a comfortable position.

My heart ached. I couldn't speak but wanting to say how much I loved her. Did she know she was going to die?

The grapes I had bought seemed an insignificant present to thank her for all the years of dedication, nursing me through childhood illness, encouraging me to write poems like my father and to be brave, to believe in myself. I held her hand while she drifted in and out of drugged sleep, desperately willing her to be well.

At this critical time Ross, aged sixteen, ran away from home.

His emotions shredded, alone with Reg, he could no longer bear the brunt of his scorn and ridicule. Ross took off on his bike, headed to Aldershot, found the first recruiting office and asked to become a boy soldier. The recruiting officer issued him the forms to join the Royal Army Service Corps Junior Leaders. Needing the consent of a parent, he took the forms back to Reg and demanded his signature. I don't know what transpired between them but Reg gave his consent. Ironically, he was not his guardian. Reg had never legally applied to be our stepfather.

My poor mother was distraught when she learnt that Ross was no longer at the Silesian College but a boy soldier. Despite all the odds, she recovered from the operation, enduring a gruelling course of radiotherapy before convalescing in a nursing home near Ewhurst, Surrey. Charles took me to see her and I shall always remember his kindness.

Mummy returned home a month later, having made a remarkable recovery. Her friend, Jane, became a constant companion, helping the healing process and allowing me to continue my freedom at the hotel. The cancer remained in remission for another forty-six years, a tribute to my mother's indomitable spirit and the skill of her surgeon.

CHAPTER 4

THE NIGHT PORTER

After ten months of enjoying independence, I arrived at eight for work to find Mrs. Adams, the housekeeper, whispering to Mrs. Ghost.

'Well, he's gone and done it this time,' I overheard her say, 'good and proper. I told him he should ease up on the whisky.'

They heard me approach and stopped talking.

'Oh, there you are, Jackie,' said Mrs. Ghost. 'Mr. Rosewell wants you to type some letters straightaway.'

I knocked on the manager's door and entered on his command, wondering what was so urgent.

'Miss Pearce, I'm going to the Labour Exchange in half an hour and I need these to be ready,' he said, giving me his drafts.

I returned to reception, to the big heavy Olivetti typewriter, and started to bash out letters about a vacancy for a night porter at a four-star hotel!

'What's happened to Mac?' I asked Mrs. Ghost.

'This morning at three o'clock he sounded the fire alarm and, as the guests came out of their rooms, he sprayed them from head to foot in foam from the fire hydrant.'

'Oh goodness!' I said, imagining the hotel guests in wet dressing gowns, nighties and pyjamas – or maybe even naked. They had not been amused by the false alarm, especially the ones parading as Mr. and Mrs. Smith. We hosted a number of these couples during the time I worked as a receptionist, who needed evidence for divorce proceedings. One of the ploys was to ring for the night porter on some pretext so he would arrive to find them in bed together.

The only fire burning that early morning was in poor Mac's leg. He had been an infantry soldier during the war and had sustained a shrapnel injury that continued to bother him. His usual nip of whisky hadn't been enough to extinguish the pain. I imagine that the loneliness of his job and his suffering became too much. He never spoke of a family. He left after breakfast with his old kitbag, suitcase and a hangover, a sorry end to a brave man.

The hotel struggled for two weeks without a night porter, a great worry for the manager, as one of the four-star ratings was for twenty-four-hour service. The post was advertised in papers, catering magazines and at the Labour Exchange. It was nearly high season and most skilled hotel staff looking for work had already found positions. A fortnight later, on a Tuesday afternoon, I was alone on duty when a tall, lanky man in his thirties appeared at Reception.

'I wish to speak to the manager,' he said, staring at me with his bulging, grey eyes.

'What's it about, Sir?' I queried.

'The job advertised for a night porter.'

'Your name, please?' I asked.

'Johnson,' he replied.

'Just a moment Mr. Johnson,' I said, plugging into Mr. Rosewell's extension.

'Send him straight in,' his familiar voice boomed.

Not a quarter of an hour had passed before Mr. Rosewell and the lanky man came out of the office.

'Miss Pearce, this is our new night porter.'

My reaction was one of incredulity because Johnson's demeanour was odd, not like the other staff, and he'd been hired on the spot. I saw him occasionally around the hotel and at the end of a late duty. He wasn't very communicative, generally limiting himself to a gruff good morning or goodnight. His eyes, though, were unforgettable. Three weeks later, on the Friday morning, following his day off, we received a telegram.

'Fallen down stairs and broken leg. Johnson.'

He never returned.

* * *

My job offered good prospects. The last trainee receptionist had qualified and found a post at a luxury hotel in the Bahamas. I sat alone in reception dreaming of such an adventure. The switchboard was silent; the only sound the ticking of the wall clock. Two hours and seventeen minutes remained before I could go off duty. A summer breeze wafted through the open window with a faint scent of roses and mown grass. I sighed and focussed again on adding up the luncheon takings.

'Afternoon, Miss,' said a male voice.

Distracted, I looked up from my task. Two men wearing dark suits stood in front of me, their footfalls silenced by the thick carpet runner. The older man had a harsh, unsmiling face, not the usual countenance of a visitor.

'We'd like to speak to your manager,' he said with authority.

Thirteen pounds carry sixpence I calculated, scribbling the numbers on a piece of paper. I put down my pen and gave him my full attention. He was about forty years old with Brylcreemed hair and gave off the aroma of tobacco mixed with Pear's soap.

'I'm afraid Mr. Rosewell isn't in today, Sir, can I help you?'

He pulled out a warrant card from the inside pocket of his jacket, which he held up for inspection.

Surrey Constabulary Police
Detective Inspector James Armstrong Maddox.

Suddenly alert, I studied the identity photograph to compare him to his physical likeness. He appeared older than the monochrome picture. His stern, unforgiving attitude fazed me. Foreboding and a sense of urgency replaced the boredom of my afternoon.

'Is there anyone else we can talk to about your night porter?' he asked.

A series of scenarios flashed through my mind about Johnson. Was he hurt? I saw him lying in a road, victim of a traffic accident. Or was he responsible for a crime? In the next scene he was in a police cell.

'No, Sir, there's nobody here until five,' I replied. 'What's it about?'

His eyebrows arched in surprise, perhaps at my age, an eighteen-year-old girl in charge of a four-star hotel. A guest walked passed reception with a newspaper under his arm, heading for the terrace.

'All right,' the policeman said after a pause, not giving anything away. 'Can we go somewhere private to talk?'

I hesitated. What to do next? My post as junior receptionist was to stay on duty until Mrs. Ghost returned.

'We can go to the accountant's office. She's not in today,' I suggested.

My hand shook as I shut the daybook, apprehensive of the interview. I left reception and the detectives followed me down the corridor.

The empty office was hot and stuffy, sunshine slanting through the mullioned windows fell in diamond patterns on the oak floor. DI Maddox asked me my name. I faltered with the formality, recovered, and his young colleague began to make notes. The detective inspector took out a leather album from his briefcase and placed it on Miss Violet's desk. Mug shots of criminals stared up at me from the open pages.

'So, Miss Pearce,' he said, 'do you recognise your Night Porter?'

I scanned the gallery of faces: sombre, grim, arrogant, mean and just plain scary.

'Yes!' I exclaimed, pointing at a photo. 'Here he is!'

Johnson glowered at me with those unmistakable, buggy eyes.

'What's he done?' I blurted out, without thinking.

'We are conducting a murder enquiry. Johnson is a suspect,' DI Maddox announced. 'How long did he work here? Do you have his address or any idea of his whereabouts?'

Unprepared for this revelation, I gasped, waiting for my brain to catch up.

'He was here for about three weeks. No, Mr. Rosewell keeps the staff records. I don't know where Johnson is now. Wait a moment,' I said, gathering my thoughts. 'We received a telegram last week saying he'd broken a leg.'

'Tell your manager to phone me,' said DI Maddox.

He handed me a printed visiting card. A frisson of fear enveloped me as I held his intimidating gaze. He represented the authority I couldn't escape.

'We've tracked him here and we'll find him,' the Inspector said with determination. He snapped the album shut and returned it to his briefcase. The policemen offered no further information, increasing my curiosity and uneasiness. Who was dead? How did they die? What had been the motive? I had experienced some weird and surprising moments since leaving home and starting work, not least of all sexual harassment, but working with a suspected murderer went straight to the top of the list. My instincts about his strangeness had been right, but I was shaken by this knowledge.

The two detectives hurried off on their mission. But where was Johnson? My lurid imagination had him hiding behind every doorway. I shivered despite the heat of the day and returned with trepidation to the unattended flashing switchboard in reception.

Mr. Rosewell and Mrs. Ghost were shocked when I revealed what had happened during their absence. Mr. Rosewell blanched when I gave him DI Maddox's card. Perhaps he was regretting the decision he had made hiring Johnson. Mrs. Ghost had one of her 'turns' and had to sit down.

'My goodness,' she puffed, 'and he seemed such a nice chap.'

Not long afterwards we were to learn the gruesome details.

Once again, we were without a night porter. Mr. Carl was appointed not long afterwards. He came with a long list of recommendations and, reputedly, had worked at the Ritz Hotel in London. He was polite and discreet, which appealed to the clientele. No alarm bells went off in my head this time but he did surprise me slightly when he arrived. He was completely bald, an unusual style in 1960. Yul Brynner, the actor, was only just making a name for himself. He had shaved his head especially for his role as the king in the musical *The King and I*, in which he starred with the famous actress, Deborah Kerr. Yul Brynner was to become the iconic attractive bald man. Carl, however, was not quite in his league.

CHAPTER 5

STALKED

The Prime Minster, Harold Macmillan, took the salute for the passing out parade for the successful cadets at the Royal Military Academy in July. Charles's proud parents sat beside me watching the ceremony. I searched for Charles among rows of cadets as they marched passed and found him beside Mike. Both looked splendid in their uniforms, the sun bouncing off their polished rifle butts and highly glossed shoes. Yet again, my mother had created a new dress for me, light and summery, perfect for the day, and a wide brimmed hat shielded my eyes from the glare. All the invited guests wore their finery; ladies sporting elaborate outfits and gentleman attired in tailored suits or uniform. At the end of the ceremony, the Adjutant rode his grey horse up the steps of Old College, a custom that had been carried out for years. It was a thrill to watch. Afterwards, we gathered for cocktails with the graduating cadets in the Indian Army Memorial Room, where regimental crests and portraits hung from the walls and silver trophies lay protected behind glass, memorabilia of the British Indian Army. Fathers congratulated sons and mothers dabbed their eyes. The energy was palpable and chattering voices made it hard to hear any conversation. The young men were in high spirits; at the stroke of midnight their army careers would commence as commissioned officers in their chosen regiments. A surge of patriotism filled me, admiration for Charles and his success. Absorbing the atmosphere in such an illustrious room, I felt honoured to be there.

Charles was posted to Blackdown Camp, near Camberley. I asked for my two weeks holiday to coincide with his summer leave and we travelled to Devon to visit Frances and her parents. I was welcomed like a returning prodigal daughter with hugs and kisses. Freddie shook Charles's hand and Frances gave him one of her long appraising looks. Everyone was polite, perhaps too polite, and I began to sense that the family was not that impressed by him. Bubbles had discreetly considered the morality of our relationship and its propriety. She allocated separate rooms, side by side, with a shared bathroom on the first floor of the split-level farmhouse, the perfect compromise.

I searched for Frances after unpacking and found her with Tom in the garden.

'Is he really your boyfriend?' asked Tom. 'Does he sail and play cricket?'

Tom was practicing his strokes with a cricket bat.

'Yes, Tom he is,' I replied. 'You'll have to ask him about all the sport he plays.'

He wandered off towards the house, clutching his bit of willow, to look for Charles.

'I've got this holiday placement the day after tomorrow, miles away in Somerset,' said Frances. 'Sorry I won't see much of you this time.'

Cooking was Frances's passion, a gene she must have inherited from her mother. A student at one of the top catering colleges, she was off to a luxury hotel for a spell in the kitchens.

'The trouble is, I only get a fortnight's annual holiday so I won't be able to come down again this year,' I said.

'It's a pity,' she agreed. 'I hadn't thought about holidays. I suppose I'll get the same when I start work. How are you finding your job?'

'It's not bad, but shift work is difficult. Great Fosters is a bit isolated and the bus service is erratic. I hardly go anywhere or see anybody when I'm off duty,' I replied. 'At least I have Charles. I'd go crazy otherwise. Anyway, I'm thinking of looking for a different career, especially after the night porter incident. We still don't know if he's been caught.'

'Hope I don't experience anything like that. He sounded

scary,' she said.

'What do you think of Charles?' I asked her, deciding on a direct approach.

'He's ok I suppose, not someone I'd have thought you'd end up with,' she said, with candour. 'Are you serious about him?'

'I have never really thought about it. I suppose I might marry him. I've started my bottom drawer, encouraged by Grandma,' I admitted. The term given to the collection of linen, china and silver items brides accumulated in preparation for their new homes.

My family expected me to marry and I had played along, although Charles might not be my groom. My grandmothers and my mother had been young brides, Nanny Rose, the youngest, my own age. All of them became young widows too. A sobering thought. Frances laughed at my serious face.

'We're only eighteen, Jackie. Live it up a bit before you commit yourself to one man!'

'Chance would be a fine thing!' I remarked. 'Besides, there's nobody at the hotel I'd ever consider going out with.'

'I've yet to find someone I like,' she moaned. 'You know you're welcome here with Charles, as long as you want to stay.'

It was good to confide in my friend. I smiled and thanked her.

'We have to return in a few days because Charles reports to his new unit. I bet he is feeling nervous,' I said. 'I'm going to visit Mummy. She's made a remarkable recovery you know. I'm so proud of her.'

The stay at New Barn Farm had been enjoyable, seeing my adopted family, but a sense of unease had undermined our stay. Charles had not been the success I had imagined, and I had desperately wanted Uncle Freddie's approval. The farmhouse receded in the rear mirror of the Austin A30. Charles took one hand off the steering wheel, placing it on my knee.

'I'll be over to see you the minute I can get away from camp,' he said with a grin.

It was clear what he had in mind: we had been celibate during our stay at New Barn Farm.

Well, almost.

* * *

'Why can't you come to the dance?' asked Charles.

'I am on late shift that night and Mrs. Ghost won't change with me,' I replied, filled with disappointment.

I'd been at Great Fosters for over a year, now confident in my role as receptionist and accounts/wages clerk. But how I envied friends who had jobs from nine-to-five and were off enjoying evenings dancing and going to the cinema, while I was stuck behind the desk in reception. The incident with the detectives had shaken me, another reason to consider a different career. It was time for a change. Perhaps hotel life was not for me. It was insular, as I'd told Frances, with no chance of meeting anyone apart from the staff, and I didn't have much in common with them. I hoped she'd have better luck in her placement. I was the only female under forty-five on the hotel staff and received a fair amount of unwanted attention from some of the male employees and hotel guests. Sexual harassment was common then and, although I had learnt to cope with my stepfather, it was harder to deal with in the workplace where men seemed to desire a reputation of their sexual prowess.

I remember Frank, one of the older waiters, who wrote me notes written in red biro with explicit descriptions of the sexual fantasies he had about me. He deliberately threw these 'billets doux,' as he called them, onto the reception counter. I had to scoop them up quickly before either Mrs. Ghost or Miss Cox found them and had heart attacks. These notes were baffling at first because I hadn't come across such crude terminology before.

In the staff quarters at Great Fosters I shared a bathroom. An old cast iron white bath skulked in a corner with a geyser above it, which belched out hot water to about the depth of an inch before it ran cold. It wasn't a pleasure staying in the tub for long with a scant amount of tepid water. One afternoon, while the others were on duty, I quickly washed and stepped out, wrapped myself in a towel, collected my belongings and walked barefoot to my room. I opened my door and there was Frank! All I had between us was a thin towel. My mind went blank with horror.

'What are you doing here?' I gasped, clutching the towel tighter around me.

'I came to see if you would like me to show you a thing or two,' he replied, gleeful at finding me in such a predicament.

'I should warn you, Frank, that my boyfriend will be here any minute, so I would clear off if I were you.'

My mind was numb with fear. I tried not to show it but my fingers trembled. I was alone and vulnerable. The sound of a car's engine broke the tense atmosphere.

'That's probably him now. You know he's a black belt in Judo,' I lied.

He glanced out of the window and laughed.

'It's only the afternoon post van,' he smiled and sat down on my bed.

Somehow I managed to find the inner strength to overcome my escalating fear and persuaded him to leave but it took another ten minutes. What a relief when I was able to shut the door behind him, but not before he had described some of his disgusting sexual habits with a rubber water bottle. After he left, I started to shake with cold induced by the terrifying thoughts of potentially being raped.

Frank continued to stalk me when he was off duty. He would throw tennis balls up at my window and keep watch on my movements. After the bath towel incident, I realised he was all talk and no danger. I simply ignored him, even when he followed me. It never occurred to me to report him. It would have been his word against mine. Sexual harassment in the work place was accepted in 1960. Women did not complain, knowing they would be judged for 'leading men on'.

One afternoon I took an incoming call from a Mrs. Cummins who wished to book a double room for five nights. I reserved room twelve for the following day. There was nothing unusual about the call so, two days later on the early shift, I was surprised to hear from the housekeeper that there must be a honeymoon couple in room twelve. My awareness of the complexities of sexual relationships certainly developed that summer.

'They make enough noise,' she said laughing.

The day before, when I wasn't on duty, Mrs. Ghost had booked Mrs. Cummins in with her companion, a woman. Mrs. Ghost's eyebrows shot up,

'Oh!' she said.

Sam, the barman, appeared at reception a couple of afternoons later to have a word with her. He was a character and well liked. I can't say the same about his assistant, spotty Brian, who made eyes at me and sulked when I rejected his advances.

'That Mrs. Cummins is running up a big bar bill. She comes in with her friend every evening and they down several Pernod cocktails. Got a bad feeling about those two,' Sam said.

Not long afterwards, I was in Miss Violet's office preparing the wages for the staff when I sensed someone looking at me. The hairs on the back of my neck were my antennae. A tall, middle-aged woman was staring through the glass panes in the door. Her eyes fixed on me. I shivered and the same feeling engulfed me as on the day the boys chased me home from school. Alarm bells went off in my head and I picked up the phone to break the intensity of her malevolent gaze.

'Mrs. Ghost, I need the daybook to check some figures. Is Miss Cox free to bring it down? I'm in the middle of doing the wages and can't leave the office.' My heart thumped as I replaced the receiver. To my relief, when I looked again, the woman had gone.

Miss Cox arrived with the daybook.

'Oh thank you,' I said to her. 'I'm sorry I couldn't come myself. Did you pass a tall woman in the corridor?'

'That's all right, Jackie,' she said, handing over the large accounts book. 'Yes, that was Mrs. Cummins.'

Why wasn't I surprised?

Carl, the new night porter, was still in the hotel at eight thirty when I came on duty a few mornings later. He was talking in lowered tones to the Manager, their conversation intense. I had just settled down for the day's tasks when Carl appeared at the desk.

'Have you heard, Miss?' he said with a wry smile.

'No, Carl, what about?'

'Those two lesbians in room twelve tried to do a runner in the night.'

'What?' I cried.

I had never met a lesbian before. Homosexuality was still taboo, for men a criminal offence punishable with imprisonment. An Act of Parliament decriminalising homosexuality between consenting men having reached the age of twenty-one would not be passed until 1967. I was naive, unaware of their practise and predilection for their own sex. To compound the scandal, the fact that the women had tried to abscond was shocking.

Carl had apprehended them and called the police. Mrs. Cummins and friend had been enjoying the free hospitality of hotels in the South of England evading being caught during moonlight flitting. Until now. There was a court hearing a few months later, which led to a conviction. Mrs. Ghost went as a witness. Disappointingly, the manager said I was too young to attend.

* * *

On a sunny afternoon in August, outside on the terrace overlooking the topiary gardens, tables and chairs had been set up for tea. I could see the guests through the reception window where I was alone preparing the bills. Frank came in to report that amongst them was a famous London hairdresser with a party of friends.

'Table five, tea for four people,' said Frank. 'Can you destroy that one, Miss?

'Why?' I asked in all innocence, wondering what was wrong with my billing.

'There will be something in it for you if you do,' he winked at me.

This was the first time that I had been asked to take part in anything dishonest and I was taken aback.

'Definitely not, Frank,' I refused, nuns' voices warning of breaking the eighth commandment echoing in my head. Bills were normally paid in cash, offering a little supplement to the waiters' earnings if the receptionist was in agreement with the scam. Frank looked disgruntled. Next time he came for a bill, I made sure I had all the duplicate copies. He gave me a mocking smile and threw down one of his revolting billet doux. It was the last straw. The time to change course had arrived. I needed to step outside Frank's world of harassment and the risk of rubbing shoulders with the likes of Johnson, the infamous night porter.

Gossip had filtered through about his capture and life of crime. Allegedly, Johnson had been living in boarding houses on the South coast. An opportunist, he thieved where he could. His landlady had caught him stealing money and had died from her injuries as a result of his violent attack. When he'd been apprehended, I hoped it was DI Maddox who had arrested him.

My God, I thought, *fancy working with a murderer*! I shuddered when I imagined what he could have done on those dark nights when I closed up reception. We were entirely alone downstairs in that old haunted house.

'So what will you do?' asked my friend, Christine, on the phone.

She was a secretary in London and one of my friends from the Convent, a lovely girl with an amazing infectious laugh. We used to collapse giggling in the library at school and Mother Mostyn would send us out in disgrace.

'Oh Chris, I don't know, but I've had enough here. I told you about the night porter, didn't I?'

'Crikey, I'd forgotten about him. Has he been caught?' she asked.

'Apparently,' I replied. 'I heard about the outcome from Mrs. Ghost. I wonder if he'll hang after the trial? You know it was a perfect cover for him to work as a night porter while he was on the run.'

'Gives me goose bumps just thinking about it, Jackie. You had a narrow escape there,' she said.

'Yes, it is an experience I don't wish to repeat,' I agreed. 'Trouble is, I can't go back home because of my stepfather, so I must find a job where I have board and lodgings.'

Chris knew about my loathing of Reg. She didn't like him either. It was only later that I learnt Reg was guilty of stalking her in London, whenever he was there 'on business', hanging around outside her place of work. Chris thought about my options.

'So that's teacher training college, nursing or the armed forces,' she deduced.

Nursing was not for me and I didn't want to be a teacher. I'd lived in Camberley since I was thirteen; retired Brigadiers and Generals surrounded us. Charles was newly commissioned, it seemed a natural step I should join up.

'I'll let you know, Chris. See you soon, when I can get some time off!'

I was in Miss Violet's office checking the previous day's accounts. Miss Violet was ensconced in her room, listening to the two thirty horseracing event at Lingfield on her wireless. Last year, when I had arrived fresh from school, she had taken me under her wing. I was quick to learn the double entry system of accounting and how to prepare the staff wage packets before they were handed out on Fridays. Miss Violet now counted on my abilities and I spent more time in her office, giving access to a telephone.

Suddenly I felt quite alone. The call from Chris had come through the switchboard in reception. I hoped no one had been listening. It was then that I made the decision, which was to alter my life, to try for a commission in the Women's Royal Army Corps. I found a WRAC recruiting office listed in the Telephone Directory, the address in Whitehall, London. *Here goes*, I thought, and picked up the phone again.

'Outside line please, Mrs. Ghost.'

CHAPTER 6

RECRUITMENT

Captain Patterson WRAC sat opposite me at the Whitehall Recruiting Office filling in my application form. I could see why she had been picked to be a Recruiting Officer; expertly groomed, feminine in her khaki uniform, composed and poised.

'Well, your education qualifications are in order and you've no police record,' she said with a hint of a smile.

I welcomed the positive start to a half an hour interview and afterwards, in another part of the building, I underwent a 'Medical', which caused a few blushes. I'd not had one before and the examining doctor was a young, handsome Royal Medical Corps Officer.

'I am pleased to say that you've passed your assessment,' said Captain Patterson when I returned to her office. 'If you wish to continue with your application you must sign these,' she said, placing a pile of forms in front of me.

The delight of success replaced the doubts I had of failing the requirements to join HM Forces. Now, I'd a chance to change direction, the perfect answer to fulfilling my dreams of adventure. *No going back*, I thought, as I completed my last signature.

'You'll be contacted shortly for your interview with a senior WRAC officer,' Captain Patterson said, and I left her office feeling a little daunted by the prospect.

Three weeks after meeting Captain Patterson, I had an appointment with Colonel Rivett-Drake, Deputy Director WRAC at Hounslow Barracks, the last hurdle to overcome before I could go to the Regular Commissions Board at Westbury. I produced my letter at the guardroom and was shown to a building overlooking the parade ground.

The corporal led the way along a corridor and knocked on a door. Inside the large office, the Deputy Director WRAC sat behind a wooden desk, and beyond through the window I could see the empty square.

'Miss Skingley-Pearce, Ma'am,' said my escort, before retiring.

After formal greetings, I was invited to sit down. The senior officer was a formidable lady wearing an air of authority. Badges of rank bristled on her khaki uniform and I doubted that she suffered time wasters.

'Why do you want to join the WRAC?' asked the colonel.

I mentioned a sense of purpose, a career with prospects and the chance to serve my country. The interview concluded with questions about art and literature. She asked me what books I had read. I wasn't going to say *Forever Amber*, the red-hot, bed-hopping novel by Kathleen Windsor that all the girls wanted to read. Instead, we discussed one of Laurence Durrell's books in the *Alexandria Quartet* series that Mummy had lent me. On the subject of art, she was slightly taken aback when I said that I loved Pablo Picasso's work. Under the careful eye of my art teacher at Farnborough Hill, I had been encouraged to take A Level Art in a year. An inspiration, she taught me to appreciate modern painters such as Picasso and Braque.

The senior officer wrote notes, and I wondered if I'd said too much.

'Thank you, Miss Skingley-Pearce,' she said, not giving anything away. 'You'll hear from me very soon. Good afternoon.'

I was dismissed.

Now all I could do was wait.

* * *

At Great Fosters, a new receptionist arrived to replace Miss Cox who had succumbed to her degenerating arthritis and left to live with her sister in Cornwall. The replacement was a pretty blonde girl in her early twenties. Nobody knew, except me, that she was receiving treatment for drug addiction. It was for this reason that she had applied for the job, to be near the rehabilitation centre. My experiences at the hotel had expanded my understanding of the complexities of human nature, knowledge which would help me later on, but nothing prepared me for her story. Sex and drugs were responsible for her hell, encouraged by the fast set she knew in London. I couldn't begin to imagine the situations she described. I admired her courage and determination to regain her health and life. I hoped she would succeed and that Frank wouldn't pester her. She and I had made decisions to change our environment and to search for a better future. I could wait no longer to start the process and wrote my letter of resignation.

The weekend of my departure, Charles chivalrously came to collect me. Everyone wished me well and Miss Violet gave me the £24 that I had saved up from my meagre weekly earnings, increased from £3 to £4.50. We piled my belongings into Charles's car and for the last time he started the engine outside the staff quarters. I glanced back at the magnificent Tudor house with no regrets. I was no longer the innocent girl who had arrived there fifteen months ago. Now independent, I had a better understanding of the world, both the good and the bad.

'I'll have you home soon,' Charles said as he turned out of the wrought iron gates at the end of the gravel drive.

'Home? I suppose Deramore Cottage is home now,' I acknowledged.

The minute we arrived in the driveway, Mummy stepped out of the French doors and her face lit up. Reg was also there to cast a shadow, interfering and supercilious. I had to leave again as soon as possible. All my hopes were pinned on passing the Regular Commissions Board. My brother had found his role in the army as an air dispatcher and was soon to transfer to the Army Air Corps. Sadly, he wasn't expected home for a while.

'We'll still see each other,' Charles said, handing me a bag.

'There's the annual cocktail party in the Mess next Friday and I've already booked us in. That is, as long as your stepfather has no objections.'

I smiled at him.

'I'd like to see him try,' I declared. 'Thanks, Charlie, I'd love to come.'

* * *

What had I done, resigning my job before I had secured a place at Officer Cadet Wing? For two days I pushed away the worry of unemployment and the possibility of staying at home until I could move on. On the third morning, the postman brought the letter that decided my future. It fell along with others on the mat. The manila envelope stamped OHMS (On Her Majesty's Service) lay face up, willing me to put an end to my misery. I ripped the flap open, daring to hope for a positive outcome. The crested paper looked official, the text encouraging.

'You have been awarded a place on the Regular Commissions Board on Monday 23 to Wednesday 25 October 1960.'

'Yes!' I shouted. My voice rang out in the hallway, ecstatic, all thought of failure erased. I read on. During the course I was to prepare a lecture, a subject of my choice, which would last for five minutes. For a moment I hesitated. The only time I'd performed any public speaking was as a narrator about Our Lady of Fatima in the school play at Farnborough Hill. I remember how nervous I had been, knees knocking and out of breath before I spoke.

'What's happening?' Mummy asked, popping her head round the kitchen door. 'Sounds like you've won the pools!'

'I've got my place at RCB!' I shrieked.

'Darling, that's marvellous,' she said, giving me a hug.

'Look!' I exclaimed, 'and I've been sent a railway warrant to Westbury station. Transport will be there to pick me up on Monday 23rd October. In two weeks' time!'

'I think we should make you a new outfit. You deserve it!' She smiled and her eyes danced. 'We'll go down to Harvey's and have a look at patterns and material.'

We had fun together choosing the fabric. I decided on a suit and found the perfect woollen material in autumn colours. Not content with making a skirt and jacket, Mummy insisted on sewing a blouse to go under it. She picked up a roll of cotton mix print in yellow, brown and black.

'This is the very thing. What d'you think?' she asked. 'And here's the pattern.'

She had been leafing through the iconic Vogue pattern book, taking time to find the finest fashion for me. The blouse was a shirt style with lapels and cuffs. I agreed, fished out some of my savings from my purse and handed it over to the sales girl. I'd come home on the understanding that I was to pay my mother thirty shillings a week for my board and lodgings. This amount had been decided by my stepfather, which no doubt, he pocketed. My savings were dwindling fast.

Mummy sewed every minute she could to finish the outfit on time, kneeling on the lounge floor with her old Singer sewing machine on a low table.

'Why don't you work from the dining room table, Mummy?'

'Oh no, dear, Reg will complain if I make a scratch.'

That man was a monster. My mother had only recently recovered from uterine cancer but her indomitable spirit was undaunted by the experience. She wanted only the best for me and, as money was tight, found all kinds of ways to achieve it. Her friends, impressed by my clothes, soon began to ask Mummy to make garments for them and insisted on paying her. The proceeds were saved and often spent on me. She was always chic and well-groomed and gifted me with her sense of style. Occasionally, rich friends gave her outfits they no longer wore and she transformed these into amazing clothes for herself.

On her birthday, to thank her for everything she did for me, it was a joy to give her something special. Elizabeth Arden had just brought out a new beauty range called *Blue Grass*. I offered her the whole set and she was delighted. I still have the empty round talcum powder box in which she kept some of her costume jewellery once the contents had been used. A faint perfume of citrus and lavender lingers on many years later.

'I'm excited about going to Charles's Mess on Friday,' I said, holding out the pins to her while she fitted my jacket, 'and I can wear the new dress you made me in the summer.' It was exquisite, the best outfit she had sewn for me. A fitted, mink-coloured taffeta dress with a boat shaped neckline, overlaid with a slim three-quarter fine organza dress, which had short sleeves in the same colour. The ensemble was accessorised with a new necklace I had bought.

But what a nightmare it was finding matching shoes – size seven was huge in those days! As luck would have it we found just the pair in 'mushroom,' but they had three-inch heels. Being tall I usually wore lower ones, conscious of my height.

'My goodness, darling,' Mummy said. 'Are you going to manage in those?'

Pointed shoes with stiletto heels were considered sexy and in fashion in 1960. I had to buy them. Years later I regretted wearing winkle picker shoes, they deformed my feet, provoking bunions. Back then I was a victim of fashion, without a care of the cost.

'You look beautiful,' said Charles on Friday evening. 'Have you grown?'

'Not too much,' I laughed, 'it's my new heels.'

He eyed the shoes that made me taller than him.

'Hmm,' he said. 'Nice ankles!'

He looked handsome in Mess dress with gold insignia and badges of rank. I linked arms, feeling the soft material of his red jacket against my bare skin. I shivered in my thin dress and three-quarter sleeved evening coat as he led me to his car.

We had to park a fair way from the Officers' Mess when we

arrived, because of staff cars depositing bigwigs at the entrance. Soldiers in dress uniform waited outside to salute and open the car doors for the senior officers and their ladies. The General of Southern Command and his wife, Lady P., were guests of honour, and everyone was expected to be on their best behaviour. The sergeant at the door gave a smart salute as we entered the Mess.

'Good evening, Sir, good evening, Ma'am,' he said.

No one had ever called me that before. Charles's rank upgraded my status and an unbidden smile played around my lips. A steward stepped forward, took my coat and we turned right into a crowded anteroom where Charles's friends were grouped together. We wove our way towards them.

'Hello, you two,' said Robin, one of the subalterns. 'Jackie, come and meet Graham's girlfriend, Sheila.'

A sweet looking girl held out her hand encased in a long black satin glove.

'How do you do?' she said with the correct formality.

We were the only unmarried girls with six young men. Plenty of wives were to be seen, entertained by the more senior officers. The volume of chatter increased until it became difficult to hear any conversation.

'Champagne, Ma'am?' asked the steward holding a silver tray of sparkling drinks in coupe shaped glasses.

'Thank you,' I said, scooping one up, anticipating the fizzy bubbles and the sophisticated taste of fine wine. Someone passed around fashionable Sobranie Black Russian cigarettes, and we puffed away in a halo of smoke. The young subalterns stiffened as an older officer joined us. He was the colonel of the regiment and seemed keen to check out Sheila and me as suitable girlfriend material for his young officers. He quizzed us but I didn't mention RCB and we were all relieved when he moved off to the other anteroom where all the top brass congregated. My glass never seemed to be empty. An hour had passed and we had only eaten a few scampi and a couple of cocktail sausages.

I suspected that in the room opposite more substantial hors d'oeuvres were served.

'Jackie, could you see what's happened to Sheila? She hasn't come back from the ladies. That was half an hour ago and I'm a bit worried,' said Graham.

I hadn't noticed her absence, instead listening to Robin and Charles talking about the historic launch at Barrow in Furness of HMS Dreadnought, the first nuclear submarine. She was the new deterrent in our arsenal against countries behind the Iron Curtain.

I gave Charles my champagne glass to hold and set off in my high heels. The doors to the Mess were wide open and cold air hit me. I immediately began to feel dizzy as I stepped out into the hallway. Graham had told me to look for the ladies' restroom on the first floor and I noticed the stairs were to my right. Blocking my ascent was a knot of people deep in conversation. One of them, a senior officer covered in gold braid, roared with laughter. His audience joined in his mirth. I didn't think it was funny, as I had to navigate my way around them. A striking arrangement of cut flowers in a silver bowl stood on a table in a recess by the stairs, the top covered in half empty glasses and ashtrays. I had to make a decision. I could either make a detour around the people and go up with the wall on the left-hand side or step off the hall runner and hold on to the banisters on the right-hand side. I was almost there and, choosing the right-hand side, stepped off the carpet. The moment my new shoes hit the polished wooden floor I lost my balance and slid under the table. All the glasses landed in my lap, followed by the flowers, silver and ashtrays. I sat in disbelief on the floor. The chattering stopped and everyone stared.

'Are you all right?' asked the senior officer who came forward with his outstretched hand, others following him. My beautiful dress was ruined and the glasses had shattered, cutting my legs and tearing my stockings.

'Yes, yes, I am ok, thank you,' I lied, mortified about making a fool of myself and wishing I could disappear, wrap myself up in an invisible cloak to hide from the prying eyes. A member of the Mess quickly retrieved the silver as I brushed the flowers and bits of glass off my dress. Several strong men pulled me up. A handkerchief was pushed into my hand to staunch the bleeding on my shin. Stewards already there, cleared up with cloths and dustpans. I grabbed hold of the banisters, blushing like mad and, as quickly as I could, climbed the stairs.

Rushing to the ladies' room, I found a free lavatory and shut the door behind me, shaking with embarrassment and shock. My trembling hands still clutched the bloody handkerchief and my head was spinning. I sat down on the toilet to take stock of the damage. Off came my shoes and ruined stockings. Perhaps my champagne stained dress could be dry-cleaned? What would Mummy say? I was wretched. I pressed the handkerchief over my cuts to wait for the bleeding to stop. After a few minutes, I replaced my shoes, took a deep breath and opened the door to use the washbasin and clean up. There was Sheila.

'Sheila, what happened to you?'

'Oh God,' she said holding her head. 'I've been so sick and I've a headache that's dire. But you've really been in the wars, Jackie!' We weren't alone; a number of military wives were looking the worse for wear.

'I'm not the only one,' I said. 'What's been going on, Sheila?'

'Oh, didn't you realise we've been drinking brandy champagne cocktails!' she announced. No wonder the nickname for this cocktail was Train Smash!

We stayed in the Ladies for another half an hour and finally crept out to see the Charles, Graham and the other subalterns all looking up from the bottom of the stairs with worried faces.

'Oh Charles, I feel dreadful about what happened. I can't ever go back to your Mess,' I said to him on the way home. He pulled the car over into a lay by and turned off the engine.

'Don't worry,' he responded. 'I was going to tell you when you come over to my parents' house for lunch on Sunday but maybe now is a good time. You won't have to go back to my Mess again because I have been posted to Dortmund. I leave in two weeks.'

'Leaving for Germany in two weeks?' I repeated, taken aback by his news.

'Oh God, I'm really going to miss you,' he said, holding me close.

The drive home was surreal, my mind filled with details of the accident, my ruined dress, his news. Jumbled up, they fizzed, like the champagne, in my brain.

'I hope that cut heals quickly,' said Charles when we eventually arrived at Deramore Cottage. 'You're going to Westbury next week and need to be in one piece. The command tasks are very physical.'

He kissed me goodnight and I clambered out of his car, still feeling dizzy. Everything was moving forward so fast, he in one direction and me in another. Fifteen months ago I had left home to work in the hotel, and now I was about to start out again. Of course, I was anxious about the challenges I would have to face, but excited, too, for the potential adventure that lay ahead. Charles would be in Germany, hundreds of miles away.

CHAPTER 7

WESTBURY

The train swayed and clattered over points. Next stop: Westbury. I gazed through the window of the compartment. A white horse, carved into a chalk hill, dominated the surrounding countryside of the Wiltshire Wold, perhaps created to mark a victory, an offering to ancient gods? My victory depended on the outcome of the next three days. A niggling doubt took away my confidence. I would need all my resources. Charles had told me what to expect on the command tasks, my lecture was prepared and I had kept abreast of current affairs. *No point worrying now*, I admonished myself. The train halted. I stood up and pulled down my case from the luggage rack.

Outside the station a group of young women gathered by a parked army bus. I pushed the niggles away, preparing to face the new challenges and, feeling more assured, strode forward to meet them. A man in uniform with two white stripes on his khaki sleeves leant out of the vehicle.

'Leighton House?' asked the corporal as I approached. His eyes swept over me. Did he mark us out of ten? I would be too tall, the story of my life. He asked our names, crossed them off a list and invited us on board. A slim, dark-haired girl climbed up behind me.

'I'm Wendy. Can I join you?'

I moved my handbag, she sat alongside and we settled down for the short ride.

'Hope the Regular Commissions Board isn't going to be too awful,' she said.

Her grey eyes watched for my reaction. Though anxious about the course, I didn't want to show my apprehension.

'What made you decide to try for RCB?' I asked her.

'Dad's in the army,' she replied. 'We had this brilliant WRAC officer who visited my school and talked about her career. I didn't apply after A levels. I wanted a bit of experience first, so worked in a boring office. I couldn't bear it.'

'Sounds a bit like me,' I said, 'except my dad was in the RAF.' I didn't tell her he was killed in the war. 'I live in Camberley, surrounded by the army. I've just resigned my job as a hotel receptionist.'

We laughed. I liked her easy manner and openness. I'd found an ally to share the trials ahead. The bus turned through a set of wide gates onto a long driveway, pulling up in front of an imposing three-storey mansion, built of limestone in the classical style, reminiscent of a Jane Austen country house.

'Gosh!' said Wendy. 'It's quite something.'

It was indeed. How many candidates filled with hope had passed through those portals? This was where I would win or lose. I knew that only a small percentage of candidates were chosen. I remained silent, killing my negative thoughts. We collected our belongings and left the corporal to his empty bus.

In the hallway of Leighton House, a large woman in civilian clothes waited with a clipboard.

'Good morning, ladies, come with me,' she said to her captive audience. 'I'll show you to your accommodation.'

Wendy and I were split up; I was to share a room with a girl called Elaine.

Elaine was shorter than me with an athletic figure. Her wavy light brown hair was cut to flick out around her face. She exuded confidence and her bubbly personality, a sure winner. Although I may have had similar qualities, she had oodles of it and I hoped some of her positivity would rub off on me. She chatted away while I tided my things into drawers. Her father was with the British Forces of the Rhine in Germany. How many more military daughters were on this selection course? By the time we reached the dining room we had become friends.

At lunch we met up with the other thirteen candidates, a mixed bunch of girls. Jo and Shirley the oldest, short service commission applicants from the Territorial Army. To them, we must have appeared a bunch of juvenile schoolgirls. Wendy and her roommate, Helen, came over to say hello. There was an instant rapport between Elaine and Wendy, perhaps because they were army 'brats'. Helen was a civilian's daughter from Suffolk, nothing military about her. She seemed rather reserved and had a way of looking down her nose which made her seem supercilious. I did not warm to her at all.

An introductory talk was scheduled after our meal. We all wanted to know what was expected of us. A uniformed officer arrived. He wore the rank of Lieutenant Colonel and had an air of authority, definitely not someone to cross. In his hand he carried different coloured tabards.

'Good afternoon, ladies,' he said.

We gave him our full attention. He represented the board of army personnel I had to impress and the niggles returned. My future hinged on getting through the assessment.

'I'm the training officer at Westbury,' he continued. 'You're going to be divided into two teams, red and blue. When you hear your name, please come up to collect your number. You're to wear these for the rest of your stay here. It's easier for the examining board to identify you,' he explained.

He recited a breakdown of our forthcoming programme. We were certainly going to be busy. He made us laugh when he said that there were no hidden microphones in the accommodation or Mess. We were too polite to ask if that was true.

Elaine and Wendy were allocated to the red team, Helen and I to the blue team. We were all a bit tense, revealed in the group photograph taken after lunch. Elaine was the only one smiling, proudly wearing a '7'. I was in the front row sitting next to Helen who was sporting '13'. My hands folded in my lap, my ankles crossed, I was wearing the '12' bib over my new suit. My hair looked good, but underneath the curls my face was pensive.

It was a relief to start the selection process. We scribbled away in a classroom, completing an essay on current affairs and general knowledge. It was as if I was back at school and Mother Mostyn hovered over me like a black crow. I knew what she would have written on my end of term report: 'Could do better'.

I raised my head from the test paper. The invigilator, a bespectacled captain in the Education Corps, looked at his watch and tapped his desk.

'Five minutes, ladies,' he said, and we wrote faster.

'Just like A Level exams,' said Wendy on the way back to the Mess.

'I've got writers' cramp,' I remarked.

'How did you get on?' asked Elaine. 'Wasn't that hard was it?'

It was all right for her, some of us lesser mortals had to struggle a bit.

'At least I finished the paper, don't know about my answers though,' I replied.

'Great,' said Wendy, looking at her watch, 'it's nearly tea time and I'm thirsty after all that mental work.'

'Could do with something stronger than tea,' said Helen, keen to join in the conversation. The rest of the candidates collected in groups and we made our way to the Mess.

Over the next days we were to be assessed on our academic, physical and aptitude abilities. Each of us had an interview with three different senior officers. My first one was with a colonel, who reminded me of my Uncle Freddie, a retired brigadier in the Royal Engineers. He too had a florid face and greying moustache and looked like a big teddy bear. I realised I had made a mistake as soon as he opened his mouth. He was more like a grizzly.

'Well, Miss Skingley-Pearce, why have you chosen to become an officer in the WRAC?' he asked, ramrod straight in his chair behind his desk. Eyebrows knitted together, he glowered. Those staring eyes unnerved me. I summoned up a smile and gave him my answer.

'To have a different career, one that offers adventure and a good future, Sir.'

He regarded me for a moment and then made a few brief notes in a file. I hoped it was better than Mother Mostyn's assessment of me.

* * *

'How's it going?' asked Elaine.

Rays of the pale evening sun fell in patches on my bed, broken up by the shadows of moving branches on the trees outside. I opened the gold compact case that Charles had given me.

'They don't give much away do they?' I replied, checking my make-up before snapping the container shut. My appearance mattered, helping to retain a mask of self-confidence.

'We're going to be really tested tomorrow,' she said, looking at her copy of the programme. 'The command tasks are first thing. It'll be awful if it rains.'

'That'll sort us out,' I said and glanced out of the window. The wind had risen, and threatening clouds had gathered to hide the sinking light.

We were not surprised next morning by the leaden sky that promised a damp day. Outside, seven of us in the blue team wore trousers, trying hard to look ready for action. Shirley's face was a picture of misery. In contrast I felt more at ease, thanks to Charles and my prior knowledge of command tasks. But when I saw the large obstacles covered in red paint laid out in front of us, my confidence wavered.

'Number 12, you're in command here. I'll give you three minutes to assess the challenge. In front of you is the Baby River Jordan. You have to get all your team plus equipment over to the other side. All areas marked in red are out of bounds,' ordered the Major appointed our team officer. 'Is that clear?'

'Yes, Sir,' I snapped my reply.

Adrenalin raced through my blood. Why was it that all my life I was the one picked first? Was it because I was always the tallest? Anyway, here I was facing the problem. Two banks of sand bags nine feet apart with vertical poles on either side represented the challenge. I was handed a long wooden plank of six feet, a bucket and some rope.

'Right go!' commanded the major, looking at his watch.

I had so little time to think it through. A mantra popped into my head as if my father encouraged me – *you can do it*. The process of resolving the challenge switched up a gear and I asked two girls to balance the plank over the 'river'.

'Sit on this end,' I ordered. Their weight made the plank, which now jutted out three quarters of the way across, steady. What do I do with the rope? I saw loopholes in the tops of the poles. Desperate to seem in control, I picked up the rope as if I had a master plan and threaded it through the hole in the first pole. I took both ends, plus the bucket, walked to the end of the plank and jumped to the other side. At least I was over with some equipment. I passed the rope again through the other loophole and tied the ends together. What now?

'Numbers 13, 15, 14 and 17, follow me,' I encouraged. One by one they walked the plank and leapt across. My spatial reasoning screeched to a halt. How was I going to get the first two over from other side? Quick thinking rescued me again.

'16 and 11, pass over the plank,' I instructed. How stupid that I had chosen number 11, one of the plumper girls, to act as anchor. She panted, her face flushed despite the cool weather and struggled with her teammate to hand it across. The rest of us made attempts to grab it. A few lay on their stomachs to get a better reach above the painted river. Unfortunately, the plank fell into the red zone, but we soon hauled it out to our side of the obstacle. I was distracted by a new voice.

'Who started this?' asked a colonel who had arrived to watch with a group of officers.

'Number 12, Sir,' replied the major.

He stared at me. Any worries I had experienced previously were doubled. I tugged the rope: it seemed secure so I asked number 16 to use her hands and feet to slide along it. My voice sounded odd, harsh and scratchy, not like mine. She inched her way over the 'river'. I held my breath. What if the rope parted company? I exhaled and relaxed. She had made it.

Now I was confronted with the biggest problem. The last of our team, number 11, had to attempt the crossing. She hung, suspended. I was in suspense too. Would she let go? Her weight pulled the rope down and her bottom nearly touched the red paint. She eased her way towards us. Her trousers, having slipped down, offering the male officers a good view of her bare waist. I grabbed her as she collapsed, triumphant, on the sandbags.

The major came over to me as number 11 completed the task.

'What kind of a knot is this?' he asked pointing at the rope.

'A sheepshank, Sir,' I replied without hesitation. It sounded impressive but I didn't have a clue. It was a bluff; did he believe me? In fact, I remembered later it was a couple of half hitches. I had learnt to do these while sailing with Uncle Freddie on his sloop. But was I sailing through the tests?

The Mess bar was an attraction each evening after the trials of the day. Exhausted candidates met up for a reviving sherry before dinner. Wendy and Elaine were already there with another girl, one of the red team we had not yet spoken with. Wendy waved her hand and beckoned me over.

'Jackie, come and meet Lesley,' she said. 'She's from Copenhagen.'

She reminded me of my school friend, Frances, with her curvy figure, golden hair and beautiful skin.

'Why Copenhagen?' I asked.

'My dad is the MA at the British Embassy.'

I looked blank.

'MA?' I asked.

'Military Attaché. He's posted back to England soon. My mother is fed up with moving every two years and can't wait to be home.'

It occurred to me this would be our military lives too, a posting every couple of years to a different unit. That was exactly what I wanted but, equally, officers' wives, were expected to follow the drum and their husbands to the outposts of the British Army.

'I'm black and blue,' she confessed, sipping a Tío Pepe. 'My command task was brutal, how about yours?'

'Tough, like yours,' I replied, only too aware of my aching limbs. 'I've had a good soak in the bath to get rid of the mud.'

'More fun tomorrow,' she said, throwing back her head with a laugh.

I ordered a Bristol Cream from the straight-faced barman. I wondered if he was secretly taking notes? He wasn't a bit like Sam at Great Fosters, who couldn't wait to crack a joke. We finished our drinks and entered the dining room, Helen tagging along behind, a long shadow.

* * *

The following day, yet another physical experience awaited me. In the gymnasium, the individual obstacle course looked like something the Marines had designed. The climbing walls high, the vaulting horse demanding and the jumps wide. Tight turns were needed to make the circuit. I had to pass this test. I hated heights but was not going to show the Physical Training Instructor my weakness. He was fit and bristling with energy. The challenge had to be completed within an allotted time and each obstacle had a score. Thank God I had long legs and could run fast. I was given a few minutes to plan my strategy. I climbed, jumped, ran and tunnelled until a whistle blew. Breathless, I skidded to a stop.

'Why did you choose that way of going around?' the sergeant asked me, ready with his clipboard to take down my answer.

'Gave more points,' I gasped.

My legs trembled and I felt a trickle of perspiration running down between my breasts. The physical test had been hard, but I was elated by my success and allowed a tiny smile of achievement to escape across my face. Not so for Shirley, number 17. When her turn came, she tore her Achilles tendon and was carted off to hospital.

The blue team, now six, continued the assessments. I remember a light airy room. We sat on chairs placed in a semicircle, an arena set for battle. Christians and Lions sprang to mind. The time for the mini lectures had arrived. I waited my turn, absorbing the delivery of the other candidates' prepared texts, while our team officer listened and scratched his critique on paper with an ink pen. Then he looked up at me.

'Number 12,' he commanded.

My notes fluttered in my hand. I couldn't afford to let him see me quivering with nerves. I took a deep breath and, taking strength from a well-rehearsed script, I stood up and began to speak about Pablo Picasso and his new controversial form of art, cubism. I loved Picasso's work, channelling again the enthusiasm developed by my inspirational art teacher. Well into my five-minute talk, I heard the tap of a pen warning me only one minute remained. For a second I faltered, then continued my résumé of Picasso's most famous cubist painting, *Les Demoiselles d'Avignon*. The nude female bodies were distorted and formed geometric shapes. It was difficult to tell from the facial expressions of the audience if they shared my passion. The Major questioned me about the concept of cubism. I imagined chocolate box Constable prints on his living room wall. Did I explain the work well enough? I did try my best for you, Pablo.

One more hurdle to jump, the final interview.

'Number 12, you are next to see Colonel White,' said our major.

The course was nearly over. My confidence regained, I glided down the corridor to the appointed room and knocked on the door. 'Enter,' boomed a male voice. Straight away I became aware of someone else sitting at the back of the interviewing room. My eyes remained on the colonel but instinctively I knew the visitor was a woman. The interview wasn't taxing and, without any difficulty, I answered his questions.

'Thank you, that'll be all,' the senior officer said, ending the interview.

Relieved that the assessment was over, I stood up and turned around. There sitting in the chair, was Lady P., wife of the General of Southern Command, witness to my dramatic fall in the hallway during the recent cocktail party at the Officers Mess in Blackdown. I had blamed my high heels, but the champagne cocktails had also contributed to my downfall. She might say something to the colonel, ruining my hopes of passing RCB. But instead she smiled at me. And was that a wink? Still not sure if my chances were diminished after this unexpected encounter, I kept the fears to myself.

A formal dinner was held for the candidates that last night. Perhaps they were checking for our social skills and table manners. Wendy and Elaine sat either side of me.

'Thank God that's over,' I said to Wendy. 'Was it as bad as you thought?'

'Crikey, yes,' she replied.

'Yes, and we still don't know if we're suitable officer material – if we made the grade,' Elaine added.

'Well, we gave it our best shot and have the bruises to prove it.' I laughed. 'We'll know in a couple of days when our results arrive by post.'

'Cross fingers we meet again at Officer Cadet Wing in

January,' said Wendy.

We raised our glasses.

'Good luck,' we echoed.

The London train gathered speed and flashed through the English countryside onwards to Reading, my stop for Camberley. Again, I saw the white horse. This time he seemed to be galloping across the hills. I'd made a bid for freedom and wanted to spread my wings like Pegasus, to fly into the unknown, to an exciting future.

CHAPTER 8

FINAL MEDICAL

I lay in bed, warm and cosy under the green eiderdown. There was no need to get up. It was only twenty-five minutes past eight. I heard the latch of our garden gate click and footsteps on the gravel path.

'The postman has arrived!' my mother called.

Now wide awake, I jumped out of bed with a groan, my muscles still stiff from the strenuous few days at Westbury. The letterbox rattled and the mail plopped on the doormat. I grabbed my dressing gown from its hook, struggled to push my arms into the sleeves and opened the door. Dreams of my new career might be shattered in the next few minutes and I could be looking for another job. Mummy had beaten me to the hall. She stood at the top of the landing holding a brown manila envelope marked OHMS. This small package held my future.

'I think this is what you've been waiting for,' she said handing it over. I hesitated to reveal its contents.

'Go on, darling, find out if you've passed,' Mummy said.

I made a couple of attempts to tear the envelope and pulled out the letter. The words blurred and then registered.

You have successfully passed the Regular Commissions Board. A place has been allocated to you at Officer Cadet Wing Hindhead...

'Yes!' I shouted, hugging her.

'I'm so pleased for you, darling,' she cried, hugging me back. We did a little jig and fell apart laughing. Her reaction was predictable; her first thought was of my wardrobe.

'You'll have to think about some new clothes, and we must go to that hat shop on Park Street,' she said, full of plans. 'We'll visit Harvey's for dress patterns. You always look elegant in the things I make for you and the new slim fashions show off your figure. I'm glad that you didn't take up Aunt Sylvia's idea. She was all for you going to Lucie Clayton's modelling school after you left the convent. D'you remember?'

Only too well. Reg had been against her proposal, probably because it wasn't his suggestion. Modelling had seemed glamorous at the time but being a clotheshorse wasn't for me. I wondered what I would look like sporting the WRAC uniform. Had Wendy, Elaine and Lesley received their results today? Why didn't we exchange addresses before we left Westbury? I wouldn't know if they had passed until I arrived at Hindhead. Elaine would be there. I was certain.

Reg mumbled congratulations when he returned from work. I avoided him as much as possible. He had laid down the rules for returning home when I resigned my job at Great Fosters and pontificated about every topic of conversation at the dining table. He'd found my transistor radio, claiming it as his own, twiddling the knobs to change stations, commenting on Elvis Presley's rubbish modern music until he heard some Beethoven. I couldn't wait to leave.

* * *

Rain was forecast. I grabbed my white umbrella with its bamboo handle and opened the front door.

'I'm off to catch the Aldershot bus for my final medical. See you later,' I announced to my mother.

'Ok, darling, I'm making your favourite for supper – apple and blackberry pie,' she answered from the kitchen. 'Good luck!'

I took the short cut opposite our house through a scrap of wooded land into Tekels Avenue. Architectural trees and rhododendrons adorned the gardens of the houses in this desirable part of town. Bursts of autumn colour glowed and shimmered from the chrysanthemums in neat flowerbeds. As I turned into Park Road a cold north wind lashed me, and I pulled my swagger coat closer, hurrying along to get to the Camberley bus station. The Aldershot bus was about to depart.

Raindrops splashed against the windowpanes. I stared out at the familiar route, York Town, Frimley. The conductor made his rounds. I offered him my fare and he gave a crank to his machine and out rolled my ticket. I asked him to tell me when we reached Steeles Road. He nodded and hung onto an upright rail as the driver negotiated a corner into Frimley High Street. A memory flashed into my head. I was fifteen years old, going to school on the bus and it was right there that I unexpectedly saw the first British transsexual woman. She wore a summer dress, had long blonde curly hair and strode with purpose along the pavement on the opposite side of the road. A passenger had shouted out:

'There she is, Roberta Cowell!'

I asked my mother later who she was. We were both baffled. How could a man turn into a woman? Mummy didn't have the knowledge to explain the hormone treatment and pioneering surgery. She only said that his 'winkle' must have been chopped off, her euphemism for male and female genitalia. Ouch! This chance encounter in Frimley made me realise later how far science and medicine had advanced in post-war Britain. Roberta Cowell had previously been a spitfire pilot, a hero of the Second World War but also had the courage to change sex and face the world ten years later as a woman. As a teenager I wanted to understand and appreciate these discoveries that would shape the future.

Before the town of Farnborough was the entrance to the convent. The bus stop I had used as a schoolgirl remained outside the gates. It seemed a lifetime ago that I'd climbed up the steep driveway, wearing my green uniform with the striped blazer and Tam O'Shanter beret. I smiled, thinking of Frances and Christine, my friends who'd made those early teenage years bearable with our antics.

The road widened and, shortly afterwards, a bold sign for Aldershot, 'Home of The British Army', appeared by the roadside. The conductor rang the bell as we neared the army barracks.

'Your stop, dearie,' he called out.

I alighted and looked for directions. Ahead, I saw 'Medical Centre' in white and red lettering on the side of a wooden building. What kind of examination would it be? Different to the one in Whitehall? Apprehensive, I took a deep breath, opened the door and entered. A middle-aged nurse in a white overall sat behind a desk. She wore a grim countenance, not unlike 'Grandma' from the Giles cartoons in the Daily Express.

'Yes?' she queried in a clipped voice. I gave her the letter for my medical.

'Go to the Officers' Waiting Room over there,' she ordered, pointing to a door on her right. 'I'll call you later.'

The room was furnished with armchairs. I sat down and propped up my umbrella. My unease mounted with abstract thoughts; hypodermic needles, phials of blood, bandages. I shrugged off these mental images, picked up a *Reader's Digest* from the table and flicked through the pages, finding an article about the sprinter, Jesse Owens. I was engrossed in his story when I heard male voices; I looked up to see two young officers in uniform. They walked in and sat down opposite me.

'Good morning,' they both said, their eyes assessing me. A hot blush started to rise up from my throat. I murmured a response and quickly looked down again at the magazine.

'Miss Skingley-Pearce.'

'Yes?' I answered, lifting my eyes to see the nurse standing in the doorway.

'Come with me,' she ordered.

I put down the magazine on the table and followed her to the office. She started to fill in a form.

'Have you brought a sample?' she enquired.

'I'm sorry, I don't understand.'

'Have you bought a specimen of urine?'

'I didn't know that I was supposed to bring one,' I replied.

Just then an orderly came into the office.

'Turner,' she ordered. 'Go and get a vase!'

He came back with what looked like a large drinking glass.

'No, you fool,' said the nurse in a loud voice, 'not that kind of a glass, a specimen vase.'

It was a wooden building, the walls paper-thin, and I imagined the young men in the waiting room hearing every word.

'Go and fill this,' she said, thrusting the object into my hands after Jenkins had supplied the right kind of container.

'Where do I go?' I asked, flushed with embarrassment.

'Oh, come with me,' she said, clearly exasperated, and marched off down the corridor, me in tow. We had to pass the open door where the two officers were seated.

'In here.'

She indicated the ablutions room and, sensing I was nervous, started to turn on all the taps. My bladder wouldn't comply; I just couldn't pee to order. Talk of bodily functions was not discussed openly at that time and I felt awkward. But the running water eventually had an effect and I managed to produce a sample. When I came out of the lavatory, she had disappeared, so I had to carry the blasted thing back to her office, the contents showing through the glass. Humiliated, I felt the heat from my burning cheeks as I passed the officers in the waiting room. Luckily, I didn't have to go back there. I was sent straight in to see two ancient colonels, the medical officers.

A hearing test came first. I stood in a corner of the room facing the wall. One of the doctors whispered words and I had to interpret them. It was like playing a game at a children's party. Colour blindness was next. Hidden among a chart of coloured dots were numbers in varying shades of reds, greens and oranges. Then I undressed for the examination of my reflexes, throat, ears and chest. The examination of my heart with their stethoscopes took a long time.

'I think you may have a heart murmur,' said one of them. 'What do you think George?' Colonel George came over and examined me again.

'Don't think so,' he said, listening for the abnormality.

I began to feel cold in my bra and pants, waiting for a verdict. I was convinced that there was nothing wrong with my heart. They, simply, were dirty old men. Tense and helpless, I was at the mercy of these omnipotent male doctors.

'That's all in order,' said Colonel George with a smile – or was it a leer?

I hadn't doubted it at all, but for a second my heart had missed a beat. 'You'll be hearing shortly about your medical,' affirmed the other one.

I dressed and returned to the office where I signed a form. Suddenly, I remembered my umbrella. But I couldn't face those officers so instead fled, leaving it behind. Charles wouldn't be pleased that I had lost one of his presents.

A few days later, I received the expected letter with my joining instructions for Officer Cadet Wing. I had passed my medical and was to report to Huron Camp, Hindhead on 11th January between 15:00-16:00hrs. A railway warrant would be provided on request. Relief and excitement filled my senses. I bathed in the success of winning a place on the course and the anticipation of seeing friends from RCB there.

Almost two months had to be endured before I started cadet training. I had a list of items to buy and needed to pay my mother for dress material. Harvey's, the department store in the High Street, had a poster in the window advertising for staff over the Christmas period. A week later, I was selling toys on the first floor. The sales girls were a good bunch and my contemporaries. I enjoyed their company more than that of the middle-aged hotel staff and we cracked jokes and teased each other. In the toy department with me was Angie, aged eighteen, who lived in York Town and had a wicked sense of humour. She recounted stories of her hot affair with Ron, a car mechanic, who took her dancing on Saturday nights.

'You should see us jiving down the Town 'all.' Her eyes lit up, ''E always buys me a *Babycham* after. Makes me knees go wobbly,' she laughed and then whispered. ''E's a good dancer 'n good at the other,' she gave me a knowing wink. ''Ere quick, Jax, we've got a customer. Bet he's going to buy a cuddly toy.'

'You're sure, Angie? He looks more like an 'Etch a Sketch' man to me,' I said, referring to the new toy craze of 1960. We pinned on our smiles and stepped forward.

Weekends were less exciting. Charles was in Germany. Our lives had changed dramatically since I had left the hotel. I was following in his footsteps but in a different direction and who knew where it would lead? When would we see each other again? Our intimacy had been curtailed when I returned to live at home. We had visited Farnham Heath a few times before his posting, our only chance to be alone. The heather in our hair had been a telling sign of what we had been up to, until we removed the evidence. But he wrote to me often and, for my birthday at the end of November, I received a present. A lizard skin handbag. I hadn't told him about the umbrella.

* * *

'Tea's ready,' called my mother.

I abandoned an airmail letter to Charles and hurried downstairs to the sitting room. On the coffee table Mummy had laid out the best china and two silver cake forks, part of a boxed set, which my father and mother had been given as a wedding present. The aroma of her favourite tea rose from the silver teapot.

'We'll let it stand for a few minutes. I'll be back in a moment,' she said and left the room.

I knew she was bringing me a surprise; the cake forks were a clue. She'd been baking all morning and I had been banned from the kitchen. She had even put out the linen napkins Nan had embroidered on the table. Would this be the last birthday I'd celebrate with her? Did she feel the same? In six weeks I would be leaving home for good and then I'd discover the limits of my abilities, physically and mentally. I just had to make the grade. Although I loved her, I never wanted to live at Deramore Cottage again. She reappeared in the doorway carrying an iced Victoria sponge decorated with sugar roses and nineteen burning candles.

'Happy birthday, darling,' she said as the tiny flames flared up to illuminate her dear face. 'Blow them out and make a wish.'

That wish was easy.

CHAPTER 9

OFFICER CADET WING, JANUARY 1961

Huron camp couldn't have been more different to the splendour of the Royal Military Academy Sandhurst. Single storey wooden huts spread out across acres of Bramshott Common, uniform and utilitarian.

'Reminds me of wartime barracks,' Reg commented, driving the Daimler through the camp gates. He was right. Originally built to accommodate the Canadian Army in the Great War of 1914–1918, Spanish Flu had struck soldiers stationed here and many had died in the epidemic, their bodies buried in the nearby churchyard of Bramshott village. In the Second World War, prior to D-Day, the Canadians were based here again, remembered with affection by the local community.

'Not what I expected, darling,' said my mother, absorbing the bleak landscape. 'I hope you are going to enjoy your course here.'

'I'm sure it'll be brilliant,' I responded, trying to assuage both our doubts.

A large sign announced *Women's Royal Army Corps School of Instruction*.

I caught my breath. The selection board and interviews had got me this far, but would I fit in? Would I be able to conform to military life? I remembered the previous July when I'd been to Charles's passing out parade at Sandhurst. For the successful cadets, this had been the culmination of two years at the Academy. I imagined that the training would be different for girls; ours was a one-year course, no combatant role for us. Guns were not for the distaff members of the army in those days.

I showed my joining instructions at the guardroom to a WRAC sergeant dressed in dreary khaki. She directed my stepfather to Cadet Wing. White painted stones marked the verges by the entrance to Headquarter Company. A large parade square appeared, tennis courts, and the ubiquitous rows of huts. I felt nervous in such a regimented and daunting environment. The road forked, we bore right to see a group of young women surrounded by luggage talking to WRAC personnel. An empty green army bus pulled away and Reg steered the car into the parking space. A slender girl in cadet uniform with red edged epaulettes detached herself from the knot of girls and made a beeline for us. I climbed out of the Daimler.

'Good afternoon, I'm Sue,' she announced, holding a clipboard. 'You are?' she queried. I gave my name and she ticked me off a list. How confident she appeared, her welcoming smile reassuring.

'I'll take you to your quarters now. You can have tea in the anteroom afterwards.' She pointed to the sign on the building behind her: *Officer Cadets' Mess*. 'In half an hour the OC will give the new intake a briefing.'

What was the OC again? Briefing?

Reg, Mummy and I collected my luggage from the car and followed Sue to hut fifty-one. She stopped outside the entrance.

'Better say goodbye now,' Reg announced, realising that he was not allowed to enter the female accommodation. He put down my case, making a show of pecking me on the cheek.

'You're invited to have tea with us,' said Sue.

'Thank you but I think we'll head home,' he replied, looking out of place, no longer the centre of attention. I knew he wanted me to ask him to stay but my silence conveyed the answer. Mummy handed over my hatbox, her eyes brimming with tears. I gave her a kiss, promising to write soon.

As soon as they had left, Sue pushed open the door to reveal a gleaming corridor.

'Rooms are allocated alphabetically,' she explained. 'Yours is further on, next to mine.'

Was her proximity going to be restrictive, noticing my every move? We tramped down the lino, lugging my case and bags, the echo of our footsteps bouncing off the walls until we came to the right one. My name stood out in black letters.

'I'll let you sort yourself out before tea,' instructed Sue. 'Don't be late.'

I had arrived, but was I going to cope with the strict rules and orders? I wondered who else was in my intake, no sign yet of the girls from RCB.

My room was at the end of the block on the left-hand side. The window looked out over a patch of clipped grass and further away onto the back of a building, the Sergeants' Mess. I hung up new clothes in the wardrobe, hats on the shelf and the rest of my belongings in the chest of drawers. I had my own washbasin, above it a mirrored cabinet where I stored my toiletries. A drop-down leaf desk with pigeonholes for files and stationery stood against the wall opposite my single bed. The room contained everything I needed, and I was sure I could make it cosier. I'd bring my homemade rug and some of my artwork next time I visited my mother. I didn't really have time to reflect on the new surroundings. Worried about being late, I checked my watch, appearance, combed my hair and hurried to the Officer Cadet's Mess.

The anteroom door stood open and, to my delight, I saw Elaine chatting to Wendy and Lesley. I rushed over to exclaim my congratulations.

'I knew you'd pass RCB!' I declared, laughing in relief.

As I remember them from those days, Elaine already wore the mantle of a leader. She, Wendy and Lesley were to become my comrades, pivotal to my well-being at Cadet Wing. Elaine, self-assured, full of fun, and because she was shorter than us, held her head high. Flicked out hair framed an open face and blue eyes. Wendy, slim and almost as tall as me, walked like a model. Nothing fazed her, she attacked every situation with humour and was to remain one of my lifelong friends. Lesley, the mother hen, had a curvy figure, masses of curly hair and possessed a gentle nature. I don't know how I would have survived without her support, given what was to come. We would all spend the next year together – and even better, they were billeted in hut fifty-one. My spirits rose knowing we would be sharing our experiences as cadets in that grim camp.

Senior cadets and new girls stood around sipping cups of tea. Sue was speaking to a large woman in uniform wearing the insignia of a major, a crown on each epaulette. Formidable, with a bearing that commanded attention, her bright red lipstick contrasted with startling white teeth. Despite her big frame she had slim legs and well-turned ankles. A pair of black court shoes encased small feet. Here was the Queen Bee. I hoped she didn't have a sting to go with that serene countenance.

'Look over there,' said Lesley. I followed her gaze.

'It's Jo and Fil, they're with Helen.'

Jo gave a wide grin, slid her glasses up the bridge of her nose and hurried to join us. Jo was one of the short service commission entrants at Westbury. The other, Shirley, had torn her Achilles tendon. Fil was one of those who had struggled over the Baby Jordan on my command task, a large girl, intelligent and great fun. The only disappointment was seeing Helen there, looking down her long nose at us.

'Did you know that only seven candidates got through our RCB?' confided Jo. 'I've got it on good authority that it was the highest pass rate for ages.'

'We must be extra special then,' said Wendy with a laugh, passing me a cup and saucer.

I learnt from Jo about our seniors and the directing staff. Sue was the Cadet Sergeant, in line for the sash of honour, awarded to the best student on the course. The red-edged epaulettes showed her success. Her intake had another six months to go before commissioning. The officer in charge of Cadet Wing was

Major Vennard, with the red lips – the OC who was about to give us a briefing. We sat on dining chairs, lined up in preparation for our induction talk. Our seniors departed. I counted seventeen remaining girls in the anteroom. No comparison to the new intake of two hundred male cadets at Sandhurst.

'What do you think about the dress code?' asked Elaine after supper. Wendy, Lesley and I were in her room pondering over our 'briefing'.'

'Hope I've enough dresses,' said Lesley. 'No trousers allowed to be worn in the Mess, skirts only on Wednesdays and at the weekends. The Mess is where we can relax. I can't see us leaving camp that often.'

'There must be a few pubs around here,' I remarked.

'Did you meet the other new girls from our hut?' asked Elaine 'Florian? Her room is opposite yours, Jackie.'

'Was she the pretty one sitting next to Helen at dinner?' I asked. Elaine nodded. 'No, I haven't, I'm sure I'll bump into her soon.'

'I said hello to Deidre,' announced Wendy. 'She's exhausted after travelling for the last two days from Northern Ireland and is going straight to bed.'

'I'm off too. Better be prepared for tomorrow,' I said.

We split up and I wandered off to my room. By ten o'clock, I lay in my strange bed thinking about the course. Did the rest of the new intake feel as nervous as me? I hadn't spoken to all of them yet, but they seemed a great bunch of girls. Jo and Sheila, another short service candidate, were older. The rest of us were novice nineteen year olds. My alarm clock gave its familiar tick and I closed my eyes. Tomorrow would have to take care of itself.

* * *

I wasn't sure what to wear on that first morning. I checked my wardrobe and pulled out a skirt and jumper, hoping the outfit would be appropriate for the day's activities. I opened my door and, at the same time, through the door opposite, a petite girl stepped out, wearing a fashionable twin set and tweed skirt.

'Hello, you're Jackie, aren't you?' she asked, 'I see it says Jacqueline on your door,' she smiled, and a dimple appeared on each cheek. 'Don't you dare call me Flo, it's Florian!'

I liked her straightaway, cheerful and outgoing. We fell in step and quizzed each other on the way to the Mess.

'It's like being back at boarding school,' she continued. 'Did you go to one?'

'I was a day girl,' I replied.

'Mmm,' she hummed. 'I wonder what they'll give us for breakfast?'

'Don't think we'll starve,' I replied when we arrived in the dining room. Cadets tucked into cooked breakfasts and animated conversation flowed as if the diners had known each other for ages.

We slipped in beside them.

At nine o'clock the new intake gathered outside the Mess, as per instructions on our programme pinned to the notice board inside hut fifty-one, otherwise known as Part One Orders. We nattered away, discussing the first thing on our agenda; a visit to the quartermaster's store. Silence descended when we saw a woman marching along the road towards us carrying a 'swagger' stick, her uniform adorned with badges of rank and wearing a pair of gleaming shoes.

'Good morning, Ladies,' she said in a bright voice, halting beside us.

'I'm the Regimental Sergeant Major. You'll call me Ma'am.'

She fascinated me. The RSM was of average height with a generous bosom. The beret captured her short crinkly hair and, through a pair of steely eyes, she assessed us. The motley crew.

'Line up in rows of three,' she ordered, and we obeyed her, shuffling and bumping into each other.

'We'll proceed to the QM stores for the issue of your uniforms. By the left quick march.'

I stifled a giggle and followed step with the 'squad'. We marched along the road past a number of wooden huts set in a landscape of bare trees and concrete paths. The 'Halt' command came as a surprise and, unbalanced, I lurched forward. I wasn't the only one. The RSM registered the shambles and raised her eyebrows. We had stopped outside a long low building where a stern looking sergeant stood by the sign *Quartermaster's Stores.*

'This way, Ladies,' she ordered, ushering us into the depository, stacked with every item of uniform. WRAC girls manned a long wooden counter set up inside the door, tape measures and notebooks at the ready. The Quartermaster, an imposing woman, took charge.

Our names called out and we stepped forward to be measured from head to foot. WRAC girls rushed about collecting the right size and article. In no time, a pile of clothing appeared on the counter. Wendy was trying on black flat shoes, the beetle crushers. What passion killers they were, too. I also looked like Minnie Mouse in outsized footwear. The final acquisition was the gas mask. I pulled mine on, the seal so tight I could feel it cutting into my flesh. I saw the QM coming over, her face slightly distorted through the Perspex goggles, to put her hand over the breathing holes. I pulled the straps, ripped off the contraption and took a deep breath.

'Just checking that it's in working order,' she said with a wry smile, enjoying the moment.

'Sign for your uniform here,' barked the stern sergeant, pointing below the long list on a buff form.

I was kitted out, but it wasn't over. I wished for a shorter surname like Fry or Day because laundered clothes had to be marked. My nametape was miles long and sewing was not my favourite pastime. Part of our allotted necessities was a small muslin bag with ties known as a 'housewife'. It contained everything I needed for the task; needles, cotton, thimble and scissors. We had been instructed to bring nametapes with us. Mummy had ordered mine from Cash's with green lettering. She had already sewn labels on my underwear and the new civilian clothes.

Another surprising handout was a packet of sanitary towels donated each month from the Lord Nuffield Fund. Spare ones came in handy for polishing our floors.

'What's the tip about bulling shoes?' I asked Florian. 'Heating up shoe polish, was that it?'

I hated the idea of all that spit and polish.

'Swop you,' she offered. 'If you set my hair, I'll do your shoes.'

I considered that an ideal exchange. She'd been admiring my thick chestnut hair, which I wore in a bob that ended in a curl either side of my cheeks. Hair could not be longer than to the top of our collars. Those beastly detached collars were torture, the collar studs leaving indents and bruises on our throats – not attractive when exposed in 'civvy' clothes.

I stood in front of my cabinet mirror to see a girl with hazel green eyes wearing a WRAC green beret. Was it on straight with the badge over my right eye? White flashes, denoting an officer cadet, were fastened to the lapels of my khaki suit, not the most flattering shape. The battle dress top fastened at the waist had two breast pockets. At my throat, the tie I'd tried to knot three times, still askew. My skirt hung in an A line below the knees. And then there were the beetle crushers! I didn't recognise myself, the first time dressed in uniform. Was that really me? What on earth was I doing here?

Our intake regrouped outside the Mess, all of us feeling awkward in our new gear. It was if we were in a film, a squad of women waiting for the action to begin.

And so, it did.

CHAPTER 10

SPRING TERM

Sergeant Lively, decidedly lively by nature, was assigned to our course. I imagined she was popular in the Sergeants' Mess, quick-witted, not as daunting as the RSM and more approachable. Both of them drilled, chivvied and whipped us into shape. First lesson: how to salute.

'I want to see a smart salute, not a rose arch,' Sergeant Lively instructed. 'Bring your arm the longest way up and the shortest way down, keeping your arm straight from the elbow, no floppy wrists.' Demonstrating the correct movement and on the command, 'Squad salute!' we copied her with stiff arms, not a floral structure in sight. The importance of walking purposefully, and never dawdling to arrive five minutes early for lectures and appointments, were drummed into us, a lesson that has remained with me.

On the vast Parade Square, we learned how to march. Wendy and I, the tallest, were chosen alternatively to be right marker. Our job was to keep eyes straight ahead or 'front' while our squad turned theirs for the command 'eyes right'. How soon we gained experience and became competent with the full drill repertoire, excluding the use of firearms. The first time I handled a gun, a -22 rifle, was at an indoor shooting rifle range in Germany. It would take another fifty-five years before women in the British Army were considered for combatant roles to fight in a theatre of war. Finally, on 25th October 2018, women soldiers dependent on their ability alone, became eligible to join all branches of the army including the Infantry and Special Air Service.

The first week, packed with lectures, drill and inspections, gave me no time to reflect on my decision to join up. To record our commitment, in a group photo of latest cadets, taken outside a large Nissan hut, I stood with Wendy and Lesley in the back row, the usual place for tall girls. Florian and Elaine sat in the front. The 'cheese' moment came, and we smiled. Elaine wore the broadest grin and Florian's dimples came out well in the resulting picture. I have to admit I looked radiant, a reflection of my contentment at having found new friends and new beginnings, a passport to the future.

We didn't have time to explore outside camp during the first weekends, as we were busy polishing, ironing and cleaning. There was a rumour of a pub called the Royal Anchor, the senior cadets' haunt, not far away on the road to Liphook, but then we were getting over our first set of vaccinations, TABT – typhoid, paratyphoid A and B and tetanus. Many experienced reactions and I reported to the Medical Centre with a particularly swollen arm.

'Quite normal,' said the Queen Alexandra's nursing sister. 'Get down and polish your floor. That'll help reduce the swelling.'

Poor Deidre developed cowpox after her smallpox vaccine and was miserable, great red blotches appearing all over her face and body. The rest of us had been immunised as children, grateful not to be suffering like her. Deidre recovered from her ordeal but, after a few weeks, packed her bags and left. I don't know whose decision it was, hers or the directing staff of Officer Cadet Wing.

Every morning started with bedmaking and cleaning our rooms. While we were in the dining room or at lectures, the seniors were tasked to inspect them; wearing white gloves to pick up microscopic dust particles and reporting the cleanliness of each junior's room. All misdemeanours were recorded in a book against our names.

> *Dust on the doorjambs*
> *Dust on lintel*
> *Smear marks on tap*

'Black' marks led to extra orderly cadet officer duties.

The WRAC officers on the directing staff of Cadet Wing also carried out more formal inspections. We had to stand by our beds with all our kit laid out in a precise pattern. The Captain on duty and the RSM were our inquisitors. The bed was made with hospital corners and every item placed exactly as shown on a crib sheet. The procedure took ages and most of us got up at six o'clock to be ready for breakfast by eight o'clock and inspection at eight forty-five. We also had to be turned out in immaculate uniforms, which unlike the kit inspection, I actually appreciated.

The officers were collectively known as 'The Office', our lecturers on a variety of subjects. Mornings in the lecture room were studious ones, scribbling away at our notes. Major Vennard threw herself into revealing the mysteries of army organisation. Captain Spurling inspired us with tackling pay and accounts, the one subject I was good at, thanks to my previous job at the hotel. Major Fleetwood-Jones expounded on the joys of military history as we tried to keep awake. To change the dynamic of an all-female staff, Dr. Feuchtwanger, professor of current affairs, was intense and engaging. The Cold War had intensified between the Eastern Bloc and Western Bloc countries. John F. Kennedy was President of the United States and relations had been severed between capitalist USA and communist Cuba. The Doomsday Clock registered four minutes to midnight and we learned, on paper, how to survive the fallout of an atomic bomb. These were worrying times, but outside the classroom we were optimistic of a peaceful outcome. Occasionally, visiting officers from the RMA Sandhurst came to lecture us on tactics. They kept us awake. It was good to see real men again.

A daily routine was established: lectures in the morning and drill most afternoons, except on Wednesdays, when we played sports in our ridiculous divided skirts. The physical training instructor took us for brisk cross-country runs over the common. We struggled through gorse and heather, breathless and praying we were getting fitter. Netball was popular in WRAC units. We had to participate in matches on camp and learn the rules. My position was defence, leaping up to deflect the danger of a goal. Our team rushed about, trying to win possession of the ball and passing it on to Elaine, our shooter. The lesson wasn't only about sport, but also taught the value of being part of a cohesive unit as team players.

Throughout our first weeks we still hadn't explored the surrounding area, and, feeling detached from the outside world, receiving mail from friends and family was a lifeline. One morning after lectures, en route to my room, I rushed into the Mess to check the post rack. An airmail letter from Charles awaited me. Eager of any news, I lifted the side flaps of the envelope as I walked back to my room and by the time I reached hut fifty-one the letter was unfolded. Four words jumped out from the page, I came to a sudden halt in the corridor astonished by an unexpected question.

'You ok?' asked Elaine. 'Not bad news, I hope?'

'No, not exactly,' I replied, taken aback. 'Charles has asked me to marry him.'

His name had come up in our conversations and they'd seen the letters with the British Forces Post Office franked letters in my pigeonhole. Wendy, standing in her doorway, overheard our conversation.

'Hurray!' they cheered. But I didn't join in. Did I want to marry him, give up my new career and become an army wife?

'Are you going to accept?' asked Wendy, seeing my expression.

'I'm not sure,' I replied, confused and undermined.

'Don't you love him?' enquired Elaine.

'I thought so, but now ...' I left the sentence unfinished. Elaine and Wendy waited for me to continue.

'I haven't seen him for three months,' I explained, 'and to be honest, I haven't missed him that much. I feel bad because we've been going out for two years and I think he assumed we'd marry. He wants me to go and stay with him in Dortmund during Easter leave.' Charles was a nice enough chap; he'd make someone a good husband. But mine? I bit my lip. How would I answer? To be married was every young woman's goal in 1961, wasn't it? But not necessarily mine. I'd chosen a different life and was enjoying it, the chance to be independent and travel before settling down to domesticity.

'You know, my parents live near there and I'm going home for Easter. If you want to see him you could stay with us,' Elaine offered.

'That's kind, Elaine, but I'll have to think about it.'

'Ok,' she said, 'let me know when you do so I can write to Mummy.'

'Thanks. I want to drop off my books and brush my uniform for this afternoon's parade before lunch,' I said. 'See you in the dining room.'

I headed for my room. I didn't know what I was going to do. His proposal had thrown up many questions about our relationship and my career. I'd wait until I came to the right decision before composing a reply.

* * *

At last, a chance to leave camp! A driving instructor arrived in a Triumph Herald and for the following weeks would teach us how to pass our test. Some of us had driven before but Juliette, from hut forty-seven, was the only one with a licence.

My first experience of driving had been in the Austin 7 at Tekels Park when I was fifteen. Charles had let me drive his parent's car once but had reprimanded me on changing gear without double-declutching. I wasn't offered another chance. There were no dramatics, though, with my driving instructor. He was calm and composed.

Once I had the hang of it, driving was fun and gave me

confidence. My instructor thought I'd pass my test with no problem, as long as I learnt the Highway Code. My ambition was to own a car when I had enough money, not possible on cadets' pay. I would have to wait until after commissioning. Elaine was waiting to buy a scooter, but her father hadn't sent the expected funds. In the meantime, Juliette offered her friends lifts in the Morris Minor she'd been given at Christmas. Wendy decided, however, that she wouldn't go out with her again because Juliette talked nonstop and didn't keep her eyes on the road. Her driving didn't comply with the Highway Code we were all studying. In the autumn term my turn would come to take the all-important driving test.

The next change to our routine was an educational trip to the Old Bailey in London. Other outings were planned: The Houses of Parliament, The Stock Exchange and Lloyds of London. For these occasions we wore civilian clothes, our best dresses, hats and gloves. One of our Captains played chaperone.

In high spirits we set off on an early train from Liphook station, savouring a whole day away from lectures and drill. I sat in the compartment with the girls from hut fifty-one, their laughter and chatter a background to my inner thoughts. I had decided that I would go and visit Charles and find out if I wanted to give up everything to become his wife. It would need to be a long engagement, male officers had to be twenty-five before they could marry unless they were granted permission from their commanding officers, and I'd have to resign and give up my career. What of love and commitment? I had to be sure. Elaine had written to her parents to ask if I could stay, offering support if it all went wrong. I stared out of the window, my eyes unseeing, unaware of our approach to Waterloo Station.

The girls took out their compacts to powder noses and reapply lipstick. Jolted back to the moment, I registered my reflection in the windowpane and readjusted my Aage Thaarup hat to a jauntier angle. It was a creation of the talented Danish

101

milliner with the eponymous label, patronised by ladies of the Royal Family. I had found it in a new boutique in Camberley and my mother insisted that I buy it, it being so chic and expensive.

The noise and crowds at Waterloo Station engulfed us. Down we went into the murky world of the underground. Escalators glided past posters advertising Lionel Bart's musical show *Oliver*. Others displayed the newest in lingerie, long corsets incorporating strapless brasseries and suspenders. The models smiled encouragingly, locked into their sculpted forms. My grandmothers had worn salmon pink, whale-boned corsets with laces, like strait jackets. I avoided anything so restricting, although I had an elastic roll on girdle like my friends. Mostly, I was content with a suspender belt and bra.

The rolling escalator ended, we regrouped on the platform and waited for the whoosh of air, heralding the arrival of the train. We stepped on board, hung on to our handbags and found seats alongside shoppers and businessmen in suits, all intent on being somewhere else.

At Blackfriars the train screeched, came to a halt and we piled out to remount the moving staircase up into the pale sunlight. Red buses and black taxis circulated along the busy roads and people hurried down pavements. We absorbed the buzz and excitement of the capital. The latest fashions in the window of a dress shop caught my eye, especially a grey suit with three-quarter length sleeves, the cropped jacket trimmed in white, and I made a mental note to tell Mummy. She would be down at Harvey's checking out the Vogue patterns in a flash.

We traipsed to the Old Bailey. The statue of Lady Justice, holding a sword in her right hand and the scales in her left, glowed in the morning sun on top of the building. Our escort did a quick head count and we followed her through the entrance to the older part of the establishment, where she showed a letter to an official who ushered us into the public gallery of Court Number One.

The atmosphere was sober and serious during the trial in progress. The plaintiff, a skinny man with a scared face, was giving evidence. He shook in the witness box as he recounted the moment he was stabbed by the defendant. The defendant, allegedly a gangster from the East End, stood in the dock. Charged with grievous bodily harm, he seemed unaffected by his possible sentence. The memory of Johnson and his buggy eyes came to mind. Would he have shown remorse, unlike the man in front of us? The ancient building where thousands of murderers had been convicted and the solemnity of the occasion affected me. Tense, I watched the stern faces in the courtroom. An oppressive mood filled the space until the defendant's solicitor made a facetious remark about the plaintiff and Elaine burst out laughing.

'Silence in court,' came the stern reproach. It was as if we'd all been reprimanded; poor Elaine, overcome with embarrassment, looked suitably repentant. We would never know the outcome as the case was adjourned. The plaintiff appeared desperate, and who knew what would happen to him? We never knew the circumstances around the attack.

We gathered outside. 'Meet you at Waterloo at 16:15 to catch the 16:27 train to Liphook,' said our Captain, looking at her watch before turning away and disappearing down Newgate Street towards the tube station. Groups of girls wandered off to discover what the City had to offer.

'Let's go to Soho for lunch,' suggested Wendy.

'Brilliant idea,' announced Florian.

'Shall we go by bus or tube?' asked Elaine.

'If we go by bus we'll see more of London,' I said. Lesley nodded in agreement.

We strolled down to Ludgate Hill in search of a bus stop. Wendy saw a tobacconist and went in to buy some coloured Sobranie cocktail cigarettes, the height of sophistication. The five of us found the right bus and climbed upstairs. She passed around the distinctive packet, I chose a pink one and we lit up. Such luxury!

We found Wardour Street, the heart of Soho, sleazy and exhilarating. Feeling out of place with eyes everywhere, our grumbling stomachs took priority. It was way past our lunchtime and we were starving. A Chinese restaurant adorned with painted red dragons over the door attracted our attention.

'Ever had Chinese food?' I asked my companions. They shook their heads.

My previous knowledge of China was limited to geography lessons at school, travel books and the 1960 film, *Suzy Wong,* set in Hong Kong. We entered the restaurant and were transported to the Orient; pictures of Chinese scenery decorated the walls, lanterns with painted panels and red tassels hung from the ceilings. A Chinese waiter approached and guided us to a table. After a long debate, we ordered our meal and then talked about the trial at the Old Bailey.

'Bet that witness was involved with drugs or prostitution, probably on the other man's turf,' said Lesley, examining her chicken chow mein.

'You've seen too many gangster films,' responded Wendy, attacking her noodles.

The scenario sounded possible there in the red-light district. I scrutinised the other diners, wondering if any of them were in the same line of business and suppressed a shiver. The noodles I had eaten were slippery and the sauce spicy, not flavours I had experienced at home. I would have preferred a ploughman's lunch in a Pub.

We still had time before our rendezvous at Waterloo station, so wandered down the street to discover a small shop selling all kinds of interesting accessories. We went in to investigate, my eyes were drawn to a pair of pretty jade earrings hidden among gold chains and brooches, little green balls suspended on two-inch-long gold earring posts, a sheer extravagance at £3.

Carefree with the taste of freedom, I bought them. I loved the way they swung below my short haircut as I moved, the cold stones caressing my neck. I had no idea how important they were to become, on the day fate intervened and rocked my world.

* * *

Our curriculum was designed not only to mould us into young officers but also to give us an opportunity to look and act the part.

A representative from Revlon Cosmetics arrived at Cadet Wing to give us a make-up demonstration. She wore a navy suit with a red blouse, matching lipstick and stiletto heels. How dowdy we were in comparison, khaki uniforms and beetle crushers. Daphne, her model, sat in front of us in the anteroom, swathed in a white cape with her face covered in foundation and powder. Her mouth twitched, trying not to laugh.

'Any questions about beauty preparations?' the rep asked.

'Yes, I've one,' replied Wendy. 'Can you tell me how to get rid of freckles?'

Major Vennard, who had joined us for the presentation, leant forward.

'I'm interested to know the answer as well,' she whispered.

The rep held the lipstick she had chosen for Daphne and considered her reply. She painted a bow on Daphne's top lip and filled in with a deep red colour.

'Lemon juice,' she responded.

Wendy, expecting her to suggest an expensive cream, raised her eyebrows and allowed a small smile to spread across her face. Lemons were not available to us on camp either, and we had no access to the cookhouse. The rep, having finished her makeover, revealed the transformed Daphne who flapped her eyelashes, heavily coated with mascara. Everyone tried to look impressed. Released from her cocoon, Daphne rushed over to sit beside her friends from hut forty-seven.

'Can't wait to wash off this muck,' she hissed.

Major Vennard stopped to talk to Wendy after the demonstration.

'I wouldn't do that if I were you, Wendy,' she said.

'I came to the same conclusion myself, Ma'am,' Wendy replied.

'Good,' she said. 'We'll just have to put up with a few more freckles.'

They burst out laughing.

Nobody bought any of the products or used citrus fruit remedies. We stuck to the familiar Ponds Cold Cream, our powder compacts and, in my case, Max Factor lipstick and mascara. I used a tiny brush to scrub the dampened black paste before stroking on lashes to give an alluring Brigitte Bardot look. Quite often I was reduced to using spit when water wasn't handy!

Juliette was leaving us. A brigadier's daughter, she had decided army life wasn't for her. We'd miss her quirkiness and her Morris Minor. Fifteen remained from the original seventeen on our intake. Who would be leaving next? There was always the possibility of being summoned to 'The Office' and given a three-month warning, which could lead to dismissal. For the moment, all was going well for me on the course, and I was off with Elaine to Camberley on a weekend pass. It had been two months since I'd been home. I pushed open the green gate to Deramore Cottage. The garden was glorious, filled with golden daffodils competing with purple crocuses in the flowerbeds. We followed the path to the front door where Mummy waited for us.

'You look well, darling,' she said. 'Come in, you two, and tell me what you've been up to.'

My mother was impressed to hear about the organised presentations held in our Mess. We were considered to be ladies and some aspects of the training at Officer Cadet Wing were similar to a finishing school. Flower arranging by the school of Constance Spry, a talk by a wine specialist from London and make-up by Revlon.

Mummy quizzed me about the course and, talking to her, I realised that I'd made the right decision. I was now part of a group of young women who wanted more out of life than the usual career choices for our generation and, despite the threat of nuclear war, the future promised to be exciting.

I didn't tell her about Charles' proposal of marriage, knowing she didn't like him and there wasn't an opportunity to discuss it privately with her. Elaine said I was going out to Germany to visit her at Easter so that solved the problem of explaining the ulterior motive. My newfound independence, although bound by army regulations, was less restrictive than marriage and the training at Cadet Wing could lead to a fulfilling career. When would I have such a chance again?

CHAPTER 11

EASTER

Before Easter leave, I wrote to my mother, needing to be honest about the marriage proposal. Furious, she responded immediately. In her letter, Charles was compared to a sparrow and me to a swan. She asked if I was sure that he was the right man for me. I wasn't – that was the reason for going to see him in Germany. Mummy still thought I would stay with Elaine. But Charles had arranged a room for me in the female wing of the Teachers' Mess. These young women were employed by The British Forces Schools to educate servicemen's children in the Dortmund catchment area. British female teachers in BAOR (British Army of the Rhine) were unkindly known in certain circles as 'The Fishing Fleet', a term used for adventurous young women who sailed to India during the Raj in search of husbands.

Ten days before Easter, I had my return rail warrant and booked seat on the military boat train from Liverpool Street Station to Harwich, leaving on the Friday evening. This was the first opportunity I'd had to travel abroad. I packed my case, said goodbye to my friends and 'au revoir' to Elaine. We'd made plans for Charles and me to stay at her home in Wetter for a couple of days.

The Railway Transport Officer at Liverpool Street Station checked my identity card and warrant. I felt out of place in civvies among the crowd of men in uniform waiting to board the boat train. I assumed many of them were national servicemen returning to or joining their units in BAOR. I hauled my case onto the train and found a compartment occupied by another woman and sat opposite her. We broke the ice when she stood up to reach into her suitcase on the rack above, tripped over her holdall and nearly landed in my lap. My chatty companion was an army wife, joining her husband in Paderborn. The four-hour journey to Parkeston Quay, Harwich passed quickly in her company.

Lights shone in the darkness from the moored ferry, the night air filled with the smell of the sea, salty and fresh. *No going back now*, an inner voice warned as I trudged up the gangway onto the deck. I parted company with the army wife and went in search of my cabin.

We sailed at midnight and I spent a sleepless night on a bunk in a four-berth cabin with three other women, most of the time kept awake by the pitch and roll of the boat. My head spun and the snoring from the bunk below didn't help my insomnia. Far out in the North Sea, I thought of my father whose plane had been shot down by a German night fighter, and the wreckage of the Lancaster, never found, lost in deep water off the Belgian coast. I wondered what he'd have said to me, if he'd approve of the path I was taking. The lack of paternal guidance tormented me. I wish I had known him. The family spoke of him as an exceptional man. I had no respect for Reg, and Uncle Freddie was too far away.

Woken by a knock on the door at six o'clock, I just had time to dress and breakfast before we docked. Tired, and with a throbbing headache, I bagged a place by a window in the lounge for my first glimpse of the Dutch coast. The cloudy sky gave a cool backdrop to the Hook of Holland and reflected my mood, leaden and unsettled. Called to disembark, I joined the stream of military passengers heading for the train station. Reassured by the presence of British army transport officers on the platforms, I found the train to Wuppertal with their assistance. Communicating in German, a language I hadn't learnt at school, would have been a problem.

My case safely stowed on board, I settled down in my seat for the next phase of the journey. The carriage was full, passengers read or chatted. I wanted to be left alone and turned my face to gaze out of the window. The train pulled out of the station at nine o'clock and started the long crossing through Holland to Germany. The flat countryside, dotted with steeply pitched roofs of houses in the villages and towns, flashed by. The swaying movement of the locomotive lulled me and I closed my eyes. I dozed, wiping out the doubts flitting around in my head.

Strident voices woke me; the train had stopped.

'Where are we?' I asked.

'Roermond,' replied the man sitting opposite.

Two German border guards pulled open the compartment door and demanded everyone's identity cards or passports. They were intimidating and brusque. I offered my documents. There was no warmth in the guard's eyes, only suspicion and mistrust. For the first time, I felt alone and unprotected. He handed back my papers and turned his attention to the next passenger. I began to relax a little when the guards, their task completed, climbed off the train and we started moving again.

It was evening when I arrived at my destination, hungry and exhausted. I picked up my case and alighted. The noise of the station blasted in my ears. Unfamiliar guttural German voices and the screeching of trains arriving and departing made a deafening assault. The sign Wuppertal Hauptbahnhof stood out in big letters near the exit. Beneath it, waiting for me in uniform, was Charles. I was genuinely relieved to see his familiar face after the long journey. He hastened forward to greet me, planted a kiss on my cheek and took the case, offering his arm with a smile, and murmuring a few welcoming words.

Outside the station a driver jumped out of a military car and opened the passenger door. He took my case to the boot while we climbed into the back seat.

'I don't like your blue eye shadow!' Charles said, inspecting me.

'Oh really?' I replied, 'it's the latest trend.'

He made a face. Too bad, I wasn't taking it off for him. My

fears of marrying him were growing. He would be as controlling as Reg.

'Have you looked for an engagement ring?' he asked.

'No,' I replied. 'Was I supposed to?'

How was I going to get out of this situation? I had nine days before my return to England. I felt like a captive bird with clipped wings.

'Doesn't matter,' he said. 'We'll look for one here.' I kept quiet and watched the road. The journey to his Barracks another thirty miles. Lights from the oncoming cars shone in my eyes obscuring the view from my window. I sensed his annoyance and to change the mood I asked him about his platoon, friends and the new Regiment. He held my hand, easily distracted.

The camp lit up like a beacon against the night sky. Turning the car through the gates, the driver continued down an avenue to the Officers' Mess. Next to it was the teachers' accommodation. We climbed out and I followed Charles up a flight of stairs to the ladies' wing.

'Here's your room,' he said.

He opened a door, allowing me to pass through, dropped my case and grabbed me. The buttons of his uniform pressed against my body.

'It's been so long,' he complained and whispered. 'We'll go to my room later.' He seemed agitated. Perhaps this side of the building was off limits to men and he didn't want us to be seen together. Or did he suspect I was having second thoughts?

'Let me show you the short cut.' he said.

On the right, outside my room, Charles pushed open a pair of wide doors, leading to the male officers' quarters. I wondered how often they were used.

'Mine is just past the stairs. I'll be in trouble if I'm found in here,' he said. 'I'll get changed and pop back to collect you in half an hour when the coast is clear.'

Nobody was around when I located the bathroom or when I

returned to unpack. I didn't meet one teacher during my stay, which wasn't surprising.

Charles had taken leave. We went out during the day and we spent the nights together in his room. However, my doubts were mounting about sharing my life with him and I avoided giving him an answer or mentioning the ring.

We'd been careful not to be found together, but the strain and guilt affected me, so I was relieved to spend a few days away from prying eyes to stay with Elaine. Charles had borrowed a friend's Volkswagen beetle for the trip to Wetter. We said little above the noise of the engine while he concentrated on driving. What would Elaine think of him? I checked the address she'd given me on approaching the Officers' Married Quarters.

'That's their house on the right.' I pointed out.

After a warm welcome and coffee, we were shown to our separate rooms, where I could have space from Charles's attention.

'How's things?' Elaine asked me, once we were alone. It was easy to see why Elaine was so bubbly; she was clearly her parents' daughter.

'Not that well, to be honest. He wants us to get engaged,' I replied.

Four days spent with him had convinced me that we had no future together. I wasn't going to comply with his views and there was something missing that I couldn't define. I questioned whether or not I loved him. What was love after all? At nineteen, my life was before me and I wanted to experience so much more before settling down.

'Hope you sort everything out, Jackie.' She laughed at my serious face. 'Cheer up, it isn't the end of the world.'

Wasn't it? I wondered.

'You still haven't given me an answer about getting married,' Charles said on Easter Monday outside his Mess, the morning I was due to leave.

'I think we should wait,' I replied, trying to put off the inevitable. 'I don't think I'm ready for marriage. I want to finish my course and have some tours of duty.'

He wasn't happy about my decision.

'Can't imagine why, you'll end up as an army wife anyway.'

'No, Charles, I want a career first.'

He believed nothing had changed and that we would continue as before. But he was wrong. I'd made up my mind.

There was little conversation in the car to Wuppertal station. He fought back tears when we said goodbye and I didn't have the heart to tell him the truth. I felt terrible, I was going to let him down and I knew he'd hate me for it. But it was the only answer. My mother was right; we were incompatible.

So, began the long journey back to England and Huron camp to start the summer term on the 4th April. Depressed by the outcome of my visit and the unavoidable end of my relationship with Charles, I felt downhearted. Reflecting on my future, I came to the conclusion that I needed to devote all my energy to passing the course at Cadet Wing.

CHAPTER 12

PARATROOPERS

An outing appeared on Part One Orders for 12th April at 10:00hrs: a visit to the Depot of the Parachute Regiment and Airborne Forces. The thought of those tough men really appealed after three months of female company at Huron Camp. One of our course subjects was military history and a lecture on Operation Market Garden was planned. Two thirds of the men deployed from the two parachute battalions had been killed in the resulting battle of Arnhem in 1944. The fighting spirit of these men had become a legend of commitment and bravery. The morning at the Para Depot promised to be an educational one from my point of view, as I wanted to learn more about those heroes who had fought and died in the same war as my father.

The WRAC driver parked the army bus outside the Officers' Mess at Maida Barracks, Aldershot. Our escort alighted and saluted the Adjutant of the Depot who appeared at the entrance of the building. He looked amused and returned the courtesy as we copied our officer. Dressed in khaki, adorned with white flashes and wearing beetle crushers, we were not as familiar to him as male combat soldiers in army boots.

After the bumpy ride from Hindhead, some of us needed to 'spend a penny'. Wendy asked the Mess Steward and he showed us the way.

'Coffee will be served in the anteroom, Ladies,' he informed us.

We removed our headgear, rushed into the WCs with as much dignity as our full bladders would allow, washed our hands, combed our beret-flattened hair and I applied a touch more lipstick.

'That colour suits you,' Wendy said. 'Come on, I'm dying for a coffee.'

We heard chattering voices and laughter coming from the anteroom. The rest of the cadets were talking to a group of Para subalterns, detailed to look after us until the lecture.

He stood out from the others. His titian hair was short at the sides and longer on top, a stray lock hung over a high forehead. The khaki battledress sporting the insignia of the Parachute Regiment clothed his fit body and two brass pips on his epaulettes defined his rank of Lieutenant. The haircut gave him a nonchalant air and his rugged face creased with smiles as he talked to Elaine. He exuded self-confidence and raw masculinity. He turned to laugh at something one of his Para friends said and his gaze fell upon me. A strange and new sensation consumed me, gripped by a profound magnetism, every cell in my body wakened to an unseen, unheard call. My heart beat faster and my knees weakened. Our eyes locked.

'Coffee, Ma'am?' the Steward said, offering me a cup.

'Thank you,' I whispered, taking it, feeling the hot flush of my cheeks, grateful to be distracted. I looked up and there he was beside me.

'Hello, I'm Rudge Penley.'

I could hardly breathe, but I managed to reply, 'Jackie Skingley-Pearce.'

'I'm delighted to meet you, Miss Skingley-Pearce,' he said, his amber eyes bright with amusement. Nothing in that room existed but him. People talked, their mouths moved but I heard only his voice and the pounding in my breast. I don't remember drinking the coffee, but the cup was empty. He asked where I lived and, on learning I had spent my childhood near Arundel, he grinned.

'Ah, a South Downs girl. I come from Portsmouth,' he said, the underlying tone of his voice seductive and smooth.

His fellow officers laughed and joked with him and he answered back with quick repartee. I was in awe of his easy manner and the bond of camaraderie he had with his friends.

'Jackie,' said Wendy patting me on my shoulder. 'We've got to leave; the lecture starts in ten minutes and we've to walk over to the lecture room.'

'Must go now, Rudge,' I said, disappointed not able to stay with him.

'How can I forget you with a name like that,' he joked.

I'll keep you pending,' I quipped, a play on his name but, given half a chance, I'd never have kept him waiting. Reluctantly, I joined Wendy and the others. At the doorway, I looked back at him; he waved as I followed the others out of the Mess. Would I ever see him again? My emotions didn't recover, and I couldn't concentrate on the lecture.

An impressive diorama showed the landscape of Arnhem. Flags marked the bridges and strategic places held by the Red Devils. The Staff Sergeant explained how the battle had unfolded. Photographs of uniformed paratroopers hung around the walls, but I could only think of the man I'd just met. I heard footsteps outside the lecture room. They stopped and, after a moment, retreated. I wondered if it was him?

It was nearly lunchtime when we climbed back on the bus to return to Huron camp. The officers were nowhere to be seen.

'You're very quiet, Jackie. It doesn't have anything to do with Lieutenant Penley, does it?' asked Wendy. 'I think he likes you!'

A smile, her answer, spread across my face. I couldn't shake the impression of the man with the dark red hair. A hundred fireflies flitted and danced through my senses.

* * *

The telephone rang in the hall after supper and the orderly cadet answered it.

'Jackie, it's for you,' she called from the doorway.

I dared to hope it might be him and scrambled to my feet. It would have been easy to find out our Mess telephone number.

'Hello?' I said into the Bakelite receiver inside the booth.

'I couldn't wait to hear your voice again, Jackie,' Rudge said in his distinctive voice, its frequency pulling me in.

'It's good to hear yours too, Rudge,' I responded, elated.

'Did you enjoy your visit to our Depot? Staff Rogers is good, isn't he? He's a specialist on the battle of Arnhem. I followed you but the door to the lecture room was closed, so I thought I'd better leave,' he said.

I heard his deep laugh and my skin prickled.

'M'mm,' I murmured, 'Staff Rogers was good.'

'You certainly all caused a stir in the camp today! How about coming out for a drink with me on Friday night?'

I couldn't believe he wanted to take me out, he was way out of my league. Officially I was still Charles's girlfriend, but there was a draft letter on my desk telling him our relationship was over.

'I'd love to,' I said, my spirits soaring.

'Ok, I'll come and collect you from your Mess at seven,' he confirmed.

I had known it was him outside the lecture room. A wonderful sense of euphoria washed over me. I was going to see him again!

That Friday, through the anteroom window, I watched Rudge climb out of a grey Ford van parked outside our Mess. He looked different out of uniform, more handsome, a picture of health and vitality, the epitome of manhood. The evening sun shone on his dark red hair turning it to burnished copper. He smiled when he saw me coming out of the Mess and, being a perfect gentleman, opened the passenger's door. I felt nervous, but he put me at ease with his amusing wit and conversation. He drove out of the camp, turned left towards Liphook, the next town, and parked outside the Green Dragon.

'I'm told the beer's good here,' he commented.

I hadn't been there before but, even if it had been a dump, it would have been the best place on earth that evening. The Green Dragon was everything an English pub had to offer; a welcoming staff, oak beams, comfortable furniture, open fireplace and a big bar. He placed his glass of draught Guinness on a table next to my shandy and sat opposite me.

'So, Jackie, what do you want out of life?' he asked.

'Gosh, nobody has ever asked me that before,' I replied, somewhat surprised by the question. 'To have adventure and to be fulfilled,' I answered, after reflection.

Rudge smiled. He seemed to approve. He was easy to talk to and in no time, I had told him about my family, my soon to be ex-boyfriend Charles, life as an officer cadet and my love of art. I asked about his interests and was impressed by his enthusiasm. He told me he took part at Easter in the one hundred and twenty-five-mile Devizes to Westminster Canoe Race with another officer from his regiment. He was self-deprecating and made light of his achievements. His passion was free fall parachuting, and he was an assistant instructor. Rudge had a confidence that came from experience, and I felt naïve in comparison. He was twenty-two and I found him exciting and attractive. He possessed a great sense of humour and we had a wonderful time on that first date, laughing and talking together.

He drove me back to camp in his van. It was a clear night; I could see a crescent moon and a sprinkling of stars through the windscreen.

'How about Tuesday evening, same time?' he asked.

Not wanting to appear eager, relieved he couldn't see my reaction in the dark, I smiled. The knot of doubt unravelled from my solar plexus.

'Yes, I'd like that,' I replied.

He turned to look at me, his face in shadow, but I could detect his grin. There were no kisses or hugs when he dropped me off outside the Cadets' Mess, too many eyes to judge and report. I watched him drive off towards the guardroom, the taillights fading into the darkness. I had become a pawn in the game of love and I'd no idea of the outcome. I stood riveted to the spot, gripped by emotion, until I could no longer hear the sound of his van roaring up the A3. Love was not kind or gentle, but had slashed through the layers of my self-protection to leave me raw and vulnerable. I had never experienced such feelings for Charles.

* * *

'Jackie, are you ok?' Elaine asked at breakfast on Tuesday morning. 'You're very quiet and look pale.'

I was unable to concentrate, unable to sleep. I was a wreck.

'Yes, thanks,' I replied. 'I've sent a letter to Charles ending our relationship. He'll be mad with me and I'm feeling guilty.'

'Oh, I see,' she said. 'So, you've made your decision.'

I nodded and drank more coffee. I'm sure she thought I was heartless, but it had to be a clean break. I couldn't pretend anymore. Rudge was the only man who absorbed my thoughts. Nervous and excited about our date that evening, the day dragged on.

His grey van was there again outside the Cadets' Mess. I'd spent ages getting ready, trying on different dresses. I'd powdered my face and hidden the dark rings under my eyes.

Rudge greeted me, and, as soon as I was in the vehicle, whisked me off to Waggoner's Wells, a beauty spot on Ludshott Common. The chemistry between us was palpable. He hadn't kissed me yet, but I anticipated the moment he would and moistened my lips. I glanced at his strong profile as he sat beside me. He seemed to sense my thoughts and smiled. He pulled over and parked the van, jumped out, came around to open my door and offered his hand. His fingers curled around mine, the first physical connection between us, and he led me on a path into the woods. Bluebells carpeted the ground, birds sang overhead in the budding beech trees, the air, fresh and cool. My heart fluttered like a trapped butterfly against a windowpane waiting to be released. Along the path we came upon a wishing well and threw pennies in for luck.

'What did you wish for?' he asked.

'Can't tell you or it won't come true,' I replied and stared into the depths at the shining coins resting together at the bottom, full moons of promise. I'd been waiting for him all my life and there he was, my wish. He had turned my khaki world into glorious technicolour. He laughed, and I looked up into his handsome face.

'Come here,' he said.

His arms embraced me. I felt the male roughness of his jacket against my skin and the softness of his shirt as he bent down to kiss me. Blackbirds serenaded us in the magic wood, their voices rich and mellow, languid notes of love. The seductive scent of bluebells drifted from the woodland floor to mingle with his muskiness and I was lost under his spell. We'd crossed an invisible bridge into a sensual world and I fell silent when we pulled apart, breathless and trembling. He must have seen my reaction but didn't take advantage of me; perhaps believing I needed more time to be sure of the next step.

'Thirsty work, shall we go for a drink?' he grinned.

I nodded, still unable to speak. He took my hand and, with a reassuring squeeze, guided me back to his van. Every nerve fizzed and tingled.

We arrived at the Fox and Pelican pub at Grayshott to find a crowd of men at the bar celebrating their victory in a cricket match against the neighbouring village. A large two-handled silver cup filled with champagne was passed around and we were invited to join in the festivities. Rudge handed it to me and held it while I took a sip. Our eyes met, and I rejoiced at my good fortune, being with him.

CHAPTER 13

APRIL LOVE

Love was undoubtedly in the air that April. Relationships blossomed for other cadets too. Just after I met Rudge, a group of young subalterns from the Royal Corps of Signals arrived from Catterick Camp in Yorkshire to attend a military transport course at Bordon. The Army School of Transport, The School for the Royal Electrical and Mechanical Engineers, lay ten miles west of Huron Camp. Among the officers on the course was Barry, a friend of Elaine's; their fathers both served in the same regiment in Germany. Barry contacted Elaine to invite her to a dance in the Officers' Mess on 18th April. Florian accompanied Elaine that night, the night I went out with Rudge. The next evening, I received a phone call, which came through to our Mess during supper.

'It's for you, Jackie,' reported the orderly cadet.

I jumped up from the table, expecting to speak to him.

'Hello,' I said, waiting for his reply.

'Guess who?' said a strange voice.

Dispirited, I didn't have a clue. I mentioned a few names of young men who had visited our Mess in the last few months.

'No, it's Michael.'

Who was Michael? Then I remembered the Sandhurst cadet wearing the mustard waistcoat, standing on Lynette's doorstep all those months ago.

'Oh Mike! How are you?'

'I'm on the transport course and heard that you were at Hindhead.'

At first, he made polite conversation, then said he'd like to see me.

'Would you like to come out for a drink with me tomorrow?'

121

Only one man consumed my thoughts, I wasn't interested in anyone else.

'Sorry, Mike, I'm on duty,' I answered, using the first excuse that came into my head. I had already arranged to go out for a drink with Rudge to the Green Dragon.

'What a pity!' he said, the second time I had heard him use that phrase.

By all accounts the dance at Bordon on Tuesday night had been a success, afterwards, Elaine and Florian were invited out again. Florian, one of the prettiest girls in our intake, had met Matt, who was to become her husband a few years later. I remember Barry's Triumph Roadster parked outside our Mess. Matt and Florian were in the Dicky Seat at the back, Elaine alongside Barry up front. They waved and drove off, looking happy. Later that evening, Wendy came to my room.

'I am worried about Elaine and Florian,' she said. 'They haven't come back and now they are late.'

Elaine, the best student on our course, would not jeopardise her position. Jo, one of the short service commission girls, was Orderly Cadet Officer and had come to warn us. We wondered if she would tell the Orderly Officer, Captain Spurling. We didn't have to wait long to hear that our friends had been involved in a car accident. Both were in hospital and the Commandant of our camp had been informed.

The news filtered down to us. The roadster had rolled over after a head on collision with another car. Elaine had suffered injuries to her back and right eye. Florian had been thrown clear and damaged her knee. The two men sustained minor injuries but, the driver of the other car had escaped unhurt. We were concerned for Elaine and Florian, missed them in hut fifty-one, the fun and their laughter, and could only wait for updates on their condition.

Florian returned two days later with her knee strapped up, but Elaine was still in hospital following an eye operation. Her father was in the country on military business and had been contacted, so at least she would have his support. Both girls were in trouble. They hadn't signed out on the night of the accident, a lesson for us all.

Mike phoned me again on Thursday when I was supposed to be on duty. He wasn't best pleased to find me absent. However, he did phone again on Saturday and this time, feeling ashamed of my lie, I agreed to meet him for a drink. He came over that evening and collected me from the Mess in his car.

'Know any good pubs around here?' Mike asked.

'There are a couple at Liphook. We could go to the Royal Anchor,' I suggested, not wanting to go to the Green Dragon where Rudge had taken me.

We spent a pleasant couple of hours over a glass of bitter, catching up on news. Since his commissioning the previous summer, he had been at the School of Signals on the qualifying course for young officers. He asked about my decision to join the army, expressed his surprise, but agreed it must suit me as I looked so well. When he mentioned Charles, I explained that I was no longer his girlfriend because there was a new man in my life. Mike said goodbye at the Mess, and I thought that would be the last time I would see him. He had been posted to a Signal Regiment in Germany. Mike was charming, good looking and fun. But he wasn't Rudge.

A few days later after the transport course, I received a bouquet of flowers which delighted and surprised me. The red and yellow tulips looked cheerful on top of my chest of drawers. I propped the card against the vase. The sender had written – 'Guess who?'

Our daily routine continued at Huron Camp. I attended lectures; made notes and sketched Rudge's face in my notebook.

'Miss Skingley-Pearce,' said Dr. Feuchtwanger, our current affairs lecturer. 'What was the outcome of the Geneva Conference in 1954 after the French were defeated at Dien Ben Phu?'

Jolted back to the lecture, my brain scrabbled for an answer. Fragments of memory pieced together the history of the seventeenth parallel, which split Vietnam into communist North Vietnam and non-communist South Vietnam. I stammered out a reply.

On the parade square, the Regimental Sergeant Major put us through our paces. We were practising 'wheeling' and I was right marker.

'About turn!' shouted the RSM.

'Quick march!'

I led the platoon. A few seconds later a roar, enough to frighten all the wildlife on Bramshott Common, rang out across the camp.

'Miss Skingley-Pearce, where do you think you're going?'

I halted. Oh God, they had about turned, and I hadn't heard the command. Alone on the square heading towards the A3, I looked and felt a complete idiot. Such was the affliction of love.

Charles wrote, utterly furious by the Dear John letter and my decision to split up. I should have had more remorse at the upset I'd caused him, but instead felt a sense of release. Was it only a few days since I had met Rudge at Maida Barracks, the man who changed my life and gave me goose bumps?

* * *

'We're having a party in the Mess next Saturday,' Sue told Wendy and me, 'and you can bring boyfriends if you like.'

Should I ask him? I wasn't sure he'd want to come; everyone would know we were going out together and he'd be on show. Rudge called after supper. He usually did when he wasn't on duty or out with his platoon.

'How would you like to come over here on Saturday for the evening?' I asked him.

'Something special on?' he enquired.

'Well, it's our Senior's party. There'll be drinks and dancing. '

'I'll come if it means I can be with you,' he replied. 'I can't get over to see you during the week, a lot going on in the company.'

We too had a busy schedule; course homework to complete, a guest dinner night to attend, and I'd been formally appointed to arrange flowers. This role after winning first prize for the flower arranging competition on the WRAC Corps Day at the Depot, Guildford in February. Unfortunately, I had missed being presented to the Princess Royal, the Countess of Harewood and at that time the Controller Commandant of the WRAC, because I didn't hear my name over the tannoy system, instead drinking coffee in the Officers' Mess. Lesley said later I should have flowers instead of pips on my epaulettes if ever I was commissioned.

Saturday evening arrived, and the boyfriends of cadets turned up, who were young officers from various regiments in Aldershot and Borden. Rudge arrived, looking suave in a dark suit and wearing a Para tie. He must have seen the joy on my face when we greeted one another. I can't remember what I wore that night, only the pleasure of dancing with him in my high heels. The carpet had been rolled back and couples began to jive or sway to the music. Rudge offered his hand for me to join them. Sheer heaven to be in his arms, he held me close and we smooched to Pat Boon's 'April Love'. *How appropriate,* I thought. At the end of the party, Rudge kissed me goodnight outside in the dark.

'See you soon,' he promised.

I believed he would and, with his reassurance, I waited for our next date. There was no rush. We had found each other and had time ahead to develop and deepen our friendship.

* * *

I wrote to my mother about him. Mummy replied immediately, delighted that I had broken up with Charles, never having liked him. She suggested that I bring Rudge for lunch one weekend. He and I had too many commitments during the week to drive over to Camberley for dinner and could only snatch a few hours together some evenings. I really wanted Mummy to meet him. My concerns were about Reg's superior attitude, but I knew Rudge would cope with such arrogance. He must have met men like that before.

Rudge also wanted to introduce me to one of his friends and suggested we visit his old 'mucker' who lived in Cove.

I put on a pencil straight shirt and silk blouse, redid my make-up and splashed on a bit of *Joy* by Jean Patou. My mother had been offered the bottle by one of her rich friends in Camberley, who believed the perfume was more suitable for a young woman like me. I picked up my jacket and walked out of hut fifty-one, passing Wendy on the way. Happiness rose up like bubbles in a glass of champagne and overflowed with the anticipation of being with him.

'Don't be late back,' Wendy said. 'We've tests tomorrow morning.'

The moment he saw me, Rudge leapt out of the van. Wendy's warning words of tests were soon forgotten as his magnetism took over.

'So, tell me about your friend,' I asked.

'I've known Bob since I joined the Paras. We share the same passion. We're both free fall parachutists,' His face lit up with a wide grin. 'You'll like his wife, Jane, she's a cracker!'

We sped along the A3 and, half an hour later, pulled up in front of a house on the Officers' Married Quarters. Rudge turned off the engine.

Apprehensive, I wondered if his friend would approve of me. My concerns dissipated on meeting Bob and Jane. They were newlyweds, and their mutual love radiated warmth.

'You must be Jackie. I've heard a lot about you,' said Jane, a glamorous woman with twinkling eyes. She beamed and glanced at Rudge. Bob's broad smile and strong handshake echoed her greeting, as if giving the thumbs up to his friend. Seeing them together, I dared to imagine being Rudge's wife. I'd denied myself the chance to become Charles's. But I wasn't sure if Rudge would ever be ready for domesticity. He was a man of action, the very characteristic that had attracted me to him in the first place.

While we enjoyed drinks, the men talked about the National Free Fall Parachuting Championships on the 13th and 14th of May, an important event that attracted parachutists around the country. Listening to their conversation, I admired the confidence and enthusiasm they shared for this dangerous and daring sport. I sensed their trust and bond of friendship. I learned later that Rudge had many friends who held him in high regard for his strength of character, enthusiasm, respect he had for others and, not least of all, his wit and charm.

'Can't make it, Rudge, have an exercise on. Damn shame,' Bob said with regret. 'But we'll be parachuting together when we go over to visit the French Paras in the summer.'

'Would you like to come along, Jackie, and watch me jump on the 14th?' Rudge asked.

'That's sounds exciting,' I answered, delighted to be included in this major part of his life, to witness the environment that made his adrenalin race.

It was an event that would change my life.

CHAPTER 14

MAIDA BARRACKS

Reg sat at the head of the table, pontificating about various things during lunch. Rudge listened with interest, addressing him as 'Sir' in the right places. He rose in my estimation for the way he handled Reg, firm but polite. But my mother's brown eyes sparkled, delighted for me.

'He is a fine young man,' Mummy congratulated, handing me a tea towel to help wash dishes after the meal. I was proud to have her approval, the first she'd given to any of my boyfriends.

'How's Charles taking the news?' she asked.

'He wants all his presents back,' I laughed. 'Who wants a set of fruit knives and forks for their bottom drawer anyway?'

'You're better out of that relationship,' she retorted. 'Rudge is in a different class completely.' She had certainly gained the correct measure of him. The visit had gone well, but I couldn't wait to leave to be alone with him.

'He wasn't that bad,' Rudge remarked as we drove away. I had known he could outwit Reg and now had the proof. We laughed and conversed the way friends do, the bond strengthening between us.

'How about I come over tomorrow before supper? We could go out for a pub meal?' Rudge suggested when we arrived at Hindhead.

'I'd love that,' I said, smiling at another chance to be with him.

I waved goodbye outside the Mess and skipped back to hut fifty-one, my feet light as air.

We cherished the moments when we could be together. Army life was demanding for both of us – I had my course, and he was training his men and taking part in exercises and sporting events.

Our relationship had deepened. We shared inner thoughts and ideals, aware of our growing intimacy. I still felt a little in awe of him, afraid my bubble of happiness would burst at any second, but the way he looked at me and his lingering touch sent out clear messages.

Late afternoon, straight after classes on Monday, we drove to Frensham Ponds Hotel. We had drinks in the bar and played the two-handed football pub game, which he won every time, being far too quick for me and, likely because of more practise. We ate pork pies and salted crisps, licked our fingers, drank beer and talked, learning more about each other. The day was almost over as we left the hotel. We parked his car by the lake, not wanting the day to end. The sunset was spectacular. Golden clouds lit up the pale blue sky, slowly turning to a deep pink leaving a flush across the horizon, a promise of another fine day.

We were looking at the changing colours, savouring the moment when Rudge spoke. 'You've such soft skin,' he said, leaning over to kiss me. When he did, it unleashed the mounting sexual desire between us, and in his strong arms, I wanted nothing more than to consummate our relationship. But this was not the right place, not the right night.

'It's getting late,' he said, looking at his watch. 'I've to get you back to camp.'

Restrictions imposed on me curtailed our time together, which we both regretted that evening. He started the engine and the radio came on. Linda Scott was singing 'I've Told Every Little Star'. We had a future together and every little star would know.

* * *

A blue envelope with 'Pegasus' embossed on the flap, waited for me in the letter rack on Wednesday morning, addressed to:

Officer Cadet J. Skindley Pearce WRAC.

Lt R D Penley
Officers' Mess
Depot The Parachute Regiment and Airborne Forces
Maida Barracks
Aldershot

8th May 1961

Darling Jackie,

Merely on impulse, I decided I wanted to write you a letter: so here I am at twenty to midnight with the smell of your perfume still lingering – lucky me.

Why did I want to write? It suddenly occured to me that you haven't seen my appaling writing or spelling so I had better let you know that the guy that has recently fallen hopelessly in love with you is almost illiterate. And I also thought that if I write to you, I might get a letter back. In fact, I'll go further, if I don't get a letter before Friday, I'll smack your arse then!

Roll on Friday Jackie – I love you!

Rudge xxxx

* * *

Officer Cadet Wing
School of Instruction
HINDHEAD
Surrey

10th May 1961

Darling Rudge,

I had a wonderful time with you on Monday and can't wait to see you again. I don't care that you can't spell and have appalling writing, because I love you.

I'd like to see you try and smack my arse! But you'll have this letter by Friday, so you won't need to, will you?!

Fondest love,
Jackie
xxxxxx

* * *

He arrived on Friday with a grin. Having proclaimed our love, a whole evening lay before us. I wanted to throw my arms about him, but I knew I couldn't right then and there – not outside the Cadets' Mess with everyone going in and out for dinner. Rudge revved the van the minute I climbed aboard, and we shot off to the Barley Mow Pub near Farnham. I remember that moment, on the brink of our love affair, my happiness and the joy of being with him. We strolled into the bar, hand in hand, and he ordered his usual draught Guinness and my shandy. I hadn't been converted to the bitter taste of stout, so velvety black with its frothy head that he favoured so much.

'It slips down like milk,' he said.

He sat beside me, every cell in my body rejoicing. He must

have sensed my heightened awareness because he grinned and laughed when we started to talk at the same time, dispersing awkwardness, before relaxing into comfortable conversation. He spoke more about the parachuting competition and agreed to come over to Camberley early on Sunday morning to take me to Kidlington. I'd arranged to go home on Saturday and knew Mummy would be pleased to see Rudge again.

On leaving the pub, it was such a beautiful evening that we decided to go for a walk. He took my hand and found a path that took us up a slight hill through a copse. At the top on a grassy area, we stood looking down at the village green and the Barley Mow.

'It's been a great evening,' he said, putting his arms around me. He gave me a bear hug, noticing the nametape sewn onto the back of my dress.

'Oh Christ,' he said mortified, 'I misspelt your name!'

He held me so tightly I could hardly breathe, his body hard as iron, mine compliant. He already knew the answer when he asked if I would go back to his room. Rudge didn't say much on the way to Maida Barracks, except that we would have to sneak in and be quiet. Women weren't allowed in the Officers' Quarters. He drove into the Barracks and around to the back of the Mess, parking his van. With a mixture of increased anticipation and apprehension of being discovered, we slipped through a side door of the building. It gave onto a long corridor with a red carpet and regimental pictures on the walls. Rudge opened his door and ushered me in, locking it behind us.

He closed the curtains. We tore off our clothes. Naked, we lay on his narrow bed. The first kiss and caress created a wild energy. I didn't want him to stop but we parted a little so that he could reach out for a packet of condoms from the bedside locker. He ripped one open. He didn't use it. Something had broken the spell that bound us.

I gasped, surprised.

'What's wrong?'

He sat up, his face etched with sadness.

'I'm sorry,' he admitted. 'I've got this problem. Her name is Gina.'

'What are you talking about?' I asked in disbelief.

After a few seconds he swung his legs out of bed, padded over to a trunk and opened it. He took out a photo, handing it to me. A picture of a glamorous woman in her early twenties, with a perfect body, far better than mine, smiled provocatively at me. What was going on? My mind was in free fall. Gina had everything, plus the art of seduction that I hadn't learnt.

'I've been seeing her for a while. She phones me up when she wants me and then comes down from London and books a hotel for us to have sex, then she ...' his voice trailed off, not ready to reveal what they did together. He was the kind of man that any woman would have wanted, charismatic and desirable. I was sure he'd had plenty of lovers, but this revelation shocked me. Was she still in his life?

'Gina is a model for fashion magazines. Ready to open her legs for any photographer after he's taken her picture,' he said with distaste. I was too astounded to respond. Perhaps it was her sexual mastery that attracted him? But he didn't love her by the way he spoke of her. Was she an addiction? What did he want of me then? Why this confession? I looked at her photograph again. She was cool, beautiful and sexy. How could I ever compete? A wave of sorrow swept over me. How complex lives can become. One minute I was on top of the world, the next I was lost. He lay beside me, apologetic, waiting for my reaction. I pulled the sheet up to cover my nakedness.

'I have no excuse. You have a lovely figure,' he whispered.

At least, in this moment, he was with me. I loved him and would do anything for him, but I felt rejected, disappointed, inadequate, too taken aback to say so. There was a vulnerability about him that touched me, as if he were asking for help. What nightmare had he got himself into? It was now mine too. How were we to resolve this?

The fading light crept though the sides of the closed curtains forming patterns on the walls. Above his desk on a mantelshelf was the photo I had recently given him, taken a year before on my eighteenth birthday. Seeing it there gave me hope, but I was no longer the girl portrayed in the picture.

'I have to get back to camp, Rudge,' I said, wanting to end the evening.

'I wish you could stay,' he murmured. I turned my back while we dressed. We tiptoed back down the corridor and nothing more was said as he drove me back to Hindhead, the silence roaring between us. He stopped the van outside the Cadet Mess.

'Night, Rudge,' I said.

'See you early Sunday morning at your house,' he confirmed, brushing his lips against my cheek before I climbed out of the van and driving off. So, he did want to see me again. But could I put myself through that once more? I walked back to hut fifty-one, trying to seize control of my bruised emotions. What should I have said? What should I have done? I convinced myself, that next time, I would be able to talk to him about her, about Gina.

CHAPTER 15

KIDLINGTON

On Sunday 14th May 1961, the overcast sky threatened rain. I wore my new green and white dress, put on my jade earrings and slipped into a pair of high heels. Despite them, I still felt small beside Rudge at 6' 6". He arrived after breakfast and, shrugging on my mackintosh, I went out to open the gate into our driveway.

'You look good,' he said.

Sensing his slight agitation, which was out of character, I smiled nervously, awkward about our last evening together.

'Need to get off as I have to repack one of my 'chutes when we get to Kidlington. Have to see a few people too.'

'I'll be home next month when I get another weekend pass. I have to go now, as Rudge can't stop,' I said to Mummy, collecting my handbag and climbing into the van, making myself comfortable beside him. I looked at Rudge in profile. A stray lock of titian hair caressed his forehead. His strong arms were bare in a short-sleeved shirt, covered in freckles and a fine sprinkling of golden hairs. He had jokingly said that in the summer all his freckles joined up. We never mentioned Friday night. But here we were together and maybe we would have another chance to make love.

'Hope the weather holds,' he said, looking through the windscreen at the clouds scudding across the sky. He put his hand on my thigh.

'Good to have you with me.'

I felt reassured and some of my doubts faded.

'You'll soon be doing this with me. I want you to share the marvellous experience that gives you freedom and makes you feel alive up there.' He laughed. His kit was stowed in the back of the van. Parachutes and harnesses, boots and helmet.

He was passionate about skydiving, the surge of adrenalin, the buzz and the danger. I wasn't sure if I could do it. I hated heights.

Rudge expected a lot, but he would be teaching me. He had my trust and it would be an adventure, so I smiled and nodded. I loved being with him, full of life and energy. When he spoke to me, I felt that I was the only person in the world that mattered to him.

'I'm going to take you down to Pompey to meet my folks next week. Would you like that?'

'I'd love to. When had you planned to go down?'

'Wanted to ask you first. How about next Saturday?'

'Yes, perfect,' I replied with a light heart. *It's going to be all right,* I thought, *he does still love me.* Perhaps we could resolve his predicament with Gina? But I couldn't speak her name.

'I'll write to them tonight and tell them we're coming. I want them to meet you.'

The sun emerged from behind a grey cloud, new leaves glistened on the trees and wild flowers dotted the hedgerows. I looked ahead and saw a strangely shaped small tree on the side of the road. I half closed my eyes; it looked like an angel with wings. I would do this as a child; make out faces from the shapes of branches and leaves in trees. This one had dark leaves, almost black, giving me a sudden feeling of foreboding.

We arrived at Kidlington airfield at around eleven o'clock. Rudge parked by a hangar where men wearing jumpsuits, their goggles hung around their necks, were busy with equipment. I imagined myself kitted up like them in this new environment, and soon realised why parachutists found the sport so exciting.

'Hi, Rudge,' said Jim, one of the subalterns from 1 Para. He came over to join us when Rudge opened the back doors of his van. 'I'm going up in twenty minutes. When are you scheduled to jump?'

'I'm just going to check in now and find out,' Rudge replied. 'You remember Jackie, don't you?'

'You bet,' said Jim and winked. He was in the Mess the day I went with the other cadets to Maida Barracks. Rudge left to search for the organiser of the event, full of expectation and enthusiasm. Jim joked with me until Rudge returned a few minutes later. He took me over to the airfield where the Dropping Zone had been laid out like a big orange keyhole. A crowd of people milled around waiting for day two of the competition to begin. An Auster took off and flew overhead.

Rudge was preoccupied with the competition but equally considerate and concerned about me while he took part, making me feel important to him.

'Will you be ok if I leave you here for a while? I need to get changed and sort out my kit before my slot. You'll see me soon. I'll be flying down to get you. I've a jump shortly and then another this afternoon. Afterwards we can go and get a bite to eat.'

'Sounds good,' I said, smiling.

I watched small aircraft taxiing along the runway. Men with parachute harnesses and backpacks hung around near the planes, parked up by the hangars. Spectators laughed and joked, enjoying the event. Small boys with model airplanes acted out battles. I felt happy spending the day close to the man I loved, sharing the experience that he loved.

Up into the patched blue sky flew the planes at differing intervals. One, and then two, parachutists fell out of them, free falling to 2,000 feet silken chutes then opening and floating down to the Dropping Zone. A round of applause erupted as one of the men landed slap bang in the middle. Here came another. The red and white chute collapsed as the man landed inside the orange keyhole. The parachutist took off his helmet and I saw the dark red hair. Rudge wore a competitor's tabard with the no 3 emblazoned upon it, his face lit up, charged with excitement, full of smiles. A young boy ran up to him 'That was wizard!' he shouted.

'Hey,' Rudge said, seeing me. 'That was fun. Did you see me up there? But I want to do better on the next run. Come and help me repack my chute.'

I watched as he laid his parachute on the floor of a hanger, folding each panel over until it was totally pleated, long ropes stretching from it like jellyfish tentacles.

'Can you come here,' he asked, 'and put your heel in that?' He anchored the ropes around one of my high heels as if he wanted to involve me in this important safety procedure. Then he pulled everything into alignment.

'Thanks,' he said, coming over to release my foot again, his hand brushing against my leg, awakening my senses. He folded the 'chute and packed it into the harness with the ripcord showing, confident and skilled as if he had repeated the same operation many times before.

'Now we're going to practice how to count seconds,' he said. 'Repeat one thousand and one, one thousand and two, one thousand and three.'

I copied him.

'Yes, that's right. That's how we count seconds up there when we've jumped before we pull the ripcord. Five to ten seconds from three thousand feet.'

Finally kitted out with his main and emergency chutes, the meticulous checks completed, he picked up his helmet.

'Would you like to come up with me?' he asked as we walked outside.

'That would be brilliant!' I answered, pushing aside my childhood fears. I wanted to stay with him, hoping flying would be a better experience than I anticipated. A cold breeze chilled me, and I was glad of my Mac. We headed towards a Piper light aircraft parked on the apron of a runway.

'Hi, Tom,' he said to the pilot. 'Can you take me up?'

'Sure Rudge, I'm ready to go,' he said.

'Can my girlfriend come too?'

'Ok, I've an extra seat,' replied Tom. 'Climb aboard.'

The plane leapt forward with the roar of the twin engines. The ground sped by and suddenly we were up into the grey sky. Through gaps in the clouds, we could look down through the small windows at the airfield, the bright orange marker of the Dropping Zone clearly visible.

'Are you ok?' Rudge asked.

'Yes, fine,' I smiled. Being with him overrode my fears.

'Nearly 3,000 feet,' the pilot said.

'Right,' acknowledged Rudge. He stood up, rechecked his harness and put on his helmet, fixing the straps under his chin.

'See you later,' he said with a nod and opened the aircraft door. The cold air whistled in. He went backwards into the void and hung onto the doorframe. Verifying his position above the Dropping Zone, he shouted to the pilot.

'Are the brakes on?' He swore. 'Bugger, they're not!' His foot slipped on the wheel used to balance before launching into space.

'Sorry,' said the pilot. 'I'll go around again.'

Rudge stepped back into the plane, which then turned, circling over the airfield for a while.

'Ready in position,' he shouted, taking up his previous stance to leave the aircraft. The plane throttled back. He put his right foot out onto the wheel and this time it was secure. He let go and fell to earth. His courage was amazing. Would I be able to just take a step into the unknown like that?

The wind had strengthened, and the clouds were thicker. This time when I looked down through the window, visibility was poor. Between smaller gaps in the clouds I noticed that the Dropping Zone was being rolled up. It looked like the competition had been abandoned.

'There he goes,' Tom said, and we could just make out the opened red and white canopy of Rudge's parachute.

Instinctively, I felt that something was not right. Was it because I felt alone without him, or because the plane was flying through turbulence? But why was the orange keyhole rolled up? I concentrated on thinking of what we would be doing later, after the competition. Maybe we would have a drink with his friends and then go out for a meal together. By now I was hungry.

The Piper landed with a few bumps on the runway and taxied along the airstrip. I thanked Tom for the new experience of flying, secretly grateful to be back on terra firma. There was no sign of Rudge or anyone else. I left the plane, a bit shaken up. A feeling of déjà vu swept over me. I had witnessed this before – this sense of foreboding, falling through space – in a nightmare. Where was he? I hurried towards the hangars where Rudge had parked his van. Rounding a corner, there in front of me, a crowd of people. My heart missed a beat; I knew something terrible had happened.

I pushed through the mass of people.

The image of Rudge lying there will stay with me forever.

His parachute lay around him like a halo, covered in his blood. He was breathing in a strange way, rasping, rattling. His eyes open, pupils dilated, but he was unconscious. I stood transfixed. He was having a fit, shaking and twitching. I don't know how long I watched him; my brain unable to process the scene. I felt ice cold. Time froze. My knees weakened, and a deep pain raked the pit of my stomach. Someone put an arm around my shoulder.

'Rudge is a strong man and he's a fighter,' a male voice encouraged.

I couldn't reply. I wanted to rush over and hold him but a woman was there beside him, an off-duty nurse from the John Radcliffe Oxford hospital. Powerless to do anything, I was only able to watch him struggling for his life. The ambulance arrived, and Rudge was moved onto a stretcher.

'Come on,' said the kind man beside me. 'We're going to A &

E, so we can find out what's happened to him.'

Over the next few hours, I sat on a chair in the Accident and Emergency waiting room with Rudge's friends and the off-duty nurse. We sat in silence, waiting for news. My mind fragmented, trying to absorb what had gone wrong. He was an experienced skydiver. Why did he land by the hangar and not on the airfield?

Eventually a surgeon came out of an operating room.

'Are you here about the parachutist?' he asked us.

'Yes,' we all said. He shook his head.

'These young men, what a waste! There is nothing I can do.'

The horror of his words seeped into every one of us.

'Jackie, if you give me your telephone number I'll keep you informed about Rudge,' said the off-duty nurse.

'Would you? Oh, thanks so much,' I whispered.

Like an automaton I opened my handbag, taking out my notebook and pen. We weren't allowed to go into the intensive care ward where he had been taken. The realisation dawned on me as I thought of Rudge, his vibrancy, his zest for life, the totally wonderful person that he was, my friend, my love, I might never see him again. His friends looked shocked and, trying to keep emotions on an even keel, practicalities took over.

'There is nothing more we can do here, but we must inform his parents,' said Peter, who had taken me under his wing.

'Does anyone know where they live?'

'Near Portsmouth,' I said automatically.

'I'll get onto directory enquiries.'

He left to find a phone. Rudge's friends stayed with me. Barely aware of their conversation, I remained in a trance.

'We'll get his things and drive his van back to Aldershot,' I heard Jim say, cutting through the cotton wool sounds. 'I'm going to call the duty officer at the Depot.'

'No Penleys in the phone book,' said Peter coming back from the phone booth.

'Maybe they don't have one,' I replied. 'Perhaps we'll have to call the police?'

'Yes, it's the only answer,' Peter agreed.

His poor parents, what a way to receive the terrible news of their son. Peter had spoken to one of the nurses who shortly afterwards appeared with a cup of hot sweet tea. It was the first thing I had had since breakfast. I had no hunger, no thirst, no feeling. Only emptiness.

'Ok,' said Jim, 'I've spoken to the Duty Officer back at the Depot and he is sorting out how to inform Rudge's parents.'

'I think I should get you back home now, young lady,' said Peter.

'I have to go to Hindhead,' I replied in a dull voice.

He led me out of the hospital and I climbed into his car without a word. Peter explained that he was one of Rudge's skydiving friends and that they had known each other for about a year. He tried his best to engage me in conversation but, numb with shock, I couldn't concentrate. The journey seemed unending. In the dark, cat's eyes marked the central white line and flashed their warning along the country roads from Newbury. I could only think of him and what we should be doing at that moment. Rudge would be drinking his draught Guinness, talking to me in that engaging way of his. And afterwards, despite Gina, we might have solved the barrier she had created between us, instead he lay damaged and broken in Intensive Care. I might never feel his arms around me again, his lips on mine. I shuddered uncontrollably as sorrow seeped into my shredded senses.

We reached Huron camp and Peter asked me where he should drop me off.

'Will you be ok now?' he asked awkwardly as I got out in front of the Mess.

'Yes, I'm ok, thanks, Peter,' I lied.

'I'll be in touch when I have news of Rudge,' he said leaving me outside.

Fatigue overwhelmed me. I pushed open the door to see my

friends laughing and joking in the anteroom, a normal night in the Mess. Life continued here as it always did. My world had fallen apart, my dreams broken.

'Wendy,' I croaked.

She leapt out of her chair the moment she saw me, calling the others.

'Lesley, Florian!'

My three friends rushed over.

'Whatever's the matter, Jackie?'

'It's Rudge, he's had an accident,' I managed to say. Then my legs collapsed beneath me.

I found myself in bed, wearing my pyjamas. Lesley, Wendy and Florian were talking.

'Do you think we should tell the Office?' Wendy asked the others.

'Oh, Jackie, you had us all worried. What's happened?'

In broken sentences, I sobbed out the truth. Rudge was unconscious with serious head injuries and I wanted to be with him.

'You need to sleep now,' said Wendy. 'You've had a terrible shock and you're exhausted.'

'How can I?' I cried.

'You can,' said Wendy.

She came over to the bed.

'Turn over,' she rubbed my back. 'Sleep, sleep,'

I could no longer stay awake. I had been beside myself since the accident that afternoon, but had held myself together as best I could. The effort of coping with the shock of watching Rudge fight for his life, my helplessness, the surgeon's words, had taken their toll on my emotional state. My mind and body finally gave in, and I fell into an abyss of darkness.

CHAPTER 16

COMPASSIONATE LEAVE

That moment of waking, the split second before memories arrive, had gone. Every detail of the accident came flooding back. I hardly remembered the return journey. Still unable to come to terms with the terrible events of the day before, I lay in bed staring at the ceiling and began to tremble. Lesley knocked on my door at seven o'clock to check that I was awake. She smiled in an effort to encourage me.

'Jackie, come on, get up and put on your uniform. We must be at breakfast in half an hour,' she chided. 'I'll come back for you when I'm ready.'

In automatic mode, I carried out my morning routine. Washed and dressed in my uniform, I stood in front of the mirror and examined my sad, heart-shaped face. Mummy had a widow's peak too. Was that an omen? What was happening to him right now? Was he still alive? I hoped his parents had received the message about the accident and were with him. I wanted to be there too. How was I going to get through this? My mind raced with thoughts, too numerous to process.

Lesley accompanied me to breakfast. I don't remember eating anything, only cadets trying to find comforting words. The routine of morning lessons, afternoon drill on the parade ground, helped to give me boundaries in which to function. I felt detached. Close friends were by my side, keeping an eye on me in case they needed to tell the Office or get help. Elaine was still in hospital and I missed her. My role was to carry on, there was no other option. As Rudge's unofficial girlfriend, I had to wait for news, reliant on others.

The following day, Tuesday, 16th May, we attended a short service in the church on camp. Officer cadets took it in turns to do a reading. That morning, it was to be my duty. After the hymn, I went to the lectern and read the pre-selected psalm, number 121.

'I will lift up mine eyes unto the hills, from whence cometh my help...'

The words blurred on the page, but I managed to read to the end. *Please, God, look after him*, I prayed. I looked up from the Bible. Friends were in tears and officers on the staff, serious and concerned. By the end of the first lecture, I was called to Major Vennard's office.

'Sit down, Jackie,' she said. 'We've heard about the tragic accident of your friend on Sunday and we're wondering if you would like leave to go and see him in hospital?'

I considered for several moments. An intuitive and unexplainable knowledge came from nowhere, perhaps a sixth sense. His spirit had already left this world, only his broken body remained to fight on in intensive care.

'No thank you, Ma'am, his family will be with him by now,' I replied. 'I don't think he'll ever wake up again.'

'If you change your mind, then let us know.'

'Yes, I will, thank you, Ma'am,' I whispered, still numb with shock.

That evening there was a dinner night to which Major Vennard and the Officers were invited. We wore our Number One dress uniform, a tight fitting dark green suit. One of the cadets was elected to be Miss Vice for these dinners. At the end of the meal, her role was to give the loyal toast to Her Majesty the Queen – thank goodness it wasn't to be me. I couldn't have faced any more duties. The cadets gathered in the anteroom awaiting the arrival of the Officers for dinner at seven thirty. I sat on a settee with Anne, one of the cadets from hut forty-seven. I'd been thinking about him all day. Should I have gone to the hospital? The tearing pain of guilt, and the seeming irrelevance of still being at Hindhead while he was dying in Oxford jarred my senses and, sobbing, I hid my face in my hands.

'Here, Jackie, have this,' said one of the girls, offering me a sherry. I held the schooner glass and at that moment a shiver ran through me. I knew that he had gone. The clock on the wall registered a quarter past seven.

'Anne,' I whispered. 'Rudge has just died.'

The room receded. The girls in uniform moved and talked but I couldn't hear them. My senses retreated to an inner space where time didn't exist. Fragmented memories floated in my mind. I saw his face, felt his touch, heard his voice, a whisper, 'bide with me', and as swiftly as they arrived, faded away.

I had no other choice but to attend the dinner night. I made conversation and continued in a state of limbo until I could be alone to let go of my anguish.

The next morning at lectures, a WRAC corporal appeared at the doorway of the classroom.

'Miss Skingley-Pearce, there's an urgent call for you,' she announced.

I made my excuses, sped over the short distance between the lecture hut to the telephone box and grabbed the unhooked receiver.

'Jackie,' I answered, my stomach sick with apprehension.

'It's Jan here from the John Radcliffe Hospital.'

'Oh!' I exhaled.

'I am so sorry, Jackie, Rudge passed away last night.'

'Yes, I thought so,' I whispered. 'What time did he die?'

'Seven-fifteen,' she said.

* * *

Major Vennard contacted my mother midmorning to tell her that I had been given compassionate leave following Rudge's death. Compliant with her wishes, I automatically packed a few things. While I waited in my room for Reg, I wrote to Rudge's parents. Several attempts later I was able to put the words on paper. Tears marked the progress of my thoughts, smudging the ink. Eventually, I managed a few lines on a fresh piece of notepaper. Expressing my deepest condolences at the beginning, I concluded with these sentences.

'I was with Rudge in the plane when he made his final parachute jump last Sunday. We had been going out together for a while and were very close friends. I loved him very much. Please can you let me know about his funeral?

My stepfather came to collect me in the Daimler.

'I'm here to take you home,' he said without any emotion or compassion, no words of comfort forthcoming from his cold heart.

It was a beautiful day returning to Camberley. We drove along roads bounded on both sides with beech, branches of trees made a guard of honour with their new leaves. Life surged everywhere, birds nesting, flowers blooming. How cruel when he wasn't here to share it with me.

Mummy threw her arms around me the minute I arrived at Deramore Cottage.

'I am so, so, sorry darling,' she said, her face wet with tears.

Reg left us clinging to each other, turned the car around and headed back to his desk in Farnborough.

My old bedroom gave me the solace and privacy I needed. Grief stood in my shadow, hungry to steal all my senses. Broken images of the accident played over and over in my numbed mind. My heart enclosed in armour, the key lost somewhere in Oxfordshire. Below in the garden, rhododendrons and azaleas bloomed, creating a vibrant carpet of colour. Green leaves dressed the silver birch trees and, beyond them, in the distance, the Hogs Back sculpted the horizon. Everything was familiar, but nothing remained the same. Nature wore her early summer ball gown and mocked me.

'Come down, darling, and have a cup of tea,' my mother called from the bottom of the stairs.

I made an effort to get off the bed. Everything felt surreal.

'There you are,' she said as I sat down beside her on the sofa. 'I just have one thing to say about your Rudge. Once there was you, and God, and Rudge, and now there is you, and God, and Rudge.'

I didn't understand at first what her wise words meant. My mother had a spiritual awareness her Scottish ancestors would have called fey. Her friend, Jane, was a Theosophist, and Mummy had embraced the teachings of Krishnamurti and his thoughts on the timelessness of love.

She spoke of my father, how he was killed, and that she too knew the moment he had died. He, like Rudge, had fallen out of his plane to his death. She told me how she had mourned him, thought of suicide, but realised that life was precious, and she had to continue for the sake of my brother and me. Her understanding, empathy and deep love broke through my anaesthetised soul and I welcomed the savageness of grief.

The Daily Telegraph arrived on Thursday morning and there was the announcement of Rudge's death. 'As a result of a parachuting accident ...' Until I read it, everything had seemed untrue. The black print burnt the words into my brain, confirming the terrible reality.

The next sequence of events was clouded by shock. Somehow, his parents received my letter on time and with only a scant address.

'Please come down today and stay with us for the funeral,' his mother had said, adding that Rudge wouldn't want people to wear black and how much they looked forward to meeting me. It was a huge boost to my morale to have his family's acceptance.

There would be challenging times ahead, but now I wouldn't be alone in my sorrow.

I worried about what to wear. Rudge had confided in me he'd been colour blind, so it didn't really matter, but I wanted him to be proud of me. In the end I chose a three-quarter sleeved cotton dress, one that I'd worn on one of our dates. It was dark grey with splashes of red, purple and white. I also took a soft black velvet hat lined with grey silk, a multi coloured silk band around the crown. I packed everything into an overnight bag, including black high-heeled shoes. One of my jade earrings was missing, probably lost during the tragic events of last Sunday.

'They brought you bad luck,' my mother said when I told her, 'and now you must throw away the other one into running water, to let go of its negative energy.' It now lies at the bottom of Blackwater River.

I took the train to Portsmouth on Thursday afternoon. I sat in a carriage by the window, a little afraid of meeting his family, thinking of how it might have been on Saturday, the day Rudge had promised to take me to visit them.

His home, close to the sea, lay on the slopes of Portsdown Hill. I imagined him growing up there as a boy, loving his environment. I found the house and rang the bell. A lady opened the door and I knew immediately she was his mother, because Rudge had looked so much like her. She had a fine chiselled face with high cheekbones.

'Jackie?' she enquired.

'Yes,' I replied and fell into her arms.

All over the house were his trophies, medals and photos, smiling at us. Rudge's father, devastated by the loss of his wonderful son, asked me many questions about his last parachute jump at Kidlington. His mother, heartbroken too, bore her grief with great dignity. She told me what a shock it had been on Sunday night when the policeman came to tell them of Rudge's accident.

'I went to Oxford to be with him. I knew his injuries were serious but didn't know what to expect. When I saw him, he looked just like Rudge, except for the blood around his nose,' she said, her face clouded with sadness. 'I was told by the doctors that, had he lived, he would have been a vegetable. The damage to his brain was extensive. He wouldn't have wanted that. I imagine him parachuting all over heaven now.'

How brave she must have been to encourage him to follow his dream when growing up, to become a soldier and a paratrooper. And how proud she must have been when Rudge became the first direct entrant from Sandhurst to be commissioned into The Parachute Regiment. Her calm acceptance of how he had died made a deep impression on me. She understood her son, his love of life and passion for parachuting. I wished I had learnt more about him, the stories of his youth and experiences that shaped the man he had become.

The vicar turned up that evening to discuss the funeral service.

'Jackie, would you like to choose a hymn for Rudge?' he asked.

I felt grateful to be included in the discussion but hadn't imagined I would be asked for my opinion.

'I'm not sure, I can only think of 'Abide with Me',' I suggested.

Rudge had said those words, 'bide with me', on that fateful day, after he had packed his 'chute. I'd received them as confirmation he cared for me.

'That hymn is far too old for him,' said the vicar. I wanted to stand up for my choice, a soldiers' hymn, but I was only Rudge's unofficial girlfriend. In the end, the family chose, 'He Who Would Valiant Be' and 'The Lord is my Shepherd'.

Relatives visited to pay their respects. I began to find the situation too much and, to escape, offered to take the family dog, Bosun, for a walk. I heard the vicar say that Rudge's coffin had arrived at Christ Church on Portsdown. I had no idea of the funeral arrangements, so I was taken aback by this startling news. He was so close; I had to be with him.

I walked up the hill with Bosun and found the church. I wanted to be alone, to say goodbye to Rudge, to pray beside his coffin, but the door was locked. Distraught, I sat on a gravestone in the graveyard looking out to the Solent. The intense pain of separation hit me. Engulfed by grief, I sobbed until there were no tears left, only shuddering breaths. We'd had such little time together; our love affair had only just begun. There were so many questions unanswered.

'Oh, Rudge, what happened up there?'

The little dog pushed himself against me, willing me to stroke him. I wondered if he knew that his friend had gone. Then from nowhere, a wave of peace washed over me. It was as if Rudge was saying 'I'm ok.' Perhaps then, he was indeed parachuting all over heaven. I looked up at the magnificent night sky. The stars above me twinkled, the moon was up and the lights of Portsmouth danced in front of my eyes.

'Time to go home, boy,' I said to Bosun.

CHAPTER 17

THE FUNERAL

Rudge's home gave me comfort; I sensed he was there with us. His gentle and caring mother understood how much I had loved her son. As I lay in my bed that night, I worried that she should be warned about Gina's photos when his effects were sent from the Officers' Mess. I slept fitfully, dreaming of him, and anxious when awake how I was going to cope at the funeral.

Early on Friday morning, his mother came into my room with a cup of tea. Tentatively, I asked her if he had mentioned me at all. She shook her head.

'No, Jackie,' she replied.

'We were planning to come and see you on Saturday,' I explained, tears welling up. She hugged me and I laid my head against her breast as if she was my mother.

'I never thought that he would make old bones,' she whispered.

I broached the subject of his old girlfriend, Gina, and the photographs, so there was no mystery in finding them. I had to do this on his behalf, but I chose my words with care.

'The family are coming here after the funeral for a late lunch,' she said. 'Will you help me with the preparations?'

'Yes, please, I'd like that very much,' I replied, grateful for something to do.

After breakfast we laid out cutlery and crockery on the dining table. We covered up the prepared cold dishes with tea towels. Then it was time to get ready. I dressed in my grey frock, feeling unusually calm. I hoped I wouldn't let his parents down by uncontrollable weeping.

A car arrived outside the house at half past one to take us to the church and then onto Porchester crematorium. Other family members arrived in their vehicles to accompany his parents. The convoy drove up the hill to Christ Church. Outside a sea of red berets, officers and men of the Parachute regiment came to say goodbye to their brother, to give him a military send off. I clasped my hands, digging in fingernails to divert the emotional pain. I had to stay calm.

In front of us, Rudge's coffin, covered with the Union Jack, lay on a gun carriage. It took all my fortitude to hold back the tears. This was the first time I had been physically close to him since the accident. It was real, final, heart wrenching. His spirit had left and all that remained of him, after the autopsy, was a mutilated body inside a wooden box. The procession slowly headed west towards the crematorium where, outside, it halted. On either side of the gun carriage, stood his close friends, his brother Para officers.

His family and friends took their places inside the chapel. There wasn't enough room for everyone who had come to pay their respects and the remainder gathered outside. The officers gently carried Rudge's coffin to the waiting trestle at the front of the chapel. On top of the Union Jack, lay his red beret. I sat with his family on the left side of the room, oblivious to everything but the beret, choking back my tears.

The vicar spoke. We prayed. We sang 'He Who Would Valiant Be'. Then I heard the words that brought me into the moment. This was part of his eulogy. The famous 'If' by Rudyard Kipling, after whom he had been named:

If anyone had filled the unforgiving minute, it had been Rudge.

The bugler sounded the Last Post as the coffin rolled forwards on runners towards the unseen furnace. The curtains closed and he was gone. My heart went with him into the flames.

Grief smothers life. Its runaway power consumes and destroys peace of mind, a fractured and broken spirit, resulting in moments so overwhelming that emotions become unhinged.

Once released, grief engulfs like a great blanket of fog. Many people attended the service and the sense of sorrow was palpable. Rudge's parents were noticeably touched by all the words of condolence. Eventually everyone began to trickle away: the men in uniform, the friends, until only the family remained. We returned to Rudge's home for lunch and afterwards his mother made herself busy in the kitchen, brewing tea and coffee. I sat in the drawing room next to one of his uncles. He told me his son hadn't come to the funeral because he was the spitting image of his cousin, Rudge.

'It would have been too difficult for some people,' he said in a quiet voice.

'I miss him so much,' I said, tears coursing down my cheeks.

'Not as much as his mother,' he replied. 'You are still young. But to lose a child is the worst thing in the world that can happen to a parent.'

I had reason to remember his truthful words many years later.

* * *

That same evening, a small family group returned to Christ's Church at Portsdown, this time to bury Rudge's ashes. There were eight of us, crowded around a small square hole in the graveyard, near to where I had sat the night before. The Vicar held a short service, followed by the prayer of committal, and placed a small wooden box into the dark earth. Something snapped inside me. I couldn't take it in. All 6'6" of him could not be reduced to inches of dust. I fled and, blinded by tears, stumbled into the empty church. The cool interior and stillness offered sanctuary and, letting go of my anguish, I fell onto a pew weeping. But I wasn't alone, he was there too. The years of prayers and hymns from previous congregations and priests had left imprints in the vaulted house of God where Rudge's body had lain in his coffin overnight. Perhaps, having returned home, his soul hovered in this sacred place, waiting for the trumpets to call him to the other side. Just the memory of him created the impression he was with me. My sobs began to subside and, breathless, I lifted my head. An inscription under a stained-glass window caught my eye. I stood up to read the words.

'To the Glory of God and in loving memory of Noel John Lake Sergeant Pilot RAFVR, died 6th September 1941.'

Twenty years before, in this parish, another family had suffered the same sorrow. How had they come to terms with their loss? My father had died, like Noel Lake, in the war, leaving my grieving mother a young widow. My grandmothers too were young when they had lost the men they had loved. What cruel fate was at work? And now, it was my turn with Rudge. I looked up at the beautiful window at the figures depicted in coloured glass and saw him.

His face was that of Christ.

CHAPTER 18

FIGHTING BACK

After a week of compassionate leave, it was time to return to my course. My mind remained jagged and raw from the events of the previous ten days. Jane drove her car along the A3. She and Mummy kept up an amusing conversation on the journey to Hindhead – mostly, I was sure, for my benefit. Familiar landmarks passed by until we reached the camp gates. A flashback of him in his grey van hit me and I fought back threatening tears.

'Are you going to be all right?' Mummy asked when they dropped me outside my quarters.

'Yes, I'll be fine. Please don't worry. I've to catch up with my studies, plenty to occupy my mind,' I replied to reassure her. But I knew it would be a challenge, and I didn't know if I could do it.

'Come home soon, darling,' she said, the frown deepening on her face.

'Yes, I will,' I said, kissing her goodbye.

Everywhere in camp reminded me of him. Outside the Mess, standing by his van waiting for me, and there, where we had danced and stolen kisses. My friends had known Rudge and would be a comfort but the pain of separation became a deep ache in my heart.

Hut fifty-one appeared deserted, my friends absent. My room looked the same, but I was not. I unpacked, changed into my uniform and checked the timetable for the afternoon. I needed focus to fill the void and loneliness without him. I resolved then to put all my energy into passing the course and becoming a commissioned officer.

Whilst I'd been away, my intake had been involved in an exercise called 'First Flight'. The officer cadets were let loose in the camp to observe different trades and work alongside the staff of WRAC privates and NCOs. Cadets took on roles as clerks, stewardesses or cooks. I was slotted in straightaway. Luckily for me, it was something I could do and I was detailed to report to Headquarter Company Office.

I sat at an upright typewriter while the chief clerk showed me the many forms with army numbers indicating their different categories. My job was to type out requisitions for petrol. The personnel in the office were helpful, I enjoyed their banter and being included, but at the same time they kept their distance, as I was a potential officer.

At teatime in the Cadet Mess, the girls greeted me but I sensed several felt awkward, not knowing what to say, as most hadn't yet experienced bereavement. Later, my friends popped into my room.

'Good to have you back,' said Elaine, fully recovered now from her car accident.

Lesley put her head around the door.

'We're all going to the pub on Saturday, how about joining us?' she asked. There were various activities over the weekend, but I didn't want to go out.

A couple of evenings later, Florian was in the ablutions block washing her smalls when I went in to have a bath.

'Jackie, I have to tell you that the girls feel a presence in your room, and they are a bit scared to come and see you,' she said, an anxious look on her face.

Was he watching over me? I wanted to believe it.

* * *

On a hot afternoon at the beginning of June, I wore khaki trousers, army boots, and carried a compass, maps and a water bottle. The rest of my intake, dressed in similar kit, waited in a group on the scrub ground of Hindhead Common, an area called The Devil's Punch Bowl. This was our first orienteering exercise, testing map-reading skills – or rather, the lack of them. I welcomed the diversion and concentrated on the task ahead, to find my way back on track, to overcome the malaise of sadness that continued to grip me.

An instructor from RMA Sandhurst stood at a checkpoint with Sandhurst officer cadets. They were also taking part but start times were staggered, girls first. We'd been divided into pairs and I was with Tricia from hut forty-seven. When our turn came, Sergeant Lively blew her whistle and we set off. Tricia and I studied the map, contours, coordinates and paths to find the other checkpoints along the route where we'd be timed and monitored. But my stride was longer than Tricia's and she was getting out of breath.

'Snake. Stop!' she shouted, pointing at the ground. I looked down and there on the sandy path was a viper. I would have trodden on it if Tricia hadn't warned me, too engrossed in the map. The snake's tongue flickered, and its body wriggled, the serpentine action fascinating me. I wasn't afraid, but Tricia was terrified.

'It's ok,' I said, as it slithered its way into the undergrowth. 'It's gone.'

I wondered what other wildlife we had scared, tramping all over the Devil's Punch Bowl, the geological feature so named because of a local legend. The story purported that the devil, when he wasn't causing havoc with the human population, threw clumps of earth at the god Thor to irritate him. The scoops he removed from the soil created the hollow bowl.

Snakes, toads, lizards or dragons could not deter me, I had to continue.

Occasionally, we spoke to male cadets as we passed through the checkpoints. The afternoon sun beat down and we were thankful for the shade of the trees and the water we carried. An hour later, we arrived at the final post. Waiting for us was Sergeant Washington, one of our physical training instructors.

'Well done!' she said, pressing the knob on her stopwatch. We learnt later we'd come first out of the girls, a small achievement which made me smile – my first smile in ages. When everyone was through we milled about, the male cadets trying to chat us up. To me they were like schoolboys, eager and friendly.

'Let's all meet for a drink,' one said.

'Why don't you come over to our Mess on Friday night?' suggested one of the girls. Names and telephone numbers were exchanged before we climbed onto the green bus taking us back to camp.

The Sandhurst cadets turned up when I was still in the anteroom. Smartly dressed to impress, they wasted no time in ordering drinks. The girls enjoyed their company, conversations struck up, jokes were told and laughter followed. I observed their fun, said little and remained outside the group, so I was surprised when a nice-looking cadet, who had introduced himself earlier as Jeremy, came over to speak to me.

'Would you like to be my partner at the Sandhurst June ball?' he asked.

I'd been to several of them with Charles. I remembered the sense of occasion and grandeur, the dancing to live bands and drinking champagne, but also the 'snogging' in the dark. Jeremy was a delightful young man, destined for great things in the cavalry. Though flattered by his invitation, I declined. Bittersweet memories of dancing with Rudge came flooding back to haunt me.

* * *

On Saturday 10th June, our intake attended the Trooping of the Colour in London. For me it was another distraction. I dressed, without pleasure, in a summer dress with three-quarter sleeves, chose a hat and pulled on my gloves. Hats were obligatory for the occasion. The two officers who accompanied us that day had also worn 'mufti'.

Despite my low spirits, the weather was ideal. The sun shone in a cloudless sky. We passed the sentries in their boxes at the entrance of Horse Guards, both stiffly at attention and looking hot in their bearskins. On through a deep archway to Horse Guards Parade Ground, old buildings and square exuding a sense of drama and history, the perfect setting to mark the Queen's official birthday. Our allotted seats were in the stands on the left-hand side of the Old Admiralty Building and we slipped in beside the spectators who were dressed in chic outfits and dazzling uniforms. In the mass of people, I suddenly felt quite alone. My frayed emotions erupted without warning, clouding my eyes with tears. I fought to hold them back, trying to focus on staying in the present, absorbing the atmosphere and taking in the scene, and trying not think how much I missed him.

Ranks of Foot Guards and the Colour Party began to appear onto the square, the red and black pattern of their uniforms changing as they marched in unison to the music of massed military bands. A series of drill sequences followed until the soldiers came to a halt and lined up ready for inspection. The massed bands fell silent. The strains from the mounted band of the Household Division took up the baton making their way ceremoniously along the Mall. At the stroke of eleven, the drum horses of the Life Guards led the procession into the arena, the drummers resplendent in their livery. Behind them rode the Queen's Escort with the Royal Family. The sun glittered on the men's swords, helmets and buckles, boots gleaming like polished jet. Her Majesty The Queen, riding side-saddle on her horse, wore the badge of the Scots Guards. That year it was the turn of the Scots Guards to troop their colour. But my mind returned to Rudge's mother's story of him carrying the colour for the Parachute Regiment on a special occasion.

The officers and men on parade stood to attention as Her Majesty rode along the lines to inspect them before returning to her place in front of the Parade Ground. A young subaltern from the Scots Guards stepped out and marched to the Colour Party to receive the Colour. For a second, he looked like Rudge, tall and magnificent, then he about turned and, with military precision, paraded the Colour between the ranks of men. Stirring military music played as the waves of guardsmen marched past the Queen. Feeling proud to be part of Her Majesty's Forces, the family I had chosen to join, my resolve deepened to pass out at the end of my training as a young officer.

* * *

Later in the week, whilst at dinner in the Mess dining room, the phone rang and the cadet orderly officer went to answer it.

'It's for you, Jackie,' she said.

I made my excuses and left the table. My throat tightened. I felt faint with sadness. He used to call me at this time, but I would never hear his voice again. I struggled to compose myself, took a deep breath and picked up the phone.

'Jackie?' A terse voice enquired.

Oh no, I registered. It was Charles. His mother had unexpectedly telephoned me two weeks beforehand, surprising me because she knew that we had split up. Her call was to ask if I had Charles' telephone number in Dortmund, because she needed to speak to him urgently. At this time, telephone calls to Germany were expensive; letter writing the preferred option to keep in touch. A day didn't go by without finding the post rack in the Mess crammed with letters for cadets. Luckily, I was able to provide the number as I still had a record in my address book. It was only then that I learned that her husband had suddenly died.

'I think we ought to meet,' Charles now said, after I had mumbled my condolences and established that he was on compassionate leave. 'We've things to discuss.'

'Have we?' I questioned.

'It's the least you can do after two years,' he snapped.

'Well, I'm going home on Saturday; you can come over after lunch. I have to go.' I hung up.

My mother wasn't ecstatic when I told her of Charles' proposed visit the moment I arrived at Deramore Cottage.

'I hope you don't mind, I didn't want him coming to the camp,' I confided. 'Anyway, it's the last time that you'll see him because I'm going to give back all his presents.'

Reg was non-committal. He had better things to do that afternoon than speak to Charles; he'd planned to clean his car. I collected the things that I'd kept in my bedroom, including the fruit knives and forks Charles had bought for my bottom drawer. I could now declutter him from my life along with his unwanted gifts.

Mummy was on the terrace deadheading her roses, I was reading a newspaper in the lounge when Charles arrived.

'Good afternoon, Mrs. Pearce.'

'I'll get Jackie for you.' I heard her say.

She came in through the French windows.

'Psst!' she said with a wicked smile. 'He's here!'

'Thanks!' I made a face back. 'I'll just get those things.'

Clutching the bag of unwanted gifts, I walked onto the terrace.

'How's your Mother?' I asked, deflecting the awkwardness.

'How do you think?' he replied with a grim face. 'She's mourning her husband.'

Yes, poor lady, I knew about bereavement. 'I can't talk to you here,' he said, looking at Reg washing the Daimler in front of the garage. 'Come for a drive with me,' he suggested.

It was the last thing I wanted, but I felt sorry for him, losing his father and coping with his grieving mother. I sublimated my own wishes out of consideration.

'I won't be long,' I called to my mother, watching us from the doorway. She waved.

At first, Charles said nothing as we drove along a wooded road towards Chobham, his face set, white knuckles clutching the steering wheel.

'What have you got to say for yourself?'

'Nothing,' I replied.

'I know about this Para, and what happened,' he spat out the words. 'I've been thinking about it and have decided that I might take you back. But first of all, I want to know if you slept with him.'

I was astounded. Take me back? Never! Any feelings of compassion I may have had dissolved.

'Yes,' I said triumphantly, 'I did!'

His face contorted. I didn't know if it was with anger, remorse or loathing. He turned the car around and without another word took me back to my house. I got out, leaving his things on the back seat. I felt liberated.

A year later, I heard he'd married a British army officer's daughter in Germany and I was genuinely pleased for him. He no longer mattered to me.

* * *

Elaine, my funny and cheerful friend, came home with me for a weekend. We left camp on Friday evening and arrived at Deramore Cottage in time for supper. Fine weather had been forecast and I had suggested that we might go swimming at the Blue Pool on Saturday afternoon.

We planned first to go shopping during the morning and set off early on foot. Outwardly everything must have appeared normal, two friends chatting together heading for Camberley town. But grief lay waiting in my path, triggers that made my heart miss a beat: a soldier wearing the red beret of the parachute regiment, the snatch of songs Rudge and I had listened to when we were together, and the smell of the perfume I wore for him.

It seemed that I must fight every step of the way to overcome the sorrow of losing him and search for distraction.

A new boutique had opened at the top of Camberley High Street and, in the window, was a white 'sharkskin' swimming costume, the latest thing thanks to Marilyn Monroe. We decided to go in for a closer inspection. A few minutes later, I was in the changing room trying it on. The costume was a bit tight, completely flattening my bosom. I put my head around the curtain and asked the salesgirl if there was a bigger size.

'No madam,' she said, 'but may I check the one you're wearing?'

I agreed, and she came into the cubicle.

'Oh,' she said, 'but it's perfect.'

I didn't think so. I looked androgynous.

'It's not very flattering,' I complained.

'Ah, just a moment,' she said, understanding the problem, and returned holding two 'falsies'. We all aspired to the full-bodied figures of Hollywood actresses and, although I didn't possess a D cup, I was prepared to see the advantage of a shapelier bust.

'Just let me insert these under the lining of the bodice,' she said. 'There, that looks better.'

My refection in the mirror showed a tall slim girl with long legs and a new curvy figure.

'What do you think, Elaine?' I asked pulling aside the curtain.

Five minutes later we were out of the shop, my new swimming costume and accessories safely in a smart carrier bag bearing the shop's logo.

At the Blue Pool, off the London Road towards Bagshot, Elaine and I lay on our towels at the grass verge by the swimming pool. We had put on our bathing costumes and left our clothes in the changing rooms. It was a beautiful afternoon and we were sunbathing, enjoying being there along with loads of other young people, some of whom were Sandhurst cadets.

'Coming in for a dip?' asked Elaine, jumping up and running

to the edge of the water. I followed her and watched her effortless dive at the deep end. Aware of eyes on me in my new white costume, I chose to climb down the steps and jump in. Delicious cooling water washed over me. I came up for air, opening my eyes to see a white foam falsie floating away. Oh no! What a disaster. Now I was left with a dilemma. Did I retrieve it in front of hundreds of eyes, or just pretend it wasn't mine? Elaine reached the other side of the pool and turned around. She burst out laughing when she saw what was making its way towards her on the surface of the pool. I swam over to her, ignoring the flotsam. The problem was that now I only had one plump breast. I crossed my arms over my chest to conceal the flattened one. Elaine and I stifled hysterical laughter, climbing out of the pool by the changing rooms. With the key on an elastic band around my wrist, I was able to enter the cabin with my clothes – but my towel was on the grass at the other side of the pool! Elaine came to my aid and brought it back. Dressed again, I picked up my swimming costume and the other falsie fell out. I confess that I left it behind, alone on the slatted seat in the changing room.

Back at Deramore Cottage, we relayed the incident between bursts of giggling to Mummy. Since then she always called Elaine my bosom friend. These happier moments were important. Laughter was always the best medicine, the antidote to grief.

Elaine and I returned to Cadet Wing for the final weeks of term and the countdown to our Seniors' departure. Not long afterwards, I received an unexpected phone call from Jim, which completely floored me. Jim had served with Rudge in C Company at the Depot.

'How would you like to come out for a drink with a few of us?' he asked. I hadn't anticipated hearing from any of Rudge's friends again. His voice took me right back to Kidlington. My mind churned with memories and broken thoughts. 'We're going over to The Dog and Pheasant at Brook this evening. I can come and pick you up.' I concentrated on answering him and not bursting into tears. I'd decided to study that night but the chance to talk about Rudge, although painful, could be cathartic. No counselling had been offered to me at Cadet Wing. I was expected to carry on and get over the trauma of my loss. I'm glad that aspect of dealing with bereavement has changed in the modern army. But back then, I was only Rudge's unofficial girlfriend.

'Yes, I'd love to,' I replied.

I felt out of place in the passenger seat of Jim's Sunbeam Alpine and among the Para subalterns at the pub. Without Rudge I was an intruder, but I was grateful for their company. They joked, laughed and spoke openly of Rudge, who had been immensely popular at the Depot and their 'mucker'. They didn't talk about the accident, only of the good times. Their support salved my broken heart, they had proven their loyalty and friendship to him. I'd never forget their kindness and concern. Jim told me that, before his death, Rudge had confided that he had met the girl he was going to marry. I clung to his words and took comfort from them, finally knowing Rudge still loved me on the day he died.

Preparations for the commissioning created a burst of activity in the Camp. Stewardesses cleaned and polished the multipurpose hall. Major Fleetwood-Jones, official flower arranger for the occasion, ordered delphiniums and carnations to decorate the stark building. At the Depot in Guildford, the WRAC band practised military and popular music to be played before and during the ceremony to an audience of Seniors' parents and friends. We juniors were to be included in the assembly to witness the event that, hopefully, we would experience six months later. The VIP who would officiate at the ceremony had been invited, his name kept secret until the day.

Sue, in the next room to mine, now sported a pair of silver edged epaulettes to mark the success of her promotion to Junior Under Officer. The rumour that she had won the sash of honour percolated around camp. The evening before the great day, Sue and her intake dined with us in the Mess, talking excitedly about their new postings and life after Cadet Wing. Tearful goodbyes were held back until they departed.

In hut fifty-one, Florian and I brushed our Number One dress uniforms and polished our black beetle crushers to the RSM's standard. We chatted with doors open, discussing the day's events and guessing the identity of the official VIP for the commissioning. Florian wore a permanent grin on her face. Being in love suited her and she, of all my friends, perhaps understood the trauma I was experiencing. She quietly gave me support with her encouraging remarks and amusing asides.

The 28th June, Commissioning Day, dawned to reveal that the VIP was none other than John Profumo, Secretary of State of War. The seniors were even more nervous of being in the spotlight and we left them with the RSM before Sergeant Lively escorted us to the hall and our allocated seats.

John Profumo had himself served in the British army and retired with the rank of Brigadier. His appointment as Secretary of State of War added to his status and we were a little in awe of him when he arrived to officiate at the ceremony. His wife, the actress Valerie Hobbs, accompanied him, looking beautiful in a striking hat and matching outfit. They appeared to be the perfect couple, but the following month he was to meet the infamous call girl, Christine Keeler, at Cliveden Reaches. The story of their scandalous affair hit the headlines two years later, resulting in John Profumo's disgrace and resignation. But that day, the day of the commissioning, we only observed his persona of importance. Our Colonel Commandant hovered around him, as did the other WRAC officers, honoured by his presence.

'So, did I really get commissioned, did it count because he took the ceremony?' One of the seniors remarked to me years later.

The ceremony took place on a perfect English summer's day.

As expected, Sue won the sash of honour and a celebratory drinks party held afterwards outside the Senior Officers' Mess. Valerie Hobbs, showing a genuine interest in our choice of career and training course, questioned us in a charming manner. Her husband and our Commandant arrived to join her, and we all shook hands with the Minister of War.

The Seniors' Commissioning Ball was held that evening at the Hogsback Hotel. Our intake was automatically invited and the remaining thirteen of us turned up wearing long dresses on the arm of our escorts. My partner that night was a Mons officer Cadet called Malcolm, roped in to make up numbers. How different it might have been.

The next day we said goodbye to Jo and Sheila, the short commission entrants on our intake, required to complete only six of the eleven months training. Sheila became a shining role model as she would be appointed the Director of the Woman's Royal Army Corps some years later.

I packed for the two-month summer break and wished my friends a happy holiday. When we returned, we would be the seniors. The summer holidays, how was I going to spend them? I had fought back to stay on track but planning the future even for a couple of months was impossible.

CHAPTER 19

SUMMER HOLIDAYS

Deramore Cottage offered a place of respite to gather thoughts before organising the rest of the summer leave. Mummy cooked my favourite meals, helping to raise my spirits with her humour and understanding, and allowing me the space I needed. Reg, disagreeable as ever, fortunately was at work most of the time.

Rudge's parents had invited me to visit them again after his funeral. I wanted to, but the emotional wounds were raw and I doubted if I had the inner strength to share their bereavement as I battled with my own. Mummy, with her experience, encouraged me to go and, after a week at home, I gathered enough courage to visit them, travelling to Portsmouth by train.

As I remembered from their kindness at the funeral, they welcomed me. Lunch was prepared, and we sat down together. They asked how things were progressing at Cadet Wing. At first, we didn't talk about Rudge but he was there with us, his photos around the room, reminding us of his attractive face and personality. Mine was on the mantelpiece too, beside one of his. My heart lurched as sorrow descended like a rock fall, imagining how a wedding photo of us might have been there one day. I fell silent, swallowing the pain. It was afterwards, when the table had been cleared and the washing up done, that his mother began to speak of him.

'There's something I want to give you, Jackie,' she said, opening a small box.

Inside was a silver badge of the Parachute Regiment, a parachute within a pair of wings with a crown and lion above it.

'I had it made into a brooch for you. It came from Rudge's dress uniform.' She took it out and placed it in my hand. I held it tightly. Here was something he had touched and something to connect me to him.

'Oh, thank you so much,' I said, my eyes no longer able to contain the tears.

She also gave me a photo of him in that uniform. It had come with his effects from Maida Barracks, a snap shot of him walking through a churchyard. He had been in the guard of honour at a wedding, Perhaps Jane and Bob's? He looked wonderful, captured forever, a black and white image on the shiny paper. The rawness of losing him deepened and I cried harder whilst his mother hugged me. Gina's photos were never mentioned.

The inquest had taken place in Oxford and discussed that day. Rudge's father remained concerned with the findings, which suggested that Rudge shouldn't have left the plane where he did, at the wrong end of the airfield. I wasn't the only one distraught. His father was clearly unable to move on from the accident. Everyone who knew Rudge wondered why such a thing could have happened. He was an experienced parachutist and an assistant instructor. A verdict of accidental death was recorded at the inquest. I wasn't asked to attend, and I doubted I could have given evidence without breaking down, but I did mentally process what might have taken place, on the day of the accident, which undoubtedly raised many questions.

He must have been annoyed on seeing that the competition had been abandoned as he left the aircraft. Did he know before he jumped? Was he still mad with the pilot for not applying the brakes to the wheel? Did he know he was off course when he jumped after the second attempt? Why did he jump at all? Was it because of me? Did he go through with it as a point of honour? His passion and skill for skydiving were unquestionable, he didn't take risks. The wind had gathered force and he had to make a quick decision whether to try and land on the airfield or make for a space between the hangars. Perhaps the wind speed had dictated his choice, which proved fatal. Having overshot the airfield, Rudge must have hit some unseen power lines when coming down to land. Was that because of his colour blindness? Red and green were grey to him. His parachute then collapsed and he fell, his skull fractured as he hit the ground. The memory of him lying there, unconscious, the blood, the sound of him trying to breathe, would haunt me forever. I had to hope the accident was an error of judgement. Tragically, it was also our karma.

The President of the British Free Fall Parachuting Club gave evidence at the inquest, as did two more eyewitnesses. Ironically, he was also to die parachuting the following year, whilst taking part in a film stunt.

Rudge's parents were the bravest people I'd ever met, dealing with their grief. No wonder they'd had a son like him. I wished I was as half as brave as them. There were often moments when I wanted to be with him, too tired to go on living. But I couldn't give in, he would have expected more of me. And, because of him, I soldiered on. At my request, his mother returned the photo I had given him. It was another connection, like the brooch, and I promised I would find a replacement for her.

* * *

Set back from the Paignton to Totnes Road, New Barn Farm nestled into the landscape. A single tarmac driveway wound through pastures and around a hillside. At the top stood the farmhouse, surrounded by a green blanket of fields. I was happy to be there again; Frances' home had always been a haven. She and her parents had played a huge part in my teenage years, they had a great attitude to life and the house was always filled with laughter. Frances was the oldest of the four children and, when I was fourteen, her parents had unofficially adopted me as part of the family. I remembered the invitation to spend the summer holidays with them in Ireland as Frances' companion. Frances was at Farnborough Hill Convent with me then, and the family lived at Heath End near Farnham.

We had a brilliant time at Dunmore East, their Irish house. An old fisherman, Peter Roach, used to take us out fishing early in the mornings. One of Frances' aunts came to stay that summer, an extremely large lady with a passion for fresh herrings. Aunt Lulu stood at the bottom of the garden, overlooking the harbour, waiting for the signal to say that we had a catch. Peter, Frances and I had strung out herring nets the evening before. Just after dawn we went out in the dinghy to haul them in. Peter reckoned that we had half a cran of them! We waved, and Aunt Lulu lifted up the enormous frying pan she held in her hand to acknowledge our signal. She turned and rushed up the garden into the kitchen, her short fat legs making haste, her skirt swishing with momentum. Aunt Lulu had the pan on the stove in seconds, ready to cook some of the 'silver darlings'. Indeed, they were delicious!

I had written to Frances at the beginning of the summer break, reminding her of our Irish holiday.

'Why don't you come down to Salcombe, you'll love it here,' Frances had suggested.

Frances and two of her friends, Anna and Mary, had just completed their comprehensive catering course in Torquay. Together they had found holiday work at The Fortescue Arms in Salcombe, where they practised their skills in the kitchen and mixed drinks at the bar.

'I'll tell Mummy, so you can stay at the farm first if you like, then join us later and we'll find somewhere for you to sleep.'

Uncle Freddie picked me up at Paignton station. I was delighted to see his smiling round face again. A small half ring of hair framed the back of his bald head – but to compensate for the lack of hair, he had a fine moustache. I was greeted with a prickly kiss.

The moment I entered the house, the wonderful aroma of cooking promised one of Aunt Bubbles' delicious meals. In the kitchen, a huge table took up a third of the room. What happy memories I have of dining there on many different occasions, surrounded by the family and their friends. Stimulating conversation flowed, peppered with repartee and much laughter. Aunt Bubbles had studied at the Tante Marie Cookery School and was an extraordinary cook. Her dinner parties were spectacular, and she was renowned at the local Women's Institute for jams and cakes. Uncle Freddie had a flagon of cider, or bottles of wine for special occasions, at the ready to go with her glorious meals.

I received a warm welcome from the family, Bubbles, Granny Daisy, and the children who were home for the holidays. Thankfully, nobody mentioned Charles and the time we'd spent with them the year before.

'Frances is enjoying herself in Salcombe,' said Freddie. 'I'll take you down there tomorrow to join her. Our caravan is on site for the summer and we thought you might like to stay there.'

Another first for me, I'd never been camping or caravanning, and it sounded just what I needed, a complete change of scene.

The following day, after lunch, Freddie and I said goodbye to the household and set off for Salcombe. We passed through the pretty town of Kingsbridge where waterside pubs and moored boats competed for space at the northern end of the tidal estuary, which flowed six miles south to the sea. Freddie sped along the narrow Devon roads in his Austin Cambridge and we talked about the family and my new career.

'Jackie, darling, I know that you've lost someone you loved, but I hope that you'll not go to a medium or spiritualist in the hope of contacting him.'

I hadn't spoken of Rudge to him or Bubbles. Frances knew and, naturally, she had told the family, but this was the first time he'd been mentioned. Freddie was a father figure to me, caring and concerned, so unlike Reg. Taken aback, I couldn't answer. I didn't know any spiritualist. Perhaps, because of the war, widows and girlfriends of dead soldiers might have considered using one. Freddie would have known about such things as an experienced officer. I just shook my head. Tears filled my eyes and I began to sob. Even though Freddie saw my distress, he talked on about death and the life hereafter. He'd seen many terrible things on the battlefields of World War Two. As a major in the Royal Engineers, he was caught with his company in an enemy grenade attack, partially deaf from that devastating explosion and carrying the emotional scars of losing some of his men. Freddie was a Christian and our meaningful conversation about belief in an afterlife helped to soothe my sorrow. He reinforced the image of Rudge parachuting all over heaven.

Our journey ended when we pulled into a campsite, a field with fabulous views of the estuary. Sailing boats bobbed on the water like a procession of swans. Their caravan looked comfortable with two double beds that folded away and a small kitchen area. When the whole family stayed for the night, the younger members slept in a tent specially brought for the occasion. It looked very cosy.

While unpacking my things into an overhead locker, I heard a familiar voice.

'Anyone at home?' Frances called out.

She put her head through the doorway.

'Good to see you,' she said, smiling at me.

Frances looked marvellous; her curvy figure, halo of blonde curly hair and dark brown eyes a striking combination. 'I've just finished working the lunch shift, so I can spend the afternoon with you,' she said.

Delighted to see my old friend, I laughed as she placed a kiss on the top of her father's head. Freddie had to return to the farm to milk the cows but, before he said goodbye, we promised to take care of everything, especially remembering to turn off the gas if we used the stove. I gave him an extra hug for allowing me to express my grief. I couldn't fully show my state of mind to my mother, she would have worried too much. Freddie had listened, concerned for my mental welfare, providing support I didn't receive from Reg. Frances and I sat for a while, catching up, then I changed into shorts and a T-shirt and together we headed into town.

Salcombe buzzed with the yachting fraternity, smart and well-heeled. Enjoying window-shopping and people watching, we made for the most popular pub in town down by the harbour, known locally as 'The Fort'. Frances and the two other girls had accommodation in the town, but Mary found it noisy, using the caravan occasionally to enjoy a peaceful night's sleep. Frances pushed her way through to the bar, me in tow until we found ourselves beside a knot of young men in sailing gear, all laughing and downing beers. It was inevitable that the group become one and a tall young man chatted me up, introducing himself as Adam. I didn't want his attention.

Frances joined Anna and Mary behind the bar. They were an efficient team. I liked Frances's friends, for their cheerfulness and quick wit and stayed for a couple of drinks and a meal of scampi and chips. At ten o'clock I said goodbye to everyone, making my way back to the caravan, declining Adam's offer to accompany me. The stars glittered in an indigo sky, strange shadows cast by moonlight falling across my path. I smiled up at the Milky Way,

'Night, Rudge,' I whispered.

The following day I tidied up and put on my swimming costume and shorts before walking to the town. Frances had the morning off and we had arranged to meet up by the harbour. She waved wildly when she saw me. Earlier in the summer, Freddie had left a dinghy tied up at the mooring for their holidays. We climbed on board and rowed over to a sandy beach on the other side of the estuary. It was lovely on the water, sailing boats tacking up and down in the light breeze. Frances had brought a basket of provisions to sustain us while we sunbathed and read our books. I should have been content; the ingredients were all there. Salcombe had a wonderful holiday atmosphere, vibrant and exciting. But being among happy young people made me feel lonelier than ever. I was detached, adrift with no anchor in a seemingly alien world without him.

Frances must have sensed how I was feeling. I enjoyed her company but was pleased to leave when Freddie and Bubbles came down a few days later to take me back to New Barn Farm before my return journey to Camberley. I said goodbye to Frances, promising to stay in touch. She seemed happy because the three girls had just met up with three male students working in different bars in Salcombe. August promised to be a romantic month for them. I couldn't imagine ever being in love again.

CHAPTER 20

AUTUMN TERM

Hut fifty-one appeared deserted when I opened the main door. No familiar voices welcomed me, and the silence hung like a curtain. I pushed on, ready to start the new term with more resolve. I struggled with my luggage, heavy with the new clothes Mummy had made for the term, dragging the large case and vanity bag down the corridor, my high heels tapping out an echo. Florian's door stood open, her back towards me as she unpacked.

'Are we the first?' I called out.

She swung round, smiled and nodded.

'Yes, glad you're here. Creepy isn't it?'

'You look wonderful,' I said, admiring the blonde streaked hair and bronzed skin.

'It's the Devon sun,' her dimples appeared as she smiled, and her blue eyes lit up with summer memories.

'Ah, so nothing to do with Matt then,' I teased.

'Well, we did see each other before he was posted to Germany,' she admitted, her smile fading.

'I bet you'll see him again,' I said, feeling a stab of envy. 'I was in Devon too over the summer, I went to Salcombe.'

'It's pretty there,' she said. 'You should've told me, I'd have given you my address.'

'Thanks, Florian, but I didn't know myself at the end of last term,' I confessed.

'How are you, Jackie?' she asked.

'I'm ok,' I admitted, not wanting to talk about myself. 'Have to unpack now, see you later for dinner in the Mess.'

I stepped across the corridor as Elaine and Wendy burst into our hut, giggling and laughing.

'Hey, you two, what's so funny?' I called out.

Florian put her head around her door.

'What a shower!' she shouted, waving at them.

It was good to be back with the gang, back to an organised schedule to help subjugate my scattered thoughts and emotions. Memories of Rudge were strongest here in camp and a deep ache of sadness could strike unbidden at any second, demanding all my strength to suppress the tears.

Lesley arrived last in a cloud of euphoria; delighted she had caught the train without any mishap and pleased to share stories of summer in Copenhagen. She completed the inmates of hut fifty-one until our juniors appeared the following day. After unpacking, we met and strolled over to the Mess.

A blue airmail letter franked BFPO – British Forces Post Office – waited for me in the letter rack. I wasn't expecting to hear from anyone in Germany and it certainly wouldn't be from Charles. A familiar name appeared on the back of the envelope. Intrigued, I opened it. Mike had written to offer his condolences, having recently heard about Rudge. *I'm thinking of you*, he wrote, *yours aye, Michael.*

I shoved the letter in my pocket. What a considerate man, I reflected. Perhaps I would write and thank him when I had the time. The next few weeks would be busy with extra duties as a senior and the challenges of the course.

The new cadets arrived looking eager and fresh faced. They were young and naïve, except for the two short commission cadets, Ann, and Shirley, who had damaged her Achilles tendon on my Regular Commissions Board. She was a hoot and my intake were delighted to welcome her. Each senior cadet had been allocated a junior to take under her wing. Mine was called Liz, a short bespectacled girl with auburn hair. Her small freckled face beamed with enthusiasm. Perhaps I had been just like her nine months ago, arriving full of expectations and excitement at Officer Cadet Wing.

For the senior intake, this was our final term. Exams loomed and the dreaded half hour lecture on a military commander of the Second World War. Major Fleetwood-Jones gave out the names on pieces of paper during her military history class. I'd hoped for Monty; an interesting character and I already had some knowledge of his Western Desert Campaign when he commanded the Eighth Army. No, mine was General Sir Claude Auchinleck. I had to research him, not having learnt anything of his military career before.

The course intensified. Major Vennard prepared other challenging tests for the senior cadets. We were called to the lecture room for a mock interview. The scene was set. An officer, acting as a WRAC private, had been found guilty of a misdemeanour and, one by one, we were called into the lecture room to deal with the situation. Proceedings were carried out under the watchful eye of the OC and members of our teaching staff. Acting was definitely required – not one of my fortes.

In the lecture room the OC commended me on my ability to reprimand the offending WRAC private, which was something of a relief. I had taken on the persona of Mother Mostyn, our stern teacher at the convent. I'm sure Frances and Christine would have been amused at my role play. There was to be more acting at the end of the term – our intake divided into two groups to put on a small play or sketch for the whole camp.

Life in the Mess continued. Dining in nights, communal meals, listening to the radio or records in the anteroom and studying in our rooms. Routine allowed me, at least in public, to control my emotions, to keep my bereavement private. I threw myself into the duties of a senior cadet, carrying out the tradition of inspecting the juniors' rooms, marking the lack of cleanliness in the black book, keeping an eye on Liz, and being her mentor. She was settling in and doing so well that I could see her as a future Queen Bee, Director WRAC. In private, grief festered like a boil until it burst, and I sobbed alone in my bed at night, thinking of him. I knew I had to go on, build a life, build new relationships. But another man was out of the question.

I replied to Michael's letter, thanking him for his condolences, only to receive another a week later. He gave me news of his family. His widowed mother had moved to Canada to live with his elder sister, Barbara, who had emigrated there a few years earlier. The younger sister, Anne, had joined Barbara not long afterwards. He had no family left in England, only distant cousins. I felt sorry for his situation, glad he had found friends in the Officers' Mess of his new Signal Regiment. Michael described his troop of linemen, 'the salt of the earth', and the hardened NCOs. He had already experienced military manoeuvres with them, laying cables for communications. His letter was an insight into life at 'The Sharp End', portrayed so well that it provided a distraction for me, isolated at Huron camp.

The demands of the course continued, and we fell into bed each evening exhausted by our exertions, both mental and physical. One night I woke, dragged from sleep by fractured shards of light. Patterns danced on the army issue curtains and bounced off the magnolia walls. I yawned, tired from another night of swotting for exams. My brain was too slow to register the strange brightness in my room.

'Fire! Fire!' a voice yelled down the corridor.

I flung out an arm to find the switch on my bedside lamp. 01:23hrs, what a time for fire drill. The acrid smell of smoke hit me. Months of practise kicked in. No time to think, just act. I drew back the curtains to shut the top window. Outside, a wall of flames licked the autumn night, tongues reaching up into the dark. Plumes of smoke swirled and curled, carrying clumps of cinders in its turbulent current. Across the patch of grass from the Officer Cadet Quarters, the Sergeant's Mess was an inferno. I gasped; my hands flying to my throat as if warding off a strangler.

'Fire, fire!' I recognised the voice of Elaine, our newly

appointed Officer Cadet Sergeant.

I was calm; detached, trained and ready to react like a proper soldier. I crammed my feet into my issue shoes, grabbed my civilian woollen coat and slipped it over my striped army pyjamas. I had to leave immediately and take nothing with me. On my dressing table lay a small box. Ignoring orders, I thrust it into my pocket, switching off the light and making for the door. The rest of the girls staggered into the corridor.

'What's going on?' asked Lesley, buttoning up her warm jacket and falling in step beside me. Her room being on the other side of the hut, she was unaware of the drama unfolding outside my window.

'Sergeants' Mess,' I replied as we reached the main door. 'It's the real thing.'

'Crikey!' she said.

We gathered outside our wooden hut with the bewildered junior cadets. Fire alarms howled out their warning and figures scuttled, forming groups in the flickering darkness.

'That's all of us,' said Elaine, stamping her feet to keep warm. 'Let's go!'

Dressed in a mishmash of clothing, we stepped out into the cold night and marched together towards the parade ground beyond the tennis courts.

'Just listen to that,' said Wendy next to me. The fire roared and spat out flying sparks.

'Unbelievable how quickly it's taken hold. Everything was fine when we went to bed,' added Florian, striding out beside her.

'Hut fifty-one present and correct, Ma'am,' reported Elaine when we reached the square. The Regimental Sergeant Major waved a torch and carried her millboard. An army greatcoat over her nightwear, she looked totally incongruous. I stifled a laugh. Gone was the officious 'task master' of the parade ground, she had become someone's maiden aunt, almost human in the broken light.

'Well done, Ladies,' she said, ticking us off her list and rushing over to another crowd of women arriving for the head count. The entire complement of the camp joined us including the senior officers, some in curlers and one holding a frightened looking miniature dachshund. A farcical tableau!

The RSM ordered us to regroup with senior officer cadets from huts forty-five and forty-seven. We murmured greetings.

'What's wrong, Helen?' asked Elaine. 'You look worried.'

'I forgot my contact lenses. I can't manage without them. Do you think our hut will catch fire?' she queried, huddled in her duffle coat. Nobody replied. I thought of my belongings too. The beautiful clothes Mummy had made me, the hooked rug I'd spent eighteen months making at the hotel, the art work from my A-Level folder on the wall and, most importantly, Rudge's letter.

The fifteen of us shuffled into two ranks and stood easy. Squads of women from different companies and courses did the same, the RSM and Orderly Officer in deep conversation, checking the lists. They split up and started the head count again.

'What do you think all that means?' asked Lesley.

'Not everyone's present?' suggested Florian.

Luminous stars filled the November night sky, the Milky Way swathed in misty mystery. I imagined Rudge up there, looking down at the unfolding drama and smiled. Great clouds of smoke continued to rise above the Sergeant's Mess. The pungency of burning wood permeated everything. Flakes of smouldering pieces fell on the square.

We had a good view of the guardroom and camp entrance from where we stood. When a car rolled up, we were all riveted. Out clambered two junior officer cadets in long dresses and two young men in dinner jackets. Oh my, they were in for it, very late back from a dance and no late pass. I was never caught in the spotlight like that. They couldn't have made a better entrance as belles of the ball if they'd tried, lit up by the pyrotechnics. The young men, confused and embarrassed, made a hasty retreat, leaving the girls to mince over in their high heels to us, the pyjama brigade. The Orderly Officer rounded them up and pointed to their place on the square, no time for reprimands. Punishment would follow when they were summoned in front of the OC.

Our limbs now cold, we wondered how much longer we'd have to stand out in the open. It seemed hours before the emergency alarm of the fire engines rang out. They stormed into the camp, lights flashing, vehicles glowing in the reflection of the blazing fire. An audible sigh of relief rose from the senior officers. The miniature dachshund barked and squirmed in the arms of his mistress, the excitement too much for him. A cheer erupted from all ranks on the square. I joined in the 'Hurrays' as our saviours clanged onwards to the burning hut.

The Duty Sergeant, properly dressed in uniform, strode towards us.

'Right, ladies, we are taking you to one of our accommodation blocks in Headquarters Company, well away from the fire. Follow me, please,' she said, breaking into a quick march. We stepped forward swinging our arms to keep warm.

Blankets and sheets were stacked at the end of each bed in the Barrack room, pillows on ticking mattresses. We bagged a bed each and fell onto it, too excited to go to sleep. We chatted about the dramatic events of the night and how the fire might have started.

'We could've been burnt alive,' said Florian. 'Our hut is the closest to the Mess. Jackie's room is at the end, so she would have had it first.' I chose to ignore that thought.

Fil, from hut forty-seven, took out a cheroot from her pocket and lit up.

'Fil, you'll get us into trouble,' said Elaine.

'Who's going to notice?' she laughed and blew out a smoke

ring. 'There's a lot more outside.'

I threw off my shoes, and, still wrapped in my coat, dragged a coarse grey blanket over me, the fabric itchy against my face. Reaching into my pocket, I grasped the box that held the silver brooch. I closed my eyes, voices around me receding and I drifted off to sleep. I was with him again; no more pain, no more separation. He held me, and I lay my face against his chest as we floated together under the canopy of his parachute.

'Jackie, wake up!' a harsh voice broke through my astral journey. I opened my eyes to see Lesley standing over me. 'It's 07:00hrs, time to go.'

Pulled back to reality, his image faded but I continued to clutch the box with his parachute wings, all I had left of him.

The Duty Sergeant popped her head around the door, her face pinched and tired from the long night.

'The fire's out, Ma'am,' she said to Elaine. 'It's safe to go back to your quarters.'

'Thanks, Sergeant,' Elaine replied.

'Was anyone hurt?' called out Fil.

The Sergeant shook her head.

'No, thank goodness, it was a near thing though,' she replied. 'I'm off to a debriefing. Good morning, Ladies,' she said, disappearing.

We stumbled out into the pale light and headed off in the direction of our quarters.

'Golly, what a sight,' said Lesley as we reached the charred remains of the Sergeant's Mess, black and grotesque in a heap next to our hut. We stopped and fell silent to take in the enormity of the devastation. The smell of smoke hung in the air, reminding us of our lucky escape.

Death lay vanquished in the debris. The fire reminded me of the legendary phoenix bird that rose from ashes to renew itself again. I had another chance to live and perhaps Rudge, like the winged horse Pegasus, was flying through the heavens with his parachute, rising up to other dimensions.

* * *

Living in an all-female environment wasn't always easy. Despite army discipline, hormones played havoc with emotions. Events were exaggerated and made more of than they deserved. I suppose, like most of the cadets, I'd had my fair share of attention from the opposite sex whilst at Hindhead. I'd declined invitations, except of course from Rudge, Jim, his Para brother, and the one time with Mike.

Shortly after the fire, one Saturday in the Mess with a crowd of girls, I noticed two young men walk into the anteroom. They had come to visit Helen and Pauline. Both girls were good friends and billeted in hut forty-seven. They introduced us to Jerry and Richard, both newly commissioned officers. Jerry scrutinised me.

'I know you, don't I?' he asked. I thought his strong masculine face was familiar.

'Really?' I replied. 'Where did we meet?'

He ran through a few possible locations.

'At Sandhurst?' he asked.

I wracked my brains and vaguely remembered him from the dances there.

'Maybe,' I answered.

Jerry began to mention characters from those days and we fell into animated conversation. Also a rugby player, he knew Mike.

'Why don't you come out to the pub with us?' he suggested.

'I can't,' I said, not wanting to tread on anybody's toes.

'Oh, please do,' he responded.

Richard and Jerry insisted that I accompanied them with Helen and Pauline and, stupidly, I agreed.

We were outside the Mess about to get into Richard's saloon car when Pauline walked off. The whole thing turned into a disaster.

'Where's she gone?' I questioned Helen.

'Back to her room. She is not coming now,' she replied, her face stiff with animosity.

The four of us left camp to go to the Royal Anchor. Frosty looks from Helen did nothing to enhance my evening. I suspected that Helen and Pauline had only recently met the two officers and that I had ruined their date. After a couple of drinks and an uncomfortable evening, the men dropped us back at camp. Helen went off without a word. On the way to my room, I heard voices from Wendy's room. Wendy had a throat infection and I thought I'd find out if she was feeling any better. I put my head around the door to see half the intake with her. Everyone stopped talking and stared at me.

'Hello,' I said to Wendy. 'How are you?' I received no reply.

'Can I see you for a minute?' I asked Elaine.

'Later,' she replied, cold as ice.

Only a totally insensitive person could have ignored the vibes in that room. I knew they had been discussing me and I definitely wasn't welcome. I left. I'd wanted to explain to Elaine, in a way our leader, that I had had no intention of upsetting Helen and Pauline. It was a coincidence that Jerry and I had met before, but I had absolutely no designs on him. Elaine eventually came to see me. Cool and distant, she expressed how disappointed she was; because of my behaviour stealing other girls' boyfriends, the girls had decided I should be put into 'Coventry' for two days.

The next forty-eight hours were unpleasant. I withdrew into myself, adding another layer of self-protection. At least Florian and Lesley didn't join in my punishment, except at meals in the Mess where not wanting to compromise them, I sat with the juniors. My appetite diminished. The ostracisation affected my relationship with Elaine and I kept well away from Pauline and Helen for the rest of the term.

I'd been labelled a Femme Fatale, which was laughable. Only one man remained in my thoughts, unattainable and incomparable.

CHAPTER 21

END OF TERM

A weekend pass offered an escape from the tension of impending exams and falling out with Elaine. My mother, noticing the change in my demeanour when I arrived, asked if everything was all right, which I confirmed. She didn't seem convinced.

'You look pale, darling, and you've lost weight,' she added, putting the kettle on the stove.

'I'm fine,' I lied and, not wishing to look her in the eye, busied myself with placing the cups and saucers on a wooden tray.

'I've news for you,' she said. 'I told Eileen you were coming home, and she and Malcolm have invited you over this evening for a drink.'

Malcolm and Eileen had bought a little cottage in Tekels Avenue. An instructor at the Royal Military Academy, he had fallen in love with the pretty girl from Rhodesia. They had been married for a couple of years. Mummy and Jane sometimes babysat for their little boy.

'That's nice,' I responded and watched her measure two teaspoons of tea into the pot.

'Yes, they want you to meet one of their friends,' she disclosed.

The invitation sounded intriguing.

'Who's that?' I enquired.

'Eileen thought you would like to meet him, that's all.'

Him? The two of them were up to something. I sensed a conspiracy and I wasn't sure about accepting.

'She's expecting you at 6 o'clock,' Mummy said, pouring boiling water into the teapot. 'It'll be good for you to go out. Why don't you have a long soak in the bath this afternoon? That'll make you feel better.'

I couldn't hide anything from her, and perhaps it would

make a change to go out and spend less time with Reg, who was reading his newspaper in the drawing room, waiting for me to take in his tea.

'Maybe I will,' I replied.

She smiled and poured out her favourite brew.

'I hope you've brought one of your new dresses with you,' she said handing me a cup. 'I've cut out the gown for your Commissioning Ball, you'll have to come home for a fitting soon.'

Mummy had confidence in me passing out, but I had to get through the final six weeks and those exams beforehand.

The wooded short walk through the cut from Deramore Cottage to Malcolm and Eileen's house in Tekels Avenue took a few minutes. It carried a sense of mystery in the twilight, wild and untamed. The air heavy, with the smell of leaf mould and toadstools, as I trod the familiar path. Autumn would soon be over and my course at an end. I had no roots, and I was alone. I climbed down the bank, my high heels sinking into the damp earth until I stood in front of the cottage wondering whether to ring the bell. I felt ready to burst into tears if anyone said a kind word. I hesitated and then heard laughter from inside, drawing me in to its warmth. I reached out my hand and pressed the button. The door swung open and Malcolm appeared, a big grin on his face.

'Come in, Jackie, and meet David,' he said, putting his arm around my shoulder. His conviviality dispelled my mood and he ushered me into the sitting room. Who was David? Was I a surprise for him too?

A young man jumped up from a chair to greet me. About twenty-five years old, a little taller than me, medium built with light brown hair, he wore the typical mufti for an off-duty officer, a sports jacket and cavalry twills, a checked shirt and military tie. His mouth creased into a smile and his blue eyes lit up.

'How d'you do?' he said formally, offering his hand. He asked how long I was home in Camberley and obviously knew I attended Cadet Wing. He'd been told something of my background, an advantage over me. I was pleased that Malcolm and Eileen cared enough to intervene and welcomed the distraction of a new face, someone who smiled at me. David revealed a little about himself. An old friend of Malcolm's, both of them Captains in the Royal Army Service Corps. Eileen came in from the kitchen carrying a tray of nibbles.

'How nice to see you again, Jackie,' she said. 'It's been a long time. So, you've met David,' she smiled. 'Come and sit down and tell us all about Hindhead.'

I can't remember what I said, probably told a few anecdotes and changed the subject at the first opportunity. The alcohol helped disperse pent up feelings and I allowed myself to enjoy their company.

'Perhaps we can go out for a drink sometime?' David suggested at the end of the evening. Why not? He seemed nice. I'd have a chance to leave camp, to get away, so gave him my phone number. Though pleased to respond to his offer of friendship, I wasn't in femme fatale mode.

The conspiracy came out later when I tackled Mummy. She had told Eileen about Rudge and how much his death affected me. Eileen, by introducing me to David, who had recently broken up with his long-term girlfriend, wanted to play matchmaker.

'I'm sure they'll get on,' Eileen had confided in Mummy. In a way we did, both suffering the same affliction; a broken heart.

David collected me a week later from the Cadets' Mess in his shiny saloon car. His arrival undoubtedly caused tongues to wag, but the girls didn't know that we were both trying to come to terms with the loss of our partners. Ours was a mutual understanding, a friendship of convenience, although our relationship could have blossomed.

'We ought to get married,' David said on our second date.

I laughed. This was no answer to our predicament. We hardly knew each other.

'Would you be my partner at the Christmas dinner on 16th December at RMC Officers' Mess instead?' he asked.

He was friendly, personable and good company. My course would be finished by then. I accepted.

* * *

Lesley had taken on the motherly role of making sure I got up in time for breakfast. Exams loomed, everyone suffered from stress. A couple of cadets had been on warnings because of their work, behaviour, failure to meet the expectations for an officer in training, classroom attainment and so on. If the call came to go to the Office, you knew it meant trouble. You could potentially be dismissed, but more frequently be put on a three-month warning. The first summons to the Office was to be told that my hair was too long and needed cutting. It was shorter by the end of the day. The second was about Rudge's accident. The contrast between the two interviews showed the high standards required of cadets but also the OCs concern for our welfare.

Early one morning mid-November, before our exams, I woke up aware that someone was opening my door. Spooked, I switched on my bedside light. The brass handle slowly turned, the door creaked open, an arm hanging in its striped pyjama sleeve, a floppy hand suspended below. In slow motion the rest of the body appeared. My hand on my thumping heart, I saw a face. It was Lesley!

'Time to get up, Jackie,' she said in a disembodied voice.

I realised she was sleepwalking and sprang out of bed to put my arm around her. With first aid training I knew not to wake her but to help and influence her movements.

'Thanks, Lesley, now it's time for you to go to your bed,' I said leading her down the corridor into her room.

'Lie down,' I commanded. She obeyed, and I covered her up with a blanket.

'Sleep tight,' I whispered.

Next morning, she had no recollection of events. Each of us reacting differently as the pressure of exams mounted. I studied late into the night, fell exhausted in my bed and had a recurring nightmare of falling down a dark cavern. I'd wake up with a start, my heart racing and head reeling.

The letter rack in the hall of the Mess was always a diversion at breakfast. The post arrived early, and we'd crowd around to check if we'd any news from outside the camp. Mike's blue airmail envelopes appeared sporadically in my pigeonhole and I looked forward to receiving them. In the latest letter he'd written to tell me he was flying to Canada to see his family at Christmas. Could he visit me before his flight? He'd planned to spend a few days in England before continuing his journey. I'd been out with David occasionally but wondered if Mike might agree to be my partner at the Commissioning Ball on 14th December. He possessed the qualities I admired, a sense of humour and kindness. He'd earned the nickname 'Auntie Agatha' amongst his peers at Sandhurst as their agony aunt. I sent him an invite. It would be good to see him again.

Back in camp, consternation reigned for a week. The cadets in our intake were booked in for driving tests. Girls needing more practise had driven around Bramshott village, along the A3, with our driving instructor. My aptitude allowed one of the other girls two extra hours from my allotted time. I felt confident of passing. That is, until the day came, and I climbed into the familiar Triumph Herald. The examiner offered little conversation, except orders, where to drive and the manoeuvres required; three-point turn, reverse around a corner and parallel parking. After the initial moment of nervousness completing the sequence before setting off, check mirrors, indicate, my self-assurance returned. No words of encouragement from wooden face, I had no idea how the test was proceeding but he couldn't fault me on reversing around a corner. I was spot on. The

Highway Code followed the practical driving test. I remember the exhilaration of success when the examiner's face splintered into a congratulatory smile. Celebratory drinks were shared in the Mess that evening. We had all made the grade.

Exam week arrived. We wrote papers, developed writer's cramp and debated afterwards how we thought we'd done. Elaine was predicted to come first and win the sash of honour, continuing to outshine us all. I regained the camaraderie of my intake, apart from Pauline and Helen, although, regretfully, the friendship between and Elaine and me never completely healed.

My twentieth birthday fell in the middle of the exams and, to follow tradition, I bought everyone a drink after dinner. My teenage years over, I was different, not the fun-loving girl I had once been. Understanding the frailty of human nature and the impermanence of all things had been my lesson for the year. I had experienced vulnerability and from this came determination to become emotionally stronger and embrace the future.

That Saturday, I went home to collect my ball gown, my birthday present from Mummy, the design and material discussed during the summer. From Harvey's Guildford branch, we'd bought blue satin and a Vogue paper pattern, strapless, and draped, Grecian style, on the left hip. But I had lost so much weight Mummy had to adjust it. I stood patiently, a beanpole.

'Did I tell you that Mike is going to be my partner at the ball?' I confided, handing over the pincushion.

'Mike?' she queried, taking in material at my waist and sliding in silver pins.

'Yes, you remember he was Charles's friend. They came here a few years ago one Saturday to invite me to a party at Mike's house in Maidenhead.' I explained.

'Ah yes, Reg refused because you were still a schoolgirl and had to study,' she said. 'Charles was disappointed. Yes, Mike, I remember him, a good-looking boy with blonde hair.'

I revealed that we had been corresponding since September

and he was coming over from his Regiment in Germany en route to see his family in Canada. Stopping for a few days for the ball, he had nowhere to stay other than a hotel. I felt sorry for his lack of a family base and hinted broadly.

'He'd better come here then,' she said, checking her handiwork. 'I thought you might have asked David.' She gave me a quizzical look.

'You'll like Mike.' I replied. 'He's good fun.'

She finished the beautiful gown by Sunday afternoon. Reg 'nobly' took me back to Hindhead in the Daimler with it wrapped in tissue paper on the back seat. I wasn't really thinking about the ball, as a busy programme continued to the end of term.

However, exams out of the way, the mood of the intake became more relaxed and we dared think about a successful outcome and looked to the future. And there was the fun of preparing our sketches.

The tailors from Wetherill and Moss Bros arrived at the camp to measure us for our officers' uniforms. We were given a clothing allowance, the princely sum of £114. 13s. 4d. The Moss Bros representative took my order and fitted my uniform. This would be the first time that we'd wear the newly designed number two dress, a lovat green suit which was more flattering than the obsolete khaki, with a close-fitting jacket that reached below the hips, revere collars, four brass buttons fastenings and the WRAC insignia on the lapels. The A line skirt straighter and fell below the knee. The list of clothing was extensive, the bill amounting to more than we received. To accommodate the kit, I had to buy a tin trunk, stencilled with my name, rank and address by the quartermaster's store, banded and forwarded each time I was posted. The uniform fitting provided a sense of achievement and pride as I settled into the idea that I would soon become a commissioned officer. We still had no idea where were would be sent.

I was called to the Office. What had I done? I thought the

worst; worried I'd failed the course until I arrived to see Major Vennard's smiling face. She asked me if I would arrange the flowers for the commissioning ceremony. Relieved of my doubts, I agreed immediately. She needed a list of flowers to be ordered and an outline of my design. I hadn't a clue and having been put on the spot, said I would consider the arrangement and inform her later in the day. What had I let myself in for? Major Fleetwood-Jones wouldn't be pleased. Responding to the limited seasonal availability of flowers, I chose a mixture of different sized autumn coloured chrysanthemums, foliage and berries, providing an outline drawing with my request, which I handed to the chief clerk for the OC. A written reply appeared in my pigeonhole that evening. My suggestions had been approved, the flowers would be ordered. I felt daunted by the task.

There were lighter moments as we briefly rehearsed the 'sketch' we were to perform in our final week. I was cast as Lady Bracknell in a spoof of 'The Importance of Being Ernest', a 'take off' of the officers and NCOs who ran our course. I'd found an old suit at home, sprinkled talcum powder in my hair to turn it white, and wore a pair of black spectacle frames for my costume. Though not very well prepared, we raised a few laughs and entertained the troops. The hall was packed with the Headquarter Staff, Warrant Officers, non-commissioned officers who were currently on courses and the junior officer cadets. Senior officers sat at the front and I'm sure that we got marks out of ten for our acting abilities. Despite our limited skills, teamwork, initiative, taking a lead and projecting confidence were credited.

Results were announced. I had come ninth in order of merit, not quite as well as I had hoped. Four of us were called to the Office and this time I knew it couldn't be anything serious because the others were the highest achievers on the course. This was to be a rewarding visit to Major Vennard's office. Elaine was made Senior Under Officer, Pauline, Junior Under Officer,

Wendy, an Officer Cadet Sergeant, I was made an Officer Cadet Corporal. We had new epaulettes to attach to our dress uniforms. Perhaps Lesley was right about flowers instead of pips for my uniform. I didn't know why I'd been chosen. I'm sure Rudge would have been amused. Certainly, I felt proud of my success. They believed in my potential, and my responsibility was to live up to their expectations. I embraced the future with renewed hope of finding adventure and fulfilment.

Finally, our posting orders arrived in manila envelopes arranged in our pigeonholes. We ripped them open, groans or cheers following. Wendy and Florian were posted to Aldershot, happy to be together but with no idea of the baptism of fire that awaited them and the problems their girls would cause, fraternising with the troops stationed there, notably the Paras. Lesley was sent to Donnington, a Royal Ordnance Corps base, and was to live in a Nissan hut. Elaine had a plum posting to the Joint Staff College in Buckinghamshire to command a detachment of WRAC personnel. I would train new WRAC recruits with Helen at the Depot. I wondered how she felt about that, not being my best friend. Our Depot was being rebuilt at Guildford, and we were being sent to Lingfield, an old wooden camp in the middle of nowhere. Home from home, another all-female prison camp – not the adventurous posting I had envisaged. I was to report there on 4th January 1962. New horizons beckoned, and unexpected experiences awaited.

CHAPTER 22

THE COMMISSIONING

The Big Day of our Commissioning approached, the culmination of our training for the past year. In hut fifty-one the excitement grew as we packed cases and cleared rooms of personal possessions. My blue satin gown hung in the wardrobe, waiting for its moment to shine. All I needed was Mike, my partner, to escort me to the Ball. I hadn't heard from him. Surely, he must have reached England by now?

His awaited call finally came through to the Mess after supper. I stood in the telephone booth holding the receiver, remembering his first call in April. Memories forced their way into my mind of spring with Rudge, the bluebell wood and wishing well. I pushed them away, not wanting to feel the pain and lost hope, and listened instead to Mike's voice.

'How are things going for Thursday?' Mike enquired.

'Ok, thanks. How was your journey?' I asked him, trying hard to forget the mental images. 'You remembered how to find Deramore Cottage then?'

'I've always remembered where you lived,' he replied.

His answer surprised me, and I changed the subject.

'Everything ok at home? How's my Mum?'

'She's well, sends her love, and asked me to say that she's looking forward to seeing you at the commissioning.'

'Did she tell you where I've been posted?' I questioned, feeling more in the present.

'The Depot,' he replied. 'Only the best young officers are normally sent there.'

He couldn't make that assumption and was probably joking.

'Not sure about that,' I said.

'You were promoted, weren't you?' I heard the amusement,

a faint chuckle down the phone. I dismissed his remark; I knew I wasn't as good as the other three officer cadets with new epaulettes.

'Can I come over and see you tomorrow?' he asked. 'I've hired a car for a week.'

'Yes, that'll be nice. You'll have to come after tea and before supper, there's masses to do, we'll be busy getting our uniforms ready. I might ask you to bull my black shoes,' I laughed, to dispel my nervousness at meeting him again.

'It'll be a pleasure,' he said.

True to his word, he turned up outside the Mess in a bright red salon car. We hadn't seen each other for eight months and were initially, reserved. I invited him in and introduced him to my friends. The Mess, full of junior cadets, gave him their undivided attention, starved of male company. Mike held his own, chatting to them but I sensed he was rather overwhelmed by the army of women.

'Why don't you get your shoes, so I can give them a good shine?' he asked with a wry smile.

'Really? I was only joking!'

He insisted, I rushed to fetch them and the polishing kit. We sat together in his car while he buffed and brushed until like jet, the shoes were burnished black. He didn't say much; quiet where Rudge had been constantly engaging. Mike looked up when he'd finished and gave me a grin. His warmth and giving nature grabbed my attention, reconnecting an old attraction.

'Here you are,' he said handing them back.

'Thanks, they're perfect,' I said in admiration. Neither Florian nor I had ever achieved that level of brilliance.

'Sorry, I must go,' I announced, looking at my watch. 'It's suppertime and then I have to arrange flowers. Hope Mummy has prepared something good for yours. Say hello to her from me.'

'Good luck,' he said.

I climbed out of my seat and watched as Mike drove the red car towards the camp entrance, remembering another time when a grey van did the same.

The peppery smell of chrysanthemums overpowered the faint aroma of polish in the hall that evening. A team of WRAC personnel had laid a red carpet down the middle of the long building and arranged seats on either side for the junior cadets, parents and friends. The WRAC band area had been set up with stands behind my flower arrangement, which stood on a pedestal facing down the hall next to the VIP seating. I added the last sprays of berries to the vase and topped up with water. The flowers splashed colour in an otherwise dull room.

'Goodnight, Ma'am,' called out a stewardess carrying a mop. 'They look good.' She nodded towards my arrangement.

'Thanks. I hope they don't die overnight. Night,' I responded as she followed the others out through the main door. I remained in the empty hall picking up the odd fallen petal and leaf. The silence became an oasis of calm, peace I'd not experienced for a long time. The course was over. I'd not given time to reflect on the significance of passing out and the sense of achievement in fulfilling my aim. Then, in the stillness I heard his words again. 'So, what do you want out of life, Jackie?'

'Adventure,' I murmured, holding back the tears, 'and it starts tomorrow.' I picked up the bucket of unwanted greenery and walked away, carrying the image of his smiling face.

* * *

December sun distilled through a veil of cloud, dispelling the threat of rain. A frenzy of activity took place throughout the camp, last preparations before the arrival of the visiting VIP.

I inspected the flowers after breakfast. They looked cheerful on the pedestal at the end of the red carpet and, fortunately, none of them had drooped. I refilled the vase, lengthening their survival for the day and rushed back to my room to sort out my uniform, to be handed back to the quartermaster's stores.

The dining room echoed with excited voices at lunch and we talked of the future and our new postings.

'You'll come and visit, won't you?' Lesley asked.

'You bet,' I confirmed. 'I'll be dying to get away from the Depot. A two-year posting to another all-female camp! And with Helen!'

'Poor you,' she commiserated. 'You'll have to get a better alarm clock too,' she said, laughing, ready to relinquish her motherly role.

At two o'clock in hut fifty-one, Elaine, Wendy, Florian, Lesley, and I checked each other's Number One dress uniform with clothes brush at the ready: our shoes polished, make-up applied, hat and gloves on, we took one last look in the mirror.

'Right,' said Elaine. 'Time to go.'

For the last time we left our quarters together, falling into step and assembling with the rest of our intake outside the Hall where the RSM waited for us. Invited guests already seated, the VIP and senior officers present. The WRAC band began to play our cue, 'Lass of Richmond Hill'. The RSM brought us to attention and by the left we quick marched into the building and along the red carpet to our allotted places on the top left-hand side of the hall. We halted, about turned, and came to attention. The moment had come. Butterflies tangoed in my stomach, but the flowers were looking good and I had glimpsed Mike sitting with my parents.

The officer presiding over the ceremony was General Sir Richard Wakefield Goodbody GCB, KBE, DSO, and aide de camp general to Her Majesty the Queen, impressive in his dress uniform, covered in medals and gold braid. The General stood in front of the band facing down the hall and beside him were the directing staff; Major Vennard, WRAC, Colonel Commandant Wilson, WRAC, and all the WRAC officers who had guided us through the course. Our Colonel welcomed everyone and invited the General to take the salute and present each of us with a small commemorative plaque, bearing our name, rank and date of commission.

The band started to play a medley of military music. The guests and directing staff sat down while Major Vennard stood with the General, handing him the appropriate awards. Elaine was first – the best on the course – and received the sash of honour. One by one, we stepped forward in order of merit and marched up to the General, halted, collected our plaque, saluted and said, 'Thank you, Sir,' about turned and returned to our spot. During the commissioning, a film crew from Pathé News recorded the ceremony. Years later, seeing the tape for the first time, I felt proud by how smart we all appeared, young and full of enthusiasm. Moments captured on film of a different era, a different world, a tribute to the women who had then chosen a different career, to become an officer and a gentlewoman and to serve their country.

The Band began to play 'Greensleeves', the slow march of the WRAC. I had attained my goal and a surge of emotion threatened my composure. The music, with its lilting tune, represented my commitment and responsibility. Officers and junior cadets stood up. My intake turned to the right and, pulling myself together, we began to march in twos, our practised paces, back up the red carpet to the entrance of the hall. Once outside we let out a great roar of delight, throwing our caps in the air. We had passed out and were officers. During the past eleven months, we had lived together and shared our experiences, made friends and learnt to get along with those who weren't. We had successfully crossed the 'Baby River Jordon' since Westbury. The course had been hard especially after Rudge's death, but it had also been my salvation.

That evening the music played while the newly commissioned second lieutenants danced and jived. Mike, a brilliant dancer, had me doing the quickstep with fishtails. It was a night to remember, a real celebration, but at one o'clock in the morning it was time to go back to camp one last time.

This ball was the final event our intake shared. Many of the girls were sad to be leaving the next day. This chapter of our lives was now over; how changed we were from those brand-new cadets who had arrived in January. All the swotting, drilling and commitment had been worth it. We were now ready to step out with confidence to face all that awaited us, fully-fledged young officers in the Women's Royal Army Corps.

CHAPTER 23

HOBBS BARRACKS, JANUARY 1962

Camberley Station, that January morning, was cold and damp. I regretted packing away my greatcoat. For the first time, I wore my lovat green uniform. My jacket held WRAC lapel badges: a rose beneath a crown and a shiny metal pip on each epaulette announcing my responsibilities as a second lieutenant. A gold and silver WRAC badge on my forest green forage cap portrayed a lioness within a circle of laurel leaves surmounted by a crown, reminding me of the corps motto *suaviter in modo, fortiter in re* – gentle in manner, resolute in deed. I dared to hope that Hobbs Barracks would offer more than I expected – two more years of solely female company, and the irritations of my fellow officer, Helen.

Mummy and Reg waited on the platform to see me off, their breath visible in the icy air. Reg had been more amenable since my commissioning. Maybe he had more respect for me but, in my opinion, still not enough for my mother. The train steamed into the station and the porter wheeled the trolley, loaded with my trunk and cases, to the guard's van. Goodbyes said, I climbed into a first-class empty compartment and waved to my tearful mother.

The carriage lurched. The train moved off, wheels turning, gathering speed onward to Three Bridges. I reflected on the weeks since Cadet Wing and my uncertain future as Surrey winter landscapes sped past the windows.

Two men had featured in my life. David, the captain in the Royal Army Service Corps whom I'd met in the autumn. Both of us were bruised from losing our respective lovers. We'd found solace in spending time together on the few occasions we went out to a pub. David needed a partner at a formal dinner night, two days after my commissioning, and I had accepted his invitation. But then I had no idea that Mike, my gallant partner at the ball, would be staying at Deramore Cottage. Mummy had invited him to remain with us until his flight to Canada on 19th December. I had been looking forward to the Christmas dinner at the Royal Army Medical Corps Officers' Mess in Aldershot, but then I had mixed feelings. Dressed in a long brocade gown and high heels, I lingered in the drawing room. Wheels crunched on our driveway, announcing David's arrival, so I grabbed my handbag and said goodnight. Mummy handed me a wrap, Reg nodded over his newspaper and with a wry smile, Mike complimented me on my appearance. David came striding up the path to collect me, impressive in his full Mess kit.

At the Mess, decorated for Christmas, the highly polished dining room table laden with regimental silver and floral arrangements mirrored the glow of lit candelabra. We feasted on the best of sixties dining, port and madeira in crystal decanters circulating clockwise at the end of the meal. Mr. Vice rose to his feet and asked us all to be upstanding for the loyal toast. No smoking was permitted at a dinner night until after this protocol. Rudge had hated smoking and I had refrained whilst with him. But now the habit returned. I liked the taste of it, especially after a meal, and gratefully allowed myself a cigarette from the offered silver box.

David, an attentive and perfect escort, could not dispel my feelings of being an outsider. Invited to the function by one of his medical officer friends, he knew members of the Mess. I knew nobody. Of course, I behaved correctly, made small talk and mingled with diners afterwards in the anteroom, longing for the evening to be over. David and I knew instinctively that this was to be our last date together. Although we'd shared a difficult and emotional period of our lives, there was no deep connection between us. Our postings were to take opposing directions, and our parting that night outside Deramore Cottage was a natural ending. I kissed his cheek and murmured a final farewell.

The front door had been left on the latch, so I crept in, locking it behind me. Feeling weary, I reached my room, climbed into bed and turned off the light. There was something between the sheets. I fumbled around and touched a rectangular shape. Switching on the light again, I pulled out a box of Black Magic chocolates from under the bedclothes. Well, only one person could have placed it there. I was astonished to find his present and amused by its delivery.

I woke late on Sunday morning and arrived downstairs after breakfast to find Mike sitting in the drawing room reading the daily newspaper.

'Have a nice time?' he asked, looking up when I entered the room.

'Yes, thanks. How did you know that Black Magic chocolates were my favourites?' I quizzed him.

He laughed. 'Oh, a little birdie told me.'

Mummy walked passed the door with a tray of glasses.

'Can you give me a hand with the canapés for our Christmas drinks party tonight, darling?' she called out, and I followed her into the kitchen.

We were alone. Mummy rolled out pastry. She asked me about my evening and then spoke of Mike.

'Don't you hurt that young man, Jackie, because he's in love with you!'

That was a surprise. Mike and I were just good friends, except when he had kissed me after the ball. I'd blamed the champagne. Rudge was still in my thoughts and I wanted to concentrate on my new career. Mike would make an ideal boyfriend, handsome, kind, considerate and good fun. For now, he was just a supportive friend and I wanted nothing more while bereavement dogged my spirits.

In charge of the canapés that evening, I handed round the devils on horseback and plates of mince pies. My mother was delighted with Mike, who mixed drinks and looked after our guests. She missed my brother Ross, who couldn't have Christmas leave from his unit to come home, Mike helped keep up her spirits with his attention and conversation.

Before Mike left for the airport he asked for a photo of me and my new address, promising to send a post card from Montreal. He stooped down to kiss me goodbye. The memory of kissing him after our dance at the Cambridge Hotel returned. I'd been attracted to him then and he hadn't changed. But I had. I wasn't ready to make a commitment or to let my heart be broken again.

The train slowed. Time to concentrate on the present. How would I fit in? A bout of flu had prevented me from arriving at Hobbs Barracks on the 4th January. A car with a WRAC driver waited for me at Three Bridges station and taking on the mantle of my new status, I returned her salute. The porter transferred my luggage before we set off on the seven-mile drive to the camp. What a forsaken place it looked. Wooden huts stretched as far as the eye could see. Hobbs Barracks was in the middle of nowhere, and like Huron Camp, was bleak and desolate. In the summer of 1974, Hobbs Barracks would be used as a film set to represent a women's concentration camp in the film *The Hiding Place*. I remember how daunted I felt, a brand-new officer arriving at my unit, knowing that I had no choice. I was trapped, but had to make the most of the experience.

'I'll take you to your quarters, Ma'am,' said the driver, 'and drop off your luggage.' We passed through the camp gates and stopped to show my identity card. I received another salute before the car continued on a winding road through the girls' lines. The Officers' Quarters were at the top of the camp, near to the Medical Centre and the Officers' Mess.

A slim lieutenant wearing glasses approached as I clambered out of the car in front of the Junior Officers' accommodation.

'Hello, you must be Jackie,' she said. 'I'm Penny. We'll have your luggage put in your room. Would you like to come over to the Mess for tea first?' she asked, shaking my hand.

'What a good idea,' I replied, relieved by her friendly manner. My nerves on edge, the camp had no allure, run down and stark. What of the members of the Mess, did they reflect the environment? I had to face meeting them and needed that cup of tea.

'I think there's some mail for you too,' Penny remarked, leading me into the hallway.

Mike was as good as his word; waiting in my letter rack was a postcard from Montreal. Despite the snow scene on the front, the picture radiated warmth. Mike, at that moment, was the only friend I possessed, his words welcoming me to this sterile place.

In the anteroom, a few of the senior officers relaxed in chintz covered sofas and chairs. Penny introduced me to attractive Major Field, the Training Officer, Captain Cain, the Adjutant, a large blond lady with glasses, and diminutive Major Symonds, my Company Commander.

'Good to have you with us, Jackie,' said my OC. 'You're fully recovered from the flu I trust? Penny will bring you over to the office tomorrow. You'll be busy, we have a new intake of recruits.'

'I look forward to meeting them,' I replied with trepidation. No more was said, there was a rule in the Mess never to talk about shop, sex, politics or religion – rules we had learnt at Cadet Wing.

A stewardess arrived with a large pot of tea and set it down on a table with the crockery. Helen, not my best friend, entered the anteroom just then with some other subalterns. She greeted me without enthusiasm, looked down her long nose and introduced me to Anne, tall, blonde and cool, nicknamed 'The Iceberg'. Sally and Zara, who had been our seniors at Cadet Wing, were also with them. Sally had been with me in hut fifty-one and had often inspected my room with her white gloves. They were welcoming, and both had met Rudge. There were ten of us young officers,

Helen and I being the newest. Perhaps my posting wasn't going to be as bad as I had thought. The subalterns gathered round me for introductions, sharing memories of their time at Hindhead.

The Depot housed three training companies, each with three platoons. Mine was 1 Company, identified by yellow flashes on uniforms and my platoon, number 2. With me in 1 Company, under the command of Major Symonds, were Penny, a lieutenant, and Zara, a second lieutenant. There was a large compliment of officers at the Depot and I met most of them that evening at dinner. Two Queen Alexander Nursing Corps officers shared our Mess. Audrey, a captain, became a good friend. On the other hand, Major Bell, her boss, was a difficult woman, as I soon discovered. I had an embarrassing moment after dinner when coffee was served in the anteroom. Under the scrutiny of the senior officers, bombarded with questions, I promptly spilt coffee over the armchair when handed a cup by the stewardess, fazed by all the attention. Not a promising start!

The move of the Depot WRAC from Guildford to the temporary accommodation at Lingfield had not been without consequence. The recent influx of six hundred girls had caused a stir in the local town of East Grinstead, receiving a certain amount of press publicity. The national and local press had given the WRAC at Hobbs Barracks a mixed report. I soon learnt which reputation was closer to the truth.

A national magazine published a story about the girls, purportedly having a whale of a time six nights a week with the male inhabitants of the town. On Tuesdays, calm descended as the girls had 'In Nights' and remained in camp. When they were in town, Public Houses were reportedly doing a roaring trade and tickets for the back row in the cinema were sold out. In the feature, one of the eighteen-year-old recruits enjoying a night out, reputedly said 'It was the best thing the Army has done since Alamein.'

A local paper refuted this publication, quoting a statement

from a War Office spokesman.

'The facts, which are themselves commonplace, have been seriously distorted. We have every confidence in the WRAC at Hobbs Barracks who conduct themselves quite excellently, are a credit to the Army.'

The head of the East Grinstead police division also supported the girls:

'The WRAC are very smart and polite and by far the majority behave in a very responsible fashion. Some of them are more high-spirited than others but this must be expected in any community.'

At the Sussex Arms, a favourite meeting place for the WRACs, a licensee's wife gave her opinion.

'They are all decent kids and I think this article has hurt them very much.'

My posting to the temporary depot could be more testing than I had imagined. What kind of girls would be in my platoon? The officers and NCOs had to maintain a duty of care to the girl soldiers, set standards of discipline and behaviour during their basic training. I hoped the NCOs in my platoon were experienced or I'd be in trouble. I was as green as my uniform.

CHAPTER 24

PLATOON COMMANDER

'Good morning Ma'am,' said Corporal Mowe, saluting me. 'Welcome to 1 Company.' Her smiling grey eyes and confident stance gave me reassurance. I guessed she had dealt with situations I hadn't yet encountered and that, in any situation, she could be relied upon.

Half an hour earlier, at half-past eight, Penny had escorted me to the Company building, another wooden hut. Major Symonds' office was on the right side, ours on the left. A small room divided us, housing an antique lavatory with a pull chain and a washbasin. All mod cons! We three platoon commanders shared a large room. Two windows shed light on the notice boards behind our desks, which tracked the progress of the course, photographs of the girls who had passed out and other necessary information. An oblong rug on the planked floor dulled the tramp of our beetle crushers and ancient cast iron radiators pumped out enough heat to make the temperature bearable.

'This is yours,' said Penny pointing to a desk in the left-hand corner. A black rotary telephone, in, out and pending trays, and a large ink blotter lay on the desktop. A copy of Queen's Regulations and a dictionary were in the top drawer together with a camp telephone directory. In the bottom drawer a selection of military stationary, each document having a specific function. I hung my army regulations shoulder handbag on the back of the chair and sat down to familiarise myself with the new surroundings, conscious of my responsibilities.

'The OC said that you should report to her when you arrive,' announced Penny. I remember feeling as if I had been summoned to see the Headmistress at the convent, anxious and unsure of the outcome. I crossed the corridor, knocked sharply on the door, marched in and saluted.

'Ah there you are, Jackie. I just wanted to say that I hope you'll settle in quickly, as your platoon has been in the care of Sergeant Handley and Corporal Mowe for the last four days. You've sixty-three girls, most of whom hail from the North of England. They've already been kitted out at the Quartermasters' Store and they start their education assessments today for their job selections. Corporal Mowe will be reporting to you at 09:00hrs and take you to the girls' barracks where they're waiting to be inspected. Sergeant Handley is already with them, she is an experienced NCO and she will serve you well. You'd better get going.' She handed me the training programme.

Corporal Mowe was as short as I was tall and, despite the disparity of our height, we hit it off straightaway. I was grateful for her support and advice. I'm sure she picked up on my apprehension at meeting the platoon on my first day. In step, we left the subalterns' office and walked down concrete paths to the girls' lines, me listening to her rundown on the progress of the recruits. Outside a large wooden hut, she opened the door. Barrack rooms led off a long corridor, one revealing girls gathered by a row of iron bedsteads.

'Stand by your beds. Attention!' commanded a strong voice. The recruits, in their new uniforms, brought their heels together, arms stiffly by their sides, looking straight ahead.

'Good morning, Ma'am,' said Sergeant Handley with a snappy salute, stepping forward to greet me. Of medium height, she was smartly turned out with a millboard wedged under her left arm. I returned the courtesy.

'Have the girls Stand at Ease, Sergeant.' I requested, and she barked out the order. I was impressed by the standard of drill they had learnt in a few days. A mixed bunch, between seventeen and nineteen years old, of different shapes and sizes, different backgrounds, different accents, they had one thing in common: they were raw recruits. Their beds were neatly made with hospital corners, items of clothing laid on top, mufti stowed away in their lockers and wardrobe. I remember this inspection, my own experience at Cadet Wing, waiting for approval from the RSM and Orderly Officer. Now here I was representing authority – quite a different perspective.

Sergeant Handley brought me up to date with the girls' training as we circulated the Barrack room. Each girl stood to attention when I arrived at her bed space to carry out the inspection. Sergeant Handley's eyes darted over their kit, quick to discover a fault, focussing on the girls' uniforms and shoes, commenting on the lack of polish and elbow grease. Two girls failed to come up to standard with their bed making. The Sergeant stripped the offending objects.

'Make it again!' she shouted.

We proceeded to the next barrack room until all sixty-three girls and their beds had been scrutinised.

'That went well, Ma'am,' Sergeant Handley commented. I was relieved to have survived my baptism of fire. She was confident in her role as Platoon Sergeant and it was important that I came up to scratch like the new recruits. Another first took place later in the lecture room when I taught my platoon the different army ranks for officers and NCOs.

All I had to do now was learn their names. I kept a notebook on my desk and wrote cryptic phrases to remind me of their traits, mannerisms and misdemeanours. At the end of their course, I had to write a character reference for each one. It was easier for the recruits as they only had to remember our three names, of course, giving nicknames. I was to learn that mine was 'Longshanks'.

On Tuesdays, the girls stayed in barracks, an opportunity for their NCOs and officers to get acquainted with them. It was a chance to talk to the recruits while they polished shoes and pressed uniforms. One of the girls in my first platoon was a highly spirited lass from Newcastle – a troublemaker, quick-witted and ready to answer back and, to Sergeant Handley's annoyance, scruffy. During 'In Nights' I gained knowledge of the girls' lives and backgrounds. Many, like me, had joined the army for a new career, travel and adventure, but some of them signed up to escape from difficult family situations or from poverty. Private Smith was such a case. Sergeant Handley asked me to speak to her. She came to my office as bold as brass with a cheeky smile and a half-hearted salute. She was indeed scruffy; hair stuck out from under her squashed beret like matted horsehair, and the new uniform hung askew on her skinny frame, as if it were a hand-me-down. She absorbed my observations and grinned defiantly, exposing the large gap between her front teeth.

'So, what is this, Private Smith?' I gave her a stern look. 'I hear that you're very disruptive during drill and both Sergeant Handley and Corporal Mowe are totally fed up. Just look at the state of you, go and see for yourself in that mirror.'

She wandered over to the mirror on the wall opposite. On seeing her reflection, her face crumpled, and she burst into tears.

'Come and sit down,' I said, feeling sorry for her. She plonked herself on a chair, and, through tears, told me how she'd been bullied at school, and that her only defence was to play the fool. Her divorced mother had little time for her, more interested in entertaining her new fellas. Talking to the poor girl, I realised what a privileged background I had compared to hers. I asked if she wanted to remain in the army or return home. She chose the former.

'If you want to stay in the army you must learn to respect the NCOs and officers but, most of all, to respect yourself,' I stated. 'Learn to have pride in yourself. Keep yourself and your bed space clean and tidy. What trade have you decided on?'

'I wanna be a cook.'

'What do you think it takes to be a good cook, Private Smith?'

'I dunno.'

'You'll need to be organised and maintain a high level of hygiene. You'll be part of a team, depended upon to do your part. You'll also have to take orders from the NCO in charge of the kitchen. Do you think you could do that?' She nodded. 'Firstly, you will have to show Sergeant Handley, Corporal Mowe and me that you can smarten yourself up. We want to see a change in your attitude. You do realise this is a warning?'

'Yes, Ma'am,' she responded quietly.

'I'll be writing a report about you and it'll count towards your placement. Why don't you go to the hairdresser on camp after payday and choose a new hairstyle? And maybe buy yourself a new lipstick at the NAAFI?' She gave me a half smile. Later, at the end of the course, she told me that it was the first time anyone had taken time to talk to her about her personal problems.

'Do we have a deal?' I asked.

'Yes, Ma'am,' she said positively.

The role play carried out at Cadet Wing had helped me deal with this first difficult interview. I soon became as seasoned as the other Platoon Commanders on camp, which was essential for the task of Orderly Officer – and that duty was about to fall on my shoulders.

Private Smith did complete her basic training at Lingfield and went on to the Army Catering Corps in Aldershot, where she became a cook. When she left the platoon, she gave me a cuddly toy animal. I had a whole collection of them from girls who had passed out of my platoons by the time I was posted away. I remember my concern for that scruffy girl and my doubts that I had the ability to help her. Thank you, Major Vennard, for giving me the tools for such an occasion.

The basic training for the girls was six weeks. It wasn't until the third week that I first joined them on the parade ground for inspection before drill. Sergeant Handley and Corporal Mowe had the platoon out on the square every day from that week, until they were practise perfect. The NCOs recounted many hilarious moments as the girls tried the infamous Waterloo corner, when in a column of three abreast, they had to wheel left and form up in ranks of twenty abreast and three deep to recommence the Advance. This was practice for their march past at the passing out parade. Pile ups and tripping over at crucial moments in the manoeuvre ended in shouts and giggles. The NCOs would get up early on those inspection mornings to ensure that the girls were properly turned out. Corporal Mowe reminded me later that the subalterns arrived at the last minute still chewing toast from breakfast. I think she was referring to me!

One particularly cold February morning, I arrived to inspect my platoon on the parade square. Corporal Mowe brought them to attention and accompanied me along their ranks. It was a good effort all round, until she caught my eye. She stood behind a tall girl, looking up at her hair. I stopped and examined the problem; hair above the collar, that was acceptable. Then I saw them below her beret. Nits! Although no more evidence emerged as we inspected the other girls, this was a potentially serious situation, given how quickly lice could spread. After the inspection, I ordered Corporal More to march the girls up to the Medical Centre while I shot off to my office to make the call. Luckily my friend Captain Sister Audrey was on duty and not Major Bell, who would have not been best pleased. The influx of sixty-three girls for head checks was time consuming for her medical orderlies. I suggested to Audrey that perhaps the infested girl should have the rest of her body hair inspected too.

'Thanks, Jackie, just what I needed today. You owe me a drink,' she chuckled.

Three girls had caught nits and were given the evil smelling shampoo and lotion to use. Audrey called me later that morning, reporting that she personally had inspected the girl in question for body lice.

'Good news, she was clean as a whistle,' Audrey reported, commenting that she was impressed by the girl's personal hygiene and clean underwear. That was a relief. But I couldn't help but scratch all day at the mere thought of head lice. After all, Aud had pointed out that lice loved clean hair!

CHAPTER 25

ORDERLY OFFICER

There were enough junior officers on camp to avoid Helen, who regarded me with disdain. Penny, Sally and Zara were particularly good fun and would share their experience if I asked for advice. But nobody could prepare me for my first Orderly Officer's Duty. If the events had not actually taken place they would be hard to imagine – 'truth is stranger than fiction' springs to mind. I vividly remember the unfolding events from the time I reported to the Adjutant at nine o'clock on Friday, 9th February, one month after my arrival at Hobbs Barracks.

All started well that first day. I visited the cookhouse at lunchtime to check on the girls, finished a day's work at 1 Company, returned to the Mess for tea, then went to my quarters to change into my Number One dress uniform ready for evening duty. After dinner a call came though from the guardroom.

'Ma'am! Ma'am! Come quick!' a hysterical Orderly Sergeant shouted down the phone. 'Private Porter has been knocked down by a bus just outside camp.'

'Is she badly injured, Sergeant Gordon?' I asked anxiously, remembering the time I had witnessed Rudge's fatal accident in Oxfordshire.

'I don't know, Ma'am, I can't stand the sight of blood.'

'Call the Medical Centre immediately and tell Major Bell that we might need an ambulance.' She was the QARANC officer on duty that night. 'I'll be with you in a few minutes.'

I grabbed my peaked cap, pulled on my gloves and rushed out of the building. Hitching up my tight green uniform skirt, I climbed on board an ancient bicycle, at the disposal of the orderly officer, and began to pedal like mad to cover the half mile to the guardroom. My mind buzzed with 'what ifs', fearing what I might have to face.

The delights of the local town of East Grinstead were a pleasure that awaited me. I had only been into town to get my high heels repaired and buy some new stockings. Four weeks after my arrival, I was still getting used to running my own platoon of sixty-three new recruits, with the help and experience of Sergeant Mary Handley and the amusing Corporal Jeannie Mowe. No time for frivolities! Out of breath, I arrived at the guardroom and Sergeant Gordon scuttled out.

'Ma'am, Major Bell says we can't have the ambulance as the accident happened outside the camp.'

'What!' I exclaimed, astounded by the news and the simple lack of compassion from a member of the medical profession. 'Right, call the hospital at East Grinstead and ask them for help. We need the St John's ambulance to come quickly.' Two weeping girls wearing civilian clothes stood in the doorway.

'Sergeant Gordon, where is Corporal Jones, the Orderly Corporal?'

With no time to wait for a reply or speak to the girls, I hurried through the open barrier of the barracks. A bus had parked diagonally across the verge, its lights piercing the dark night, engine still running. Light reflected from the guardroom windows cast long shadows across the road, almost obscuring the scene of the accident. A crowd had gathered round a body lying on the ground. Two young men directed traffic and, as I approached, the knot of people parted. A stocky man wearing the uniform of a bus driver stepped forward.

'I saw this group of girls at the side of the road and as I got closer one of them stepped out in front of me. I swerved to avoid her, but she took a knock from the side of the bus,' he explained, visibly shaken.

A young girl lay prostrate in the road. I crouched down, relieved to see she was alive and conscious. A pale, pinched face looked up at me.

'How are you feeling?' I asked.

'Cold,' she answered.

'Where does it hurt?' I enquired.

'Don't know, Ma'am,' she replied, shaking.

'Don't worry the ambulance will be here soon, you'll be all right.' She bled from cuts on her knees, but there were no other signs of injury. I'd completed my first aid training at Officer Cadet Wing, but was grateful that the real medics would be arriving any second. I didn't want to examine her under those conditions.

'What's your name?' I gently asked.

'Sandra. Hold my hand,' she pleaded and reached out to find mine. Just then Corporal Jones, the Orderly Corporal, appeared beside me.

'Sorry, Ma'am,' she said out of breath. 'I was called out to the cookhouse. Can I help?'

'Yes, get a blanket from the guardroom, will you? Take the details from the bus driver and find out who was with Private Porter tonight in case we need to follow this up.' Corporal Jones shot back to the guardroom, returning with a grey blanket to cover the girl's shivering body. A few minutes later the ambulance arrived, blue light flashing and sirens screaming. The onlookers, now satisfied by the events, climbed back on the bus. The Orderly Corporal completed writing down relevant details in her notebook.

'Good luck,' said the driver. 'Hope she'll be ok.' I looked up and thanked him.

'Please don't leave me,' said the poor girl, still clinging to my hand.

'Corporal Jones, phone Major Symonds, the Field Officer on duty. Tell her what has happened, say I've gone in the ambulance with Private Porter to East Grinstead Hospital and I'll report back when I can.'

'Right, Ma'am,' she said, turning to cross the road.

The ambulance men carefully lifted the whimpering patient onto a stretcher.

'Ok Sandra, just let go of my hand for a minute, then we can get you into the ambulance and off to hospital to make sure you're all right.' Sobbing, she took her hand away.

'You coming too, Miss?' asked a friendly ambulance man. I nodded and climbed in.

'Well she's a lucky girl,' said the doctor in Emergency one hour later. 'No broken bones, a few cuts and grazes, but we'll keep her in overnight for observation. She'll be black and blue tomorrow though.'

Waiting at the hospital for news of the injured girl brought back painful memories of doing the same for Rudge in Kidlington. I wished I had been with him in the ambulance, able to hold his hand as I had done for Sandra Porter. This was the first time I had visited a hospital since his accident. Perhaps wearing my uniform stopped me from allowing the old wounds of grief to reopen. Cold and tired, I wanted to return to the warmth of the Mess, a cup of coffee and the roaring fire. The problem was how to get there. Taxi, perhaps? But I had no money with me. I hadn't planned on a night out! Instead I asked one of the nursing staff if I could get a lift.

'Wait a moment, please, I'll see what I can do,' she promised.

I popped to the ward where Private Porter had been taken. The ward sister informed me that the patient had been sedated and was asleep. I left, assured of her well-being.

'You going to Hobbs Barracks, Miss?' enquired a male voice. I looked up from reading an old Woman's Own magazine in the waiting room and saw a man who, for a second, I thought was my Uncle Harry. Slightly stooped, he was about sixty years old. His smiling kind face topped by grey hair; a pair of horn-rimmed glasses framed friendly brown eyes.

'Yes, please,' I replied.

'I've just dropped my daughter off for night duty and I'm

going home to Lingfield, so I'll be passing the Barracks. Sister said you were a bit lost,' he remarked.

'You could say that,' I said without rancour, immensely grateful.

I picked up the grey army blanket, which seemed out of place in this white and green hospital ward. It was important to take it back, otherwise I would be charged for a replacement. Thanks to the kindness of Bert and his Hillman Imp, I got back to the guardroom in time for the last girls returning to camp by eleven fifty-nine.

The personnel on duty were relieved to hear that Private Porter hadn't been seriously injured. The two girls with her on the side of the road were really shocked by the accident. Corporal Jones had taken their statements. They wouldn't be playing 'chicken' in future. Sergeant Gordon now more composed, reprieved from having to deal with blood, stood ready with the charge sheet for any of the girls who dared to be late returning to Hobbs Barracks that night.

'I'll leave you to it, Sergeant,' I said, exhausted by the evening events. 'I'm going to lock up the Officers' Mess and write my report. Please inform Major Symonds that I'm back and Private Porter is ok but staying in hospital overnight. Let me know if anything more crops up.'

Little did I know what was in store for me during the following hours!

George, a private from the Pioneer Corps, passed by on his cycle as I left the guardroom, the only man on the camp of six hundred women. He carried out essential repairs at the Depot. Tall, lanky and in his forties, he seemed like a Greek god to the inmates, and was simply known as George. He asked if he could escort me. We were heading in the same direction to our different quarters. Hitching up my skirt once again, too dark for him to see my suspenders, I climbed back on the old bike and we pedalled up the badly lit, tree lined road to the Officers'

Mess. Our dynamos whirred against the tyres making the lamps glow intermittently. The wind had got up and the temperature dropped even more.

'Cold tonight, supposed to be worse tomorrow,' announced George. Just what I needed for the next two days of duty. It was too late for that coffee and in any case, the roaring fire would be out and the kitchen staff would have returned to their billets. I turned off in front of the long single storey wooden building. The sign Officers' Mess shone in the light of my cycle lamp and I parked the bike against the step.

'Night, Ma'am,' said George as he pedalled towards his quarters.

'Night, George,' I called out and went in through the double doors.

I retrieved a torch from the fuse box in the hallway. Starting at the far end of the building I checked that all the windows were shut, and the lights switched off in the anteroom. A fireguard protected sparks from the last few embers of the dying fire. I closed the door behind me content everything was in order. Now in the dark I returned along the corridor to the front entrance. The beam of my torch shone, picking out the letter rack and pigeonholes for the officers in the hall. There was mine right at the bottom: 2/Lt J. Skingley-Pearce. Perhaps there would be a letter from Mike tomorrow? He wrote more frequently, and I enjoyed hearing his news from Germany. Hobbs Barracks was isolated, creating the sense of being cut off from the rest of the world. Mike's letters were like a message in a bottle washed up on a barren island.

I stood in the Mess hallway to hear the tinkling of a bell. There it was again, coming from the kitchen. The entrance was directly in front of me. Opening the door, I was about to throw the light switch when, in the beam of my torch, I saw hundreds of iridescent eyes. Looking directly at me were rats – huge rats. I screamed and, as a reflex action, switched on the main light.

For a split second I saw, above the pantry door, an enormous rodent with his tail hanging down over the bell extension, vibrating as he ate. I screamed again. The alarmed, squeaking rats disappeared up behind the wooden slatted ceiling and into the rafters. In a surreal moment, all that remained of them were their tails, hanging down like stalactites. The adrenalin in my bloodstream increased my fight and flight mode. Nobody had told me about the rats. I ate all my meals in the Mess, I could die of some awful disease. They were disgusting.

'Ma'am! Ma'am! Are you all right?' shouted a male voice.

'Oh! George, thank goodness it's you.'

'Bloody Hell!' he exclaimed. 'I thought you were being raped and murdered. I could hear your screams the other side of the camp.'

'George, the rats!'

'Oh, *them*,' he said, 'you'll get used to them!'

Not me. For the next week I walked, if I couldn't borrow the orderly officer's bike, to the Snack Bar outside the guardroom to buy an egg and cress bap plus a Kit Kat chocolate bar. The owners were making a fortune from the influx of residents in Hobbs Barracks. A week later, hunger finally won over my high principles and I was tucking into roast beef with all the trimmings, followed by chocolate pudding in the Mess dining room. Bugger the rats!

That night asleep in my room, dreaming of giant rodents, something woke me; the high-pitched whine of a fire alarm. The Orderly Officer's duty was to ensure that everyone paraded on the square as quickly as possible. I leapt out of bed, throwing on my clothes. First to hand was my Number One dress, but in haste I took my beret instead of my peaked cap. I began to shout *fire! fire!* as I ran down the corridor. The junior officers appeared in nightwear at their doorways.

'Where's the fire, Jackie?'

'Not sure,' I shouted. I rang the Field Officer, Major Symonds, my company commander. She took a while to answer.

'Ma'am, the fire alarm has gone off. I am evacuating the Junior Officers Quarters.'

'Right, I'll do the same here and will meet you on the square. Make sure the RSM knows and the orderly NCOs. Where is the fire?'

I rang the guardroom. A sleepy voice answered.

'Corporal Jones, see if you can get hold of the RSM. Tell her that a fire alarm has gone off and we are to parade on the square for a head count immediately. Have you had any reports of a fire, can you see one?'

'No, Ma'am.'

'We'll have to check this out before we call the fire brigade. Phone Sergeant Gordon at the Sergeants' Mess and see if she can confirm it's the real thing.'

The Orderly Corporal was now wide awake.

The junior officers had grabbed coats and left for the parade square. By now hundreds of women were emerging from their different quarters, the insistent ringing of the alarm penetrating the hubbub of voices.

'Well that was fun, Ma'am,' the RSM said sarcastically half an hour later. 'No fire and not even a practice fire drill! By the way, Ma'am, you're improperly dressed.'

Oh damn! Six hundred women plus the headquarters staff had lined up in their platoons and companies, all shivering on the parade ground at two in the morning. Someone had played a prank, which did not go down well. The RSM had taken it personally and was going to root out the culprit – God help her if she was found. Senior officers started to return to their beds, clutching jewellery boxes and the odd small lap dog. How disgruntled they were, appearing in curlers before the other ranks, shades of the real fire at Hindhead. I could still remember the drama, the acrid smell of smoke and the arrival of the fire brigade at full tilt.

Feeling weary after the early morning events, I got up at quarter to eight and dressed in my lovat green uniform. On the bike again, I pedalled around to the cookhouse to inspect the girls' breakfast.

'What would you like to try, Ma'am?' said Staff Sergeant Higgins, standing behind a huge stainless-steel counter on which different dishes were displayed in big trays.

'Scrambled egg, please, Staff.'

One of the best parts of being Orderly Officer was sampling food in the cookhouse. Girls chatted away at long tables. Cooks wrapped in steam from the kitchen. Great urns of tea stood at the end of the counter, slabs of butter, acres of toast, jars of marmalade neatly laid out in rows. Cereals, baked beans, every kind of egg, bacon and sausage, fried bread completed the menu. My breakfast appeared on a white plate with eating irons. I took a mouthful. A sudden thought overtook me. Rats. I wondered if they had them too. I put down my fork, feeling sick at the thought of them running free under the cover of darkness throughout the camp.

I moved towards tables where the girls were tucking into breakfast. Some of mine were there, not looking too happy, probably because of their disturbed night. I asked if the food was all right. Before they answered, one of them joked about losing her beauty sleep, followed by a complaint.

'It would be better if we 'ad some chips wiv it,' said Cockney Private Huggett.

'Well, you might be lucky at lunch then,' I replied, walking back to the serving counter. I needed a cup of coffee to keep awake, comforted by the fact that it would at least be made with boiled water!

'Thanks, Staff,' I said, as she handed me a cup. 'Good breakfast.'

I sipped the hot drink, feeling more alive, ready to face the day. 'See you at lunch,' I said, placing the empty cup on the counter. I left the cookhouse to mount my bike once again and return to the Junior Officers' Quarters, where I ignored all the comments from my fellow subalterns about the false fire alarm. They were planning their weekend; some of them off to see relatives and friends. Only three out of the ten had cars and would offer lifts to those without wheels. A group had been invited to a party that evening at the Royal Intelligence Corps Officers Mess in Maresfield, thirty miles away. A quiet Saturday night loomed for me.

During the day, I went to the cookhouse again to inspect lunch. Girls, dressed in their civilian clothes, had dolled up for their weekend of fun in town. Piles of food adorned the steel counter, chips the main attraction. Satisfied everything was going well, I left them to it and went down to the camp gates, buying myself lunch from the snack shop.

Not many people were around camp late afternoon, allowing me to retire to my room and carry on knitting the sweater I was making to ward off boredom, turning on my transistor to listen to Radio Luxembourg. All was well, until, in the middle of Chubby Checker's 'Let's Twist Again', I heard the phone ring in the corridor. I checked my watch. Six thirty.

'Ma'am come quick,' bellowed the familiar voice of Sergeant Gordon. 'There are Teddy Boys outside the camp, shouting and causing a nuisance. They won't go away.'

Brilliant. This was just what I needed. Already changed into my dark green uniform, I put on my hat and greatcoat, slipped on my gloves ready to ride the trusty bike down to the guardroom. I approached the red and white barrier pole that Sergeant Gordon had closed across the camp entrance. I stopped, dismounted and took a long look at my adversaries. Crowds of yobs wearing drainpipe trousers and slicked down 'DA' hair sat on motorbikes outside the gates.

'Cor, you're a bit of all right, darlin!' said one.

I pulled myself up to my full height of five foot nine and

three-quarter inches, with an added couple of my peaked cap.

'Right, you have exactly five minutes to leave these premises before we call the police,' I said, keeping calm but shaking in my shoes. 'The decision is yours.'

I raised my arm and pushed back the sleeve of my coat to look at my watch. I stood my ground and stared at them. They were a rough lot but fortunately they'd enjoyed enough fun, revving up their bikes they finally sped off into the dusk. The Orderly Sergeant came out of the guardroom.

'They were a real pest,' she said.

Pity you couldn't have sent them on their way, I thought, my inward angst dissipating with their departure.

Panic over, I returned to my room to write to Mike, my pen pal since he had returned to Germany after Christmas. He wrote amusing letters and I appreciated someone who understood military life, to share the ups and downs of the camp. A couple of hours later the phone rang again. This time it was the calmer voice of Sergeant Gordon.

'Ma'am, you need to come because there is a woman here with her family and they won't leave until they speak to the officer in charge.'

'What's it about?'

'Sorry, Ma'am, she wouldn't say.'

'Ok Sergeant, I will be down shortly,' I said reluctantly.

The routine was established; pull up skirt, climb on bike, pedal like mad. What delights awaited me this time? Inside the guardroom were three women. Sergeant Gordon introduced me to Mrs. Wells, along with her sister and mother. They looked agitated.

'We want to speak with you in private,' said Mrs. Wells.

It seemed important, but there was nowhere I could take them in the guardroom, except into one of the cells. Two were kept for military personnel who had committed serious offences. The four of us crowded into one of them, a tiny room, and sat on the bed. The blankets and sheets neatly folded up at the foot of the mattress.

'Can you tell me what this is about, Mrs. Wells?' I asked the distressed woman.

'It's my husband, he's having an affair with one of your women,' she accused. Her mother and sister comforted her as she sobbed into a handkerchief.

'Do you know her name?' I asked, wondering how I could deal with the situation.

'Yes,' she spat out a name. 'She's a stewardess.' I didn't know the girl. At least she wasn't a recruit. I made a mental note to ask the Orderly Sergeant.

'What do you want me to do about it, Mrs. Wells?'

'Stop it!' she blurted out. 'They are out together now.'

'I will speak to the girl when she returns to camp. Have you spoken to your husband?' I asked. She nodded. I didn't feel very hopeful that I could change anything. Mrs. Wells carried on crying and bemoaning her lot. When the women finally left camp, I asked Sergeant Gordon if she knew the stewardess.

'Oh yes, she works in our Mess, nice girl. Sorry to hear she's got tangled up with a married man.'

Yes, I was too. Married men were off limits, in my opinion.

I checked the clock on the guardroom wall. Nine forty-five.

'I'll stay here and wait for the girls to return to camp and see the stewardess,' I said to the Orderly Sergeant. Corporal Jones offered me coffee, which I gratefully accepted. I was beginning to feel hungry after my self-imposed diet, and the coffee kept me awake.

From ten o'clock the girls started to appear and sign in after their night out. We were doing well and by eleven-thirty most of them had returned, though there was still no sign of the stewardess. The last few stragglers fell through the guardroom door, giggling, but quickly sobered up on seeing me in the room. They were my girls, not drunk, just a bit tipsy, celebrating the approaching end of their basic training, with only a week to go before passing out. I asked if they had enjoyed the night off. They laughed, agreed and linking arms, sauntered off to walk back to their lines.

'Just two left to sign in,' confirmed Sergeant Gordon.

The clock ticked to ten minutes past twelve.

'They're late now, Sergeant,' I remarked. Just then the stewardess and Mr. Wells came into the guardroom.

'It's my fault that she's late,' he said as the stewardess signed in.

'I'm sure it is, Mr. Wells,' I commented. 'Don't you think you have caused enough trouble this evening? I suggest you go home to your wife, and we don't want to see you here again.'

He was taken aback by my knowledge of his name and married status. The stewardess looked worried. Her boyfriend had been rumbled and we were not sympathetic to his apology. Looking dejected, he briefly said goodbye to the girl and left to face his wife. I called the stewardess and took her into a cell, the interviewing room of the evening.

'Do you realise the problems that you have caused?' I pointed out. 'His wife was here earlier with half of the family complaining about you.' She burst into tears. After a heart to heart chat, she promised that she wouldn't be seeing Mr. Wells again. I doubted it. Loneliness was her problem, Hobbs Barracks her prison, and she had rattled the cage, desperate to have some fun. She was yet to meet a male she liked of her own age and had been flattered by the attentive Mr. Wells. I understood her situation. Perhaps she appreciated my empathic approach. My counselling skills were improving and possibly the reason for her promise.

The last of the girls arrived late with some silly excuse and Sergeant Gordon put her name on the charge sheet. Later, she would appear in front of her Company Commander for punishment. I said goodnight to the duty NCOs and, tired from the day's events, returned to my room to write a report about the stewardess and the visit of Mrs. Wells.

Blissfully, there had been no disturbance during the night, and I woke up on Sunday morning grateful that I only had another twenty-four hours of duty. All seemed to go well for the first part of the day. I followed the expected routine, apart from eating in the Mess. My report grew in size after the events of the last few days. One good thing happened on Sunday afternoon – Private Porter returned to the care of the Medical Centre.

It was about nine o'clock when a call came through. One of the girls in Holding and Drafting Company had tried to commit suicide by taking a bottle of aspirin. Another situation I would have to face for the first time.

'Which barrack block is she in?' I asked Sergeant Gordon on the phone. 'Ok got that, please send Corporal Jones down there to meet me, call Major Bell and warn her about the overdose.' I rushed out of the Junior Officers' Quarters and jumped on the old bike. I sped down to the girls' lines to find the poor girl lying in her bed, clutching a teddy bear. One of her friends hovered over her.

'How many tablets have you taken?' I asked the distressed girl. She mumbled. On her bedside locker lay the empty aspirin bottle. Corporal Jones arrived breathless.

'Shall I get the ambulance, Ma'am?' she gasped.

'No, too late, we must keep her awake.'

'Can you find her coat and shoes?' I asked her dithering friend.

'Let's get her up,' I insisted. The poor girl was floppy, incoherent. We managed to sit her up and slip on her outer clothing and footwear.

'Come on now, stand up and walk,' I cajoled. Corporal Jones and I linked our arms through hers, but the girl wouldn't let go of her teddy. We supported her along the three hundred yards to the Medical Centre. When we arrived, the door was open, a shaft of light cutting through the dark night. Silhouetted in the doorway was the unmistakable figure of Major Bell.

'I have got my stomach pump ready for you!' she called out. I'm sure she was rubbing her hands. Poor girl, she was going to have a tough time on top of everything else. There must have been a good reason why she had attempted to take her life. We struggled up the six steps into the Centre. Major Bell then took charge of her, shutting the door. Corporal Jones and I turned back to collect my bike and carry onto the guardroom for the girls signing in. Suddenly the door of the Medical Centre flew open again, a teddy bear flying through the air.

'We do not keep animals in this establishment, Miss Skingley-Pearce,' boomed the voice of Major Bell.

Taken aback by her lack of compassion for that poor girl and shaken by her action, I was unable to answer before she closed the door again.

Monday morning dawned, and I could not wait to hand over my Orderly Officer's duty. I paraded in front of the Adjutant at nine o'clock with a thick stack of papers, my report for the weekend. I complained about the rats, but Captain Cain wasn't interested.

'Oh yes we know about them, Jackie, and we have requested rodent control,' she commented, taking my report and making a sarcastic remark about the false fire alarm fiasco. She cursorily glanced through the pages, as if these events were to be expected and as a trained officer I should be competent to deal with them. And I was!

CHAPTER 26

MARCHING FORWARD

The girls in my first platoon had completed their basic training. Smartly turned out, they stood 'at ease' behind me, assembled on the Square for their passing out parade. A small percentage of the original recruits had left for various reasons, mostly because they were unsuitable. The six-week course had given them self-confidence. Assessed and selected for preferred trades and skills, they would receive further training, some posted to other branches of the army. While they had been at Hobbs Barracks, they'd learned to work as a team, to embrace military life and the camaraderie it offered. It had not been without hard work for the platoon NCOs to bring them up to scratch or for me to interview everyone, to write their reports, and get to know them as individuals. I was proud of all achievements.

I'd taken my place on the Parade Square at the head of my platoon, determined to lead with poise and not forget my commands. Sergeant Handley and Corporal More would be mortified if I let them down, if I fluffed it. I was their officer and my mistakes would reflect badly on them. The recruits from other companies passing out that day were also present on the square with their officers and NCOs. For Helen and me, this was a new challenge. I hadn't bothered to ask if she was nervous too. I concentrated on standing properly 'at ease', feet apart, straight arms with hands clasped behind my back. The WRAC band began to play *The Great Little Army*, and the Parade Commander brought us all to attention.

'Parade, by the left, quick march!' she ordered.

I stepped out, swinging my arms, assured that Sergeant Handley and Corporal Mowe followed with the girls. We marched forward in step, in column of route, three abreast. I gave the command: '2 Platoon, eyes right!' and saluted our Commandant who stood on the podium. Parents and friends of the girls sat along the edge of the Parade Ground, cameras clicking as we marched past. Another first achieved and, later, I received the thumbs up from Sergeant Handley. A rewarding moment.

The camp fell silent after the mass exodus of girls. Block cleaning duty came next, in preparation for the new intake of recruits. Stewardesses rattled around with buckets and mops. Corporal Mowe brought her guitar when all was shipshape. A few of the other NCOs joined us and we sat in one of the Barrack rooms to listen to her repertoire of songs, the favourite being the number one, Frank Ifield's 'I Remember You'. Lighter moments were shared; the barriers between our ranks lowered as we yodelled along and fell about laughing. My friendship with Jeannie Mowe was forged from those days.

A week's leave followed for the Company and I went by train to visit Rudge's parents. It was never easy to go there. I wore the Para insignia his mother had given me, and her eyes lit up when she spotted it. I wondered if the heartache would ever lessen. He had left a great hole in our lives. There was no number of first experiences at Hobbs Barracks that could dispel my grief.

* * *

Living in an all-female environment was far from ideal. I hardly left camp, not having transport. Occasionally, Penny took me in her Mini to East Grinstead, to the Felbridge Arms for a drink after shopping in the High Street. These outings were curtailed when Penny, engaged to her sweetheart, John, left the WRAC that summer. After their marriage the bridal couple planned to live in deepest Surrey. A new second lieutenant called Poppy would replace Penny in the Company Office. The Depot was a transitory place with a consistent changeover of recruits, postings in and out for officers and non-commissioned officers.

A highlight in our calendar was the forthcoming marriage of Sally, one of our subalterns, to a REME officer in July. The ceremony and reception would be held in a pretty village not far from the camp. The entire complement of the Officers' Mess had been invited to her wedding and we debated what to wear. I loved the story of their romance; how they had met at Bordon Camp when Sally had just been commissioned, reminiscent of Florian and Matt. Sally's posting to Lingfield wasn't a hindrance because her family lived close by, where they could meet up. I remember the joy on her face when she announced her engagement, and I congratulated her, but was secretly jealous of her happiness.

The senior subalterns in our Mess organised a party at Easter, roping me in to help decorate the Mess. A number of officers from nearby regiments had been invited and Sally brought her fiancé. The older officers at the Depot always loved meeting younger male officers, capable of drinking any of them under the table. As I recall it was a sociable evening, but I wasn't in the mood for a party and left just after eleven o'clock, already in bed when one of my friends came into my room.

'Jackie, what are you doing? Get up! Everyone misses you,' she exclaimed.

I really didn't want to go back but she insisted and, reluctantly, I dressed again. I danced and chatted for a while but was pleased when it was time for the guests to leave. One of the lieutenants had taken a shine to me and wrote several times after the party, asking for a date. I wasn't interested. He was a shadow of Rudge, the man who lived inside my head.

However, I did appreciate letters from Mike and the flowers he sent on Valentine's Day. We had become closer friends through our correspondence and now he finished his letters *with love, Michael*. I fell into the habit of referring to him as Michael from then on. He asked if I would like to visit him in Germany at the end of May during his fortnight's leave. He could arrange accommodation with the SAAFA – Soldiers, Sailors Airmen Families Association – Sister. I was touched by his invitation; he understood the isolation I felt at Lingfield. The adventuress in me jumped at the chance to travel and to rediscover the man who, since I was seventeen, had always been in the background. I remembered him, my gallant partner at the Commissioning Ball and our houseguest at Deramore Cottage, as protective and caring towards me. What did I have to lose? After deliberation, I replied and, accepting his invitation, requested leave from my Company Commander.

A new intake of recruits arrived. My role training them was more straightforward the second time round, and I had established a working relationship with my NCOs. Although I had a good team, the repetitiveness of inspections, reports and drill for the next two years did not thrill me. I needed a break. On the day the signed and approved leave application arrived on my desk, I wanted to scream, 'Yes!' acknowledging my successful pass to new horizons.

And then I was confronted with the anniversary of Rudge's death. I slipped into the chapel on Camp, a refuge from the daily routine. Outside, the platoons were being drilled on the parade ground and I could hear the faint shouts of the NCOs. I knelt in a pew, closed my eyes and prayed. His smiling face rose in my mind with that look of approval I remembered, as if he was willing me to move on, to find happiness again. But I was afraid to expose my fragile heart to another man. I feared rejection and, even more, I feared the possibility of another loss.

Sally and Zara had discussed the reason for my loneliness with the other junior officers, and later Sally confessed that they felt sorry for me. Penny encouraged me to visit Michael in Germany. So, with a new passport, a packed case and some trepidation, I left camp to catch the London train. Let out of my wooden cage I wanted to sing, extolling the sense of freedom, connecting to the outside world again beyond Hobbs Barracks.

The journey was less complicated than the previous year. I knew the ropes, not concerned about finding the right train at the Hook of Holland. I mulled over Michael's letters, the growing intimacy of his sentiments, drawn to the music of his words, I found myself attracted to him, as I had previously been in Camberley. Physically strong, with the body of a sportsman, Michael also possessed the qualities I valued; honesty, humour and kindness. I knew he cared for me, but no boundaries had been drawn. Where would we sleep at the SSAFA Sister's flat?

On the early evening of the 30th May the train arrived at Herford station. I recall that first glimpse of Michael through the compartment window, waiting for me on the platform, eyes searching the crowded coaches. He looked fit and tanned in casual clothes; open necked shirt and slacks. His face set with concentration until he caught sight of me alighting from the train and broke into a smile. My apprehension grew – although I was pleased to be with him, we hadn't seen each other for five months. Our weekly letters, full of anecdotes and personal accounts of our regiments, had fostered a deeper knowledge of one another, but I was still anxious of his expectations. He strode forward, welcomed me with a kiss on my cheek and led me to his car, all the while making small talk to hide the shyness that crept between us.

Sister Jan opened the door to her spacious flat. Tall, with dark hair and eyes that shone with health, I judged her to be about twenty-five years old. She greeted me in a gentle voice and I stepped inside, content to have arrived, to find such a kind and considerate hostess. Everything would be fine, I convinced myself, and I began to relax. Michael hovered behind, carrying my case, and followed as Jan showed me to my room. She left us together with a bright smile, departing to prepare supper with Martin. Alone with Michael I suddenly felt awkward, even more so when he explained that Martin, a fellow officer from the regiment, would also be staying at the flat as he and Jan were having an affair. What had Michael said to Jan about us? Where had he arranged to sleep? On the sofa? My young body ached to be loved again, but I battled with unharnessed emotions. Sensing my unease, Michael gave me a sheepish grin saying he would help in the kitchen while I unpacked.

I remember meeting Martin for the first time. He had charisma, an air of confidence and sex appeal. His eyes twinkled when Michael introduced us, but the femme fatale within me did not respond. We had gathered in the sitting room, the men pouring drinks, handed around glasses of lager and, with the German toast 'Prost', we sat down together to enjoy aperitifs. Transported to a different world, no longer tied down by rules and regulations, I had time to unwind and make new friends. The loneliness that shadowed me began to dispel. I was delighted when Martin and Michael announced a planned trip to a Schützenfest at the weekend including us girls. The event would take place in a small town on the River Weser where Martin's troop was on summer camp. Martin explained that for many rural communities these festivals marked the cultural highlight of the year. Local breweries donated specially brewed beer, cakes were baked, and flowers adorned the wagon for the King of Marksmen, which was paraded through the town at the beginning of the Schützenfest. A great excuse for a party! While the men had decided to camp overnight and fish in the river, they reassured us that we would be staying in a hotel.

Exhaustion from the journey, and my unsettled nerves, suddenly hit me. Jan noticed how quiet I'd become and asked if I was feeling all right.

'Just tired,' I replied. She left the table and brought back a packet of pills.

'Here have one of these, they'll keep you awake,' she promised.

I'm not sure what she gave me, but it had the opposite effect. My eyelids began to close. Michael stood up and helped me to my feet.

'You must rest,' he said, guiding me to the bedroom. I felt unsteady on my feet. He helped unzip my dress and I mumbled something about managing myself. I heard him leave the room. I must have slept for a while, a knock on the door woke me and Michael came in.

'How are you?' he asked. I registered the concern in his voice. I wasn't surprised to see him because I had noticed his sports bag in the corner. But, we still hadn't discussed the sleeping arrangements.

'I'm fine now, thanks. Sorry I was such a wet blanket,' I murmured, switching on the bedside lamp. He sat on my bed, watching me, and then deliberately leant over and kissed me. I must have looked awful with no make-up and dishevelled hair, but he didn't seem to care.

'You're so beautiful,' he declared, 'but I can't fight a dead man.'

I realised at that moment, with those words, how much I loved him. He had always been there, waiting for me. Maybe he knew me better than I knew myself. My mother's words rang in my head. 'Don't you hurt that young man, he's in love with you.' She likened his character to my father's, generous of spirit and amusing. He also resembled him, with fair hair and blue eyes. With him now, a sense of wholeness filled the vacuum that had consumed me for so long. His troubled eyes were fixed on mine and conveyed his sincerity.

'I will only make love to you when you tell me that's what you want too,' he whispered, switching off the light. He undressed, put on pyjamas from the sports bag, and climbed into bed. It seemed to be the most natural thing for him to do. He kissed my forehead and turned, ready to go to sleep.

A veil lifted. The sadness of losing Rudge had affected me deeply and I thought that I could never love another man. Rudge would have wanted me to be happy, and now, I thought, perhaps I had another chance. At the same time, I had doubts. Was I betraying him and his memory? The warmth of Michael's body reached mine. It had been over a year since I had been with Rudge. The prospect scared me as I remembered that disastrous evening. I couldn't bear the thought of another rejection. What would it be like with Michael? Did he have any hang-ups? Was there a Gina? Hope smothered doubt, bridging the gap between us. I snuggled into him.

Morning light filtered through the curtains. Where was I? For the space of a heartbeat, I was confused, until I remembered. My head in the crook of his arm, I felt the rise and fall of his breath. In sleep he held me, his body warm, protective. 'Thank you,' I whispered, remembering how he had swept away my fears. He had turned towards me when I had wrapped myself around him. He had gathered me up in his arms, holding me for a long time until he had asked again.

'Jackie. Are you sure this is what you want?'

'Yes,' I had whispered with certainty, my senses awakening from their frozen sleep.

Michael stirred, opened his eyes, looked at me and smiled.

'Morning, Angel Face,' he said. 'Ouch, my arm has gone to sleep!'

We laughed, all awkwardness lost. I had found my anchor, the man who had pieced me together, who loved me despite my past, who was not only my lover but also my best friend. A new adventure had begun and, filled with happiness, I looked forward to our trip together.

* * *

Two days later, we piled into Michael's Fiat, full of plans, heading north. We stopped for a snack at a family owned 'Kneipe' by the roadside. The ambience inside the pub was 'gemütlich'. It was a German word I had learnt from Martin – difficult to translate, a feeling of warmth, of being cosy, comfortable, cheerful. It expressed exactly how I felt sitting close to Michael, his arm around me. Despite the pleasant summer's day, we ordered homemade oxtail soup, recommended by the pub owner's wife. The rich meat and sauce with chunks of bread was the best 'ochsenschwanzsuppe' I have ever tasted. Perhaps finding love again was the secret ingredient.

Continuing our journey, I sat in the front passenger seat taking in the scenery, forests and fields, rivers and valleys, vast vistas, quaint villages and bustling towns, which fuelled my curiosity and imagination. The Brothers Grimm's stories were created in this landscape. Hamelin lay to the East, where the Pied Piper had played his tune. Dark forests conjured up memories of my mother reading 'Little Red Riding Hood', 'Hansel and Gretel' and 'Sleeping Beauty'. I, too, had been awakened by a kiss, my heart locked up for a year, surrounded by pain and shielded by dark shadows. But, like Sleeping Beauty, a prince had found me, prepared to hack away my sorrow. Now wide awake, I looked forward to whatever the future had in store.

In the small town on the Weser, south of Bremen, the fair had been set up in the square. Painted horses waited for children to climb onto the musical carousel. Coloured lights strung across trees and lamp posts ready to come alive after dark. Beer tents overflowed with people enjoying themselves. Stalls selling bratwurst, frites, pastries and cakes, catered for hungry customers. The 'Schützenfest' had begun and I couldn't wait to join in the festivities. I had so much to celebrate.

Jan and I signed into the only hotel. The men were going to pitch camp down by the river. In fact, I learnt later, they were short of funds and couldn't afford two rooms for the four of us. Young male officers were renowned for their poverty, unless they had a private income. The tailor had first call on their pay as most subalterns spent years paying off the cost of their uniforms. Unlike female officers, they needed expensive Mess kit, and of course, they had high Mess bills. Those were the days of no credit cards and only authorised overdrafts.

Jan and I weren't too disappointed, preferring a feather bed to a canvas one as the men hadn't even brought a tent and plans for all night fishing didn't appeal. We joined Michael and Martin at the Schützenfest, where a number of Martin's soldiers congregated, eyeing Jan and me up and down, checking out the 'Sirs' girls. I received a wink from one of them. *Cheeky bugger,* I thought, although I was amused. We sat at a long wooden table covered in stein glasses filled with beer. The music of an oompah band exploded in the hall, booming out the rhythm of the drinking song 'Eins, Zwei, g'suffa!' People linked arms and swayed to the music, shouting out the chorus. We drank 'Pils' and ate bratwurst and chips, deafened by the music but enjoying the fun. Martin's soldiers were keen to press drinks on us, and the local people were welcoming. The evening turned into a noisy night, the first time I had experienced German hospitality, an insight into their culture. Not used to quantities of alcohol, especially local beer, I began to feel a little tipsy. More glasses had been ordered and lined up on the table, turning the event into a drinking contest. Jan caught my eye, we had the same idea, to leave the men to the beer. We departed amid cries of protest from the soldiers. Michael and Martin insisted on escorting us back to the hotel. The two of them talked about finding a field to set camp by the river. On that occasion, I was glad to escape accompanying Michael.

Tired, slightly drunk and ready for bed, I thought the men mad to continue with the fishing venture, wondering where they would end up. Coloured lights from the square flashed against the curtains. I lay cocooned by a feather mattress, hearing laughter and shouts from below and closed my eyes. Shortly later, I was rudely woken from a deep sleep, to what sounded like a body falling downstairs.

'Jan, Jan, wake up!' I called to her inert shape in the next bed.

'What's the matter?' Her voice groggy from slumber. Another crash brought her to a sitting position. 'What's going on?'

'I think someone is being murdered!' I gasped.

Jan switched on a bedside lamp, both of us rigid with fear. A howling sound came from the corridor, as if the 'victim' was in great pain, then words, German words strung together, broken up and indistinguishable. The howl turned into snatches of the 'Ein Prosit' song. I sighed with relief, realising the 'victim' was a drunken German trying to mount the stairs. He failed miserably, fell and continued to try again. The singing would stop abruptly as he lost his footing. Finally, after what seemed an age, we heard snoring and assumed that, defeated, he slept where he lay. Grateful that our door remained firmly locked and Jan was with me, this wasn't quite the adventure I had imagined!

All was calm the following morning, with no sign of the night visitor when we left our room to breakfast. Despite bags under our eyes from the lack of sleep, a cup of coffee and a brötchen soon restored our spirits. Michael turned up, his haggard face gaunt with tiredness. Managing a half smile, his eyes studied me. I jumped up, slipping my arm through his. He smelt of smoke and damp grass. Jan and I bombarded him with questions. Where was Martin? Eager to see where they had spent the night, we asked if they had caught any fish. I wondered if any drunken Germans had interrupted their sleep. From the look of him, Michael hadn't had a lot.

The sun shone obliquely through the windows as Michael drove the Fiat along a road running parallel to the Weser. He pulled down the visor to protect his reddened eyes against the glare. After a few minutes, he turned off the tarmac, parking the car on a grassy track beside a field leading to the river. Two khaki camp beds stood out against the green of the riverbank. Martin hunched over a fishing line that dangled in the water.

'Guten Morgen,' we called out to him. He looked up and nodded, his face unshaven and his countenance as rough as

Michael's. Michael had given us an account of the night's activities; fighting off mosquitoes, no doubt drinking more beer and, in the dark, holding fishing lines while waiting for elusive bites.

The two men began to dismantle their miserable camp, pulling out the metal rods and rolling up the canvas of their beds. Suddenly, I came aware that we were not alone. In a far corner of the field, under a canopy of trees, lay a group of bullocks. One by one they rose on sturdy legs and ambled down the gentle slope to investigate the intruders. By the time the men had piled their kit into the car, come back to collect us and checked nothing had been left behind, the bullocks had surrounded us. Though used to cattle, thanks to Uncle Freddie teaching me how to milk cows, bullocks were another matter, restless and intimidating. But Martin strode into the herd.

'I'm going to wrestle with this one,' he announced.

'Don't be stupid,' retorted Jan.

What followed was sheer folly. With disbelief I stood and watched him grab a neck lock around a hefty looking beast. In no time Martin lay on his back under the animal, succumbed to its superior strength.

'Get out of here,' he shouted, digging his thumb and index finger into the bullock's nostrils. 'He's going to be bloody angry when I let go of him!'

'Idiot!' screamed Jan.

The bullock laid his brisket on Martin's chest, squeezing the air out of him.

Jan and I backed off towards the electric fence and the gate out of the field. Michael hung around in case he was needed. Martin released his hold of the bullock's nose. It pulled back, bellowed and cantered off. Michael rushed to pull his friend to his feet who, grimacing, held his side.

'I'm ok, Jan, really!'

'No, you're not,' she spat out, furious with his behaviour.

'Come here and let me have a look at you.'

Leaning on Michael, Martin stumbled back to the car where Jan examined him and diagnosed broken ribs.

'Serves you right too, you could have been killed,' she snapped.

A rather subdued band of friends returned to Herford.

Throughout the following days, Michael and I spent all of our time together. Nothing could daunt our spirits. We walked to nearby cafes, talking, holding hands and spent passionate nights in our room. Jan gave a party just before I left and invited a number of Michael and Martin's friends. I remember one of them taking a photo of Michael and me together on the sofa. Michael later showed me a copy. There was no doubt we were in love, his left arm draped around my shoulder holding me close, our eyes only for each other. The hardest part was saying goodbye. It could be months before we would see each other again.

The day of my departure, Michael drove me to the station. He didn't jump out straightaway to open the door and retrieve my case, but instead, he took out a small leather box from his pocket and gave it to me. Inside was a gold, platinum and enamel brooch of Mercury, the messenger of the gods, insignia of the Royal Corps of Signals, affectionately known as 'Jimmy'. I felt overwhelmed – I knew he didn't have any money. He'd probably had taken out a bank loan to buy it from the jeweller, Garrards of London. His touching gesture made saying goodbye even more poignant. I felt proud wearing his brooch, just as I had done for Rudge.

CHAPTER 27

POSTED

The ugly wooden camp took on a different image now that summer had arrived. The sunshine washed the dull huts in brilliant light. June brought more recruits. Sergeant Handley, Corporal Mowe and I did our best to lick them into shape. There were a few fun moments involving an inter-company sports afternoon. Corporal Mowe and I, the short and the tall, ended up in a three-legged race. We laughed so much that there was no hope of winning, it was an effort just to hobble over the finishing line.

My spirits lifted with the memory of the holiday. Michael wrote every day and the pile of letters grew. Only six months into my two-year posting, it would be another year before Michael knew where he would be sent. We fervently hoped for an opportunity to meet up again before long.

The new subaltern came to replace Penny. Poppy was full of fun and had an Austin 7 car. Even better, she came from Fleet, near to Camberley. When we could escape at weekends, she drove me home, collecting me on the return trip. What a joy to be out of camp. I had not realised how institutionalised I had become. I wanted to keep spreading my wings, to fly to pastures new.

Mummy was delighted to hear that Michael was now my boyfriend. She had worried about me since I had lost Rudge. Her concerns were then transferred to my brother's safety. Posted to Aden as an Air Dispatcher, he was throwing out supplies from the back of a Hercules aircraft in that inhospitable country. Little could she know that, a year later, his plane would crash behind enemy lines and it was lucky that he, the pilot and two others made it back to camp. This was the time of the Aden Emergency.

Terrible stories emerged of two SAS soldiers killed in the Radfan Mountains in an operation against the Yemeni National Liberation Front strongholds. They were assassinated, beheaded and their heads displayed across the border.

Army life continued routinely for me at Hobbs Barracks. In the Officers' Mess, the kitchen staff worked flat out preparing for a Regimental cocktail party. Our Director Brigadier, Dame Rivett-Drake, and many other key WRAC officers had been invited. The Brigadier had been promoted the year before, a few months after she interviewed me at Hounslow.

Prior to the event, we subalterns were detailed to look after the senior guests. Late in the afternoon of the cocktail party, I slipped on the new dress Mummy had made: close fitting, ice blue, with three-quarter sleeves and made of shantung silk. I pinned on my Jimmy brooch and joined my sister officers to host the party. A crowd of people milled about on the Officers' Mess lawn, Mess staff busy with trays of Pimms and gin and tonics. Zara and I grabbed a drink and looked around for an interesting person to talk to. Everyone was dressed in 'mufti' so we had no idea who the visiting senior officers were, apart from Brigadier Rivet-Drake.

'You're wearing your Jimmy on the wrong side,' said a cultivated voice. I turned to see an attractive lady of about forty years old in a chic cocktail dress.

'Jimmy always comes in, and not out, so it should be worn on the left-hand side of your dress.'

'Oh thanks, Ma'am,' I replied, undoing my brooch and readjusting its position.

'We haven't met before, I'm Major Paget-Clarke from Postings Branch,' she introduced herself, asking for my name. A delightful and very amusing lady, she made my hosting job a pleasant one. I later learnt that, prior to joining the WRAC, she had been a Tiller girl. She revealed that the training to be a dancer was far harder than anything experienced in the Army! This meeting with the entertaining Major would change the direction of my career.

Shortly after the cocktail party, the Adjutant called all the subalterns to her office, not happy with the form filling of Nominal Vetting applications.

'Incomplete and messy,' she complained. 'All of you, except Jackie. She's the only one who fills in forms correctly.' That was a surprise! I expect it was because of all the paperwork I had been trained to do at Great Fosters. Helen scowled. After the Adjutant dismissed us, we hurried to the Mess for coffee break before returning to our offices or the parade square. A number of newspapers were delivered to the Officers' Mess every day. As subalterns we were expected to keep up to date with current affairs and events. On the 18th July, a Stanley Franklin cartoon appeared in the Daily Mirror portraying a line-up of sexy-looking WRAC girls in front of a plane just landed in Germany, being addressed by a tall thin WRAC Officer and a very fat WRAC RSM. The caption read:

> 'Mr. Profumo is anxious to make it clear we are here for responsible military tasks … VERY anxious.'

A number of similar cartoons were published in daily newspapers about that time, lampooning the WRAC's role in BAOR. Questions had been asked in the House of Commons.

HANSARD, 16th July 1962

Mr. Profumo

The role of the W.R.A.C. in B.A.O.R., as elsewhere, is to carry out responsible military tasks and thereby release soldiers for service with fighting units. At the same time, our troops in Germany undoubtedly benefit from their companionship.

As I recently explained to the House, there are practical limitations to the number of W.R.A.C. who may be stationed in

Germany; partly because B.A.O.R. is an operational command, and partly because of accommodation and administrative problems, which are of prime importance in safeguarding high standards of discipline and conduct in the Corps.

There are at present 366 members of the W.R.A.C. serving with B.A.O.R. I hope to send a further 150 members of the Corps in the course of the next eight months. If, as a result of the improved recruiting of the Corps, further opportunities arise for sending more W.R.A.C. to Germany, I shall certainly consider them.

The cartoons, although scathing, amused me and I wondered if some of my recruits would have the opportunity to serve in Germany but, not, indeed, as comfort for the troops! It didn't occur to me that I might be posted there, being too young and inexperienced.

Summer dragged on. The heat bounced off the parade square and tempers frayed. Everyone needed a break. Sally's wedding was a great distraction. Formally resigning her commission, she was soon to become an army wife. Her own training gave her the ability to interact with the soldiers' wives, be an unpaid social worker to the families, even more so when her husband and his men were on exercise. Her knowledge of the army would make it easier for her to accept the continuous two-year postings from one army quarter to another. The long absences of her husband on manoeuvres and the expectancy of hosting dinner and lunch parties were other considerations. I knew that could be my destiny, too, if Michael ever proposed. But I wasn't sure that I was ready to give up my career.

The wedding was held on a perfect English summer's day. A great marquee had been erected on the lawn of the family's home. We sat at round tables under the canvas, dressed in our finery. I wore my ice blue silk dress and a hat I had fashioned out of pale blue net. Speeches were made, delicious food was eaten and glasses of champagne were sipped before we waved goodbye to the happy couple, off on their honeymoon.

At the Depot, Maggie, a young captain had arrived to replace Sally, posted hurriedly from Yeovil. We struck up an immediate friendship. Highly amusing, intelligent and good at her job, nobody but me knew that she was in disgrace. Her affair with a male sergeant at her last regiment had not gone unnoticed. Though given another chance, she confided that they were still meeting up. Their affair continued during leave, but their assignations took place miles away. A croft in the Highlands of Scotland was a favourite place of theirs. Love has no boundaries, and I was to wonder if they ever had the chance to be together officially. Did they both leave the army? The last I heard of Maggie, she had been posted to Singapore. Sally's happy marriage and Maggie's clandestine affair couldn't have been more different. The pursuit of happiness came at a price – when you broke the rules.

Another chance to meet Michael came unexpectedly. He wrote with the hopeful news that in August he had been detailed to courier documents to the South of England. I waited for confirmation before allowing myself the pleasure of anticipating our reunion.

Zara, Poppy and I were feeling the heat despite our summer uniforms; shirt sleeves rolled up above the elbow with ironed cuffs and lovat green straight skirts. Beavering away, filling in forms for our girls, the silence was broken only by the odd rogue housefly and the scratching of ink pens. Suddenly my telephone rang.

'Jackie, I have some news for you.' I recognised the Adjutant's voice. 'You've been posted to 14 Battalion WRAC HQ BAOR and you leave on Monday 15th September.'

I couldn't believe it. How did that happen? I had only been at the Depot for eight months.

'Honestly, Ma'am? That's a wonderful surprise!'

'Congratulations, you'd better come and see me to learn more about your posting order.'

'Yippee!' I shouted, breaking the studious sound of pens marching across the army forms.

'What's happened?' asked Zara. Poppy looked up from her work.

'I've been posted to Germany!' I exclaimed.

'You lucky thing!' they chorused, envious.

I skipped out of my office, composing myself to salute to some recruits on the way to Headquarter Company. My head filled with the startling news. *Michael's never going to believe our luck. Thank you, Mr. Profumo!*

In the Adjutant's office, I beamed at Captain Cain as she handed me my posting order.

'You're very fortunate, Jackie,' she said. 'You'll be the first WRAC officer under twenty-one to be sent to BAOR.'

My posting must have had something to do with Major Paget-Clarke, who I had met at the cocktail party. Perhaps she believed she had posted me away from the man who had given me the Jimmy brooch! The Secretary of State for War was, of course, the real instigator of my departure. I bubbled with happiness for the rest of the day. Blurting out my posting to Sergeant Handley and Corporal Mowe, who would soon have to train up another 'subbie', I broke the news to the rest of the junior officers at dinner, to Helen's chagrin.

Later that evening, the telephone rang in the corridor outside my bedroom.

'Orderly Officer speaking,' said Zara. 'Just a moment,' I heard her say.

'Jackie, it's for you,' she said, knocking on my door.

It wasn't usual for me to receive phone calls, so I was delighted when I picked up the receiver to hear that familiar voice.

'It's me!'

'Oh Michael, where are you?'

'I've arrived in England and as it's a Bank Holiday weekend I'll have a couple of days off tomorrow, so that means I can come and see you. Can't wait!'

'Me neither! Where will you stay? Maybe here? I'll see if it can be arranged. God knows what it will do to the Senior Officers' blood pressure!' I laughed.

It had been three months since we had been together; we had corresponded and shared the minutiae of our lives. The more I knew him, the more I loved him for his integrity and absolute honesty. We didn't mention Rudge again. I would never forget him; he had changed my life and, in part, had made me the woman that I had become. But Michael, with his quiet understanding, patience and love had unlocked the armour around my fragile heart.

How was I going to arrange accommodation for him? I went straight round to the Medical centre to see my friend, Audrey, who was the QARANC sister.

'That's no problem because my boss is on leave,' she said. 'He can stay in the empty MRS ward in the basement.'

Aud was a great friend and, with that problem solved, I only had a few hours to wait. How would he feel surrounded by women when he arrived? Would we have a chance to be alone, so I could tell him my news before anyone else did?

I left my office the next day at five o'clock and hurried to the Junior Officers Quarters to take a bath before his arrival. I had just stretched out full length in fragrant warm water when a female voice shouted, 'There's a man in the Mess!' I heard the exodus of the subalterns, their footsteps running down the corridor. An eerie silence hung after their departure. I took my time, calmly stepping out to dry myself, buzzing with anticipation, putting on a summer dress, doing my make-up before wandering over to the Mess.

In the anteroom, the senior officers pressed Michael with drinks and quizzed him. Now they knew it was me that he had come to see. Young officers listened to his every word. He smiled when he saw me. I could read his face – *help me out here*! The poor chap was overwhelmed. We would have gone out for a meal but after the stiff drinks the idea was abandoned, especially as he was invited to dine in the Mess. Time elapsed before we were alone, escaping outside after coffee to smoke a cigarette.

'That was quite a welcome,' he remarked. 'I'm dying to kiss you. I feel like a prized goldfish in there, being stared at in my glass bowl!' He grinned. 'So, what's this news you have to tell me?'

'I've been posted to Rheindahlen! I shall be there in a couple of weeks!'

His face was a picture. 'Bloody marvellous!' he exclaimed.

I stayed in his room that night, creeping out at dawn before the camp stirred. The medical orderly had taken his order for breakfast the evening before, delivered to his room at eight o'clock. He told me later that she knocked on the door exactly on time. 'Morning, Sir,' she had said, carrying in the tray and eyeing him up as she spoke. 'Scrambled eggs, bacon, sausages, toast, orange juice and coffee.' He was impressed.

Michael spent the morning in the subaltern's office, meeting Sergeant Handley and Corporal Mowe. They joked and laughed with him. I wondered if they could see that we had slept together – we both looked tired. Nothing got past them.

Michael had to leave at lunchtime to meet his driver for the return trip to Germany. Saying goodbye this time was easier. We would soon be stationed in the same country, although two hundred kilometres apart.

The Depot had enabled me to gain confidence through those first experiences as a young officer. I had come to terms with losing Rudge, although I still thought of him, and I had found Michael. The new posting filled me with hope. I felt privileged to have been chosen to join the British Army of the Rhine. No apprehension this time, I was ready for new challenges and the opportunity of living in a mixed Mess.

CHAPTER 28

BRITISH FORCES OF THE RHINE

This was the first time I'd flown since Kidlington. The Britannia started its descent to RAF Wildenrath airfield. On board military personnel travelling to BAOR buckled safety belts. The plane lost altitude and I took a deep breath, remembering that day in May, the clouds, the turbulence. Rudge. To avert my thoughts, I gazed out of the window to see a different view, a view of the future, the tree covered terrain of North Rhine Westphalia. Adventure awaited me below and I'd be seeing Michael again, though I felt nervous of my new posting and responsibilities. The screeching of brakes and contact of wheels on tarmac announced touch down.

In the arrivals hall of the airport, I espied the familiar sight of a WRAC officer in the same lovat green uniform that I was wearing.

'Hi, I'm Pam, welcome to Germany!' she said, stepping forward to greet me. I wondered if anyone else was taking note of the first WRAC reinforcement for the troops! On first impressions, Pam, a lieutenant a couple of years older than me and the senior subaltern in the Company, looked a fairly serious girl. In fact, she had a great sense of humour and we were to become good friends. Like me, she was tall and slim. I picked up my blue suitcase, she grabbed the matching vanity case and we made our way to the exit. I appreciated her company, unnerved by the foreign environment and the surreptitious glances from soldiers waiting for transport.

Outside, a male driver in uniform jumped out of a Volkswagen to help with my luggage. We climbed on board. Pam and I chatted in the back of the vehicle while she pointed out landmarks. We passed the Joint Headquarters building known as the Big

House, a vast complex. Flags fluttered in the September breeze in front of the main headquarters of British Forces in Germany and NATO Northern Army Group. The impressive building made me realise how privileged I was to be posted here, but also how much I had to live up to. My eyes took in the enormity of Rheindahlen Garrison town. Pam recounted some statistics of the station. There were sixty-five barrack blocks for British military and German civilians, over 1,100 married quarters, primary and secondary schools for the children of servicemen, churches, cinemas and a swimming pool built to Olympic standards, playing fields with pavilions, NAAFI buildings, shops, stores, and officers' messes with single quarters, five dining halls, an officers' club, clubs for warrant officers and sergeants and for other ranks. The complex had been designed to accommodate over 7,000 British and Allied servicemen. Too much for me to take in at first, and my orientating skills all forgotten, I was relieved when the driver finally pulled up outside E Officers' Mess, my new home.

Pam took charge. She made sure the driver carried my two cases into the foyer of the one-storey building and ushered me through its portals. Remarking that we were in time for tea, she asked me to join her, pushing open a door where a hubbub of voices assailed me, and I found myself in the anteroom. At least twenty male officers were sitting in armchairs, drinking tea, reading newspapers and talking. Silence fell when we walked in. Heads turned towards us, faces appeared over papers. Pam took no notice of their stares, but I felt the heat rising from my collar as the blushes rose. I looked away with embarrassment to focus on tea things laid out on a table. Not used to male attention en masse, I sensed them weighing me up, the new girl in the Mess. Pam poured out two cups of tea.

'Toast?' she asked, making some for herself, the Gentleman's Relish ready to hand. I couldn't eat a thing with twenty pairs of eyes boring into me, so declined. Pam, at ease in their company, had already been living in the Mess for some months. I doubted that such ease would develop in me, having spent my last eighteen months in an all-female environment. But I had to face them. Pam carried the tea and toast on a tray and, more composed, I followed her, my head held high. She approached a group of young men in uniform seated around a low table, three lieutenants from the Royal Army Intelligence Corps, later to become 'my brothers'. They stood up to shake my hand as Pam introduced us. I began to relax. Invited to join them, I found them friendly. Bob, David and Nigel were particularly good company. They soon discovered that I had a boyfriend in Herford and, therefore, knew that I was 'spoken for'.

'This is The Ladies' Royal Wing,' joked Pam a little while later, showing me the way to my room. The WRAC accommodation was at the back of the Mess, set apart from the male quarters. A door opened onto a long corridor, bedrooms off to the left. There were six of us billeted here, my room at the end. Pam opened the door to let me in.

'I'll come for you at eight. Dinner time,' she said. 'I'm just next door if you need anything.'

My tin trunk had been delivered and stood in a corner, sent on by the quartermaster's store at Hobbs Barracks. No longer pristine, small dents had appeared on its sides – signs of transportation, but also signs of new ventures. I looked out of the window to get my bearings. Beyond a lawn and a couple of fir trees, I could see the back of B Mess, accommodation for the unaccompanied Senior Majors and Colonels. I found out later that a couple of 'Int' Corps subalterns were also billeted there. One of them, James, would be part of our circle.

I unpacked, opening drawers and cupboards, deciding at the same time what I should wear for dinner. This room was much bigger than mine at Hobbs Barracks and the 'ablutions' were nearer. I bounced on the bed to check the softness and came to the conclusion that I had a pretty decent quarter. After washing and dressing in a fine black and blue wool dress, I began a letter to Michael whilst I waited for Pam. She knocked on my door and, when I opened it, looked quite different out of uniform, more feminine and less officious. She complimented me on my new dress, the cut and style – yet another triumph from my talented mother – and led the way to the dining room. I had gathered more confidence to meet the other officers, but wasn't prepared for the sight that awaited. Pam opened a door in a long-panelled wall to reveal an immense dining table around which sat the entire compliment of E Mess. I remember cringing with shyness on entering the room. The officers wore civilian clothes, dark suits and ties. Four older female officers in sombre dresses. Everyone stopped eating and talking to stare at me. How I wanted to run away!

'Here's your napkin,' said Pam, handing me the white folded damask square, kept in individual numbered pigeonholes in a rack just inside the door. 'And you can sign in this book for wine if you want some with your meal.' I didn't, not wanting to prolong the dining process, and followed her around the table to the two empty places on the other side.

When we sat down, the murmur of voices recommenced. My cheeks flushed from embarrassment and my appetite waned. Sitting opposite me was a pleasant looking young man with a craggy face. He looked up from his dish of Hungarian goulash, nodded and greeted Pam. After the waitress had served me, aware of being watched, I tried to swallow, hoping my table manners came up to scratch. Coffee was served after dinner in the anteroom and the pleasant young man made a beeline for me, brushing a lock of chestnut hair from his forehead as he approached.

'I'm Hamish,' he said, holding out his hand. Pam did the honours and introduced me. A good conversationalist, he made us laugh with his witty repartee. It was so different being in a mixed Mess. Would it get easier? I sensed the men were sizing me up, predictably defining me as a lesbian or tart. I made my excuses shortly afterwards and returned to my room to finish the letter I had started to Michael.

'Please call me on this number any evening this week,' I wrote to him with an urgency that surprised me. I needed to hear his friendly voice again. 'And don't forget to give me your Mess phone number, either!' I sealed and addressed the blue airmail letter. I could cope with my new environment and had resilience, but I also wanted Michael's support in those initial few weeks.

At eight-thirty the following morning I was to report to my new Company Commander, my first day as a platoon commander in 14 Battalion WRAC. I prayed I wasn't going to let anyone down. In preparation for this new challenge, I hung up a shirt, checked my uniform and shoes, and set my alarm clock for seven o'clock.

* * *

Breakfast became another ordeal. Pam was already seated at the dining table when I arrived, dressed in my brushed uniform and polished black court shoes. I clutched my napkin and self-consciously walked around to sit next to her. Hamish was opposite again in his battle dress uniform wearing the badges of the Special Airborne Forces, parachute wings and three pips on each epaulette. My heart missed a beat.

'Tea or coffee, Ma'am?' asked the German stewardess, distracting me from the image of my paratrooper. *He's not Rudge*, I told myself.

'Tea, please,' I heard my voice respond.

My sister officer did her best to allay my worries of joining the new unit during the short walk to the WRAC lines. In a strange way I was looking forward to being with an all-female environment again. The male officers were daunting, apart from the Intelligence Corps subalterns who, with Pam and me, were the youngest members of the Mess.

In no time, we arrived at our Company. The office, just inside the building on the left, hummed with activity. Typewriters clattered, and phones rang. Sergeant Bryant, chief clerk, stood up, smiling, and welcomed me to 14 Battalion.

'Major Godin is expecting you, Ma'am,' she said, assessing me, her professional face giving nothing away.

'Let me show you where to find your office first,' suggested Pam. 'Then I'll take you to meet the OC.'

Pam and I had separate offices facing each other across a short corridor. They flanked the larger one of Major Godin's. Without ceremony, Pam knocked on the OC's door and announced my presence. Surprisingly, I wasn't at all apprehensive. Senior WRAC officers had interviewed me many times before. Major Godin rose up from behind her desk to greet me and with welcoming words put me at ease, the new member of her team. Under her command I was to receive the best guidance. Pleasant looking, the OC was smart, always even-tempered and fair-minded. She was a good boss, allowing me to carry out my job without interference unless, of course, it was necessary. She lived in the twin Mess opposite ours, which meant that we only saw her during working hours.

On that first morning she gave me a rundown of my duties and responsibilities. I had been given a detached platoon of women based at Field Records, a twenty-minute drive away, a driver at my disposition. My job sounded more important and exciting than I had imagined. Commanding a detached platoon carried that extra prestige and to have my own driver was a bonus. I realised that I had been given a plum posting. However, I had little idea of my girls' role and asked pertinent questions about the platoon. Major Godin directed me to Major Whelan, their employment officer, stationed at Field Records. The OC also reminded me to be on time for the interview scheduled with our Colonel after lunch. It was going to be a full day.

'Coffee, Ma'am?' enquired Corporal Lee, one of the clerks, when I was alone in my new office. 'NATO standard?' This, I learned, meant coffee with milk and two teaspoons of sugar.

My phone rang for the first time.

'Your driver's here, Ma'am, to take you to Mönchengladbach,' said Sergeant Bryant.

'Forget the coffee, Corporal Lee, I'm going out.'

I put my head around Pam's door.

'Looks like I'm off to meet my platoon.'

'Good luck,' she said, glancing up from her paperwork.

A khaki green Volkswagen beetle with a British Forces Number plate waited on the top road. A German driver opened the door for me.

'Field Records?' he enquired, in heavily accented English.

I felt like a VIP ensconced in the back, dressed in my lovat green uniform. What would Helen say about me now? 'You always get people to do things for you,' she had remarked at Hobbs Barracks. She was right this time. I had a chauffeur to take me to work.

My detached platoon was located just outside the town of Mönchengladbach at Nicholson Barracks. The girls, either machine operators or clerks, worked alongside the men at Field Records. The men outnumbered them ten to one. There were about thirty girls including Warrant Officer Class Two Mrs. Halliday and Sergeant Forbes. Sergeant Major Halliday, a mother hen, guided and protected the brood of girls under her care. We shared common ground there and had a healthy respect for one another. She was the first widowed NCO that I had met. I didn't ask details but was told that she had reapplied to return to the WRAC after her soldier husband's death. She had no children.

I met Major Whelan, the girls' employment officer on that first visit. I liked him immediately. A quiet, well-mannered man, he offered me coffee and, while we drank the NATO standard in his office, he spoke highly of the girls. He and Sergeant Major Halliday had a good working relationship, important for smoothing the way for any potential problems.

One of my duties was the weekly visit on Fridays, primarily to take the pay parade and to be available if any of the girls needed to see me on regimental or welfare issues. Sergeant Major Halliday kept me informed of any problems. All started out well.

Other responsibilities I shouldered were for the stewardesses working in E and B messes at the Garrison. Known as batwomen, they cleaned the WRAC officers' rooms, polished shoes and ironed shirts. Another of my duties was to collect additional deutschmarks from each officer for this service to supplement the stewardesses' pay. I hated this job. There was always one of the old frustrated majors who complained about the batwomen not doing their job properly, the worst being Major Marion Smith, a staff officer who worked at the Big House in some highly sensitive post. She had two yappy miniature dachshunds, trained to alert her at the fall of a male footstep in the Ladies' corridor, out of bounds to men.

My fellow brother subalterns in the Mess fast became friends. Bob, a sweet guy, was in love with an English girl, Andrea. Personal issues weren't discussed in the Mess, there were too many people around. Needing someone to talk to, we arranged for him to visit my room. He managed to complete the gauntlet of walking the whole length of the ladies' corridor without being seen but Major Smith's dogs started their ear-piercing barks. I stood at my door, waiting for him, and quickly he stepped into my room. Bob had just sat down in my armchair and started to pour out his heart when came a knock on the door. I motioned Bob to stand behind it, hiding him from view. A harder knock accompanied Major Smith's sharp voice.

'Jackie, I need to speak to you about my batwoman.'

Squeezed between the tallboy and the door, Bob froze. I

opened the door halfway, conscious that he could be squashed.

'I've come to complain, she won't be getting a single pfennig from me this month,' she nagged. 'And you can tell them all to buck up their ideas.' Her two dogs entered my room. Oh no, they would sniff Bob out and both of us would be on a charge and a fast posting out. My heart raced at the thought of Bob's discovery. I daren't look guilty, as if I was hiding a man in my room.

'Yes, I will deal with that, Ma'am,' I said as casually as possible, nodding in agreement with her. I held onto the door handle, not inviting her in. She must have suspected something because that was the first and last time she ever came to my room. The dogs were everywhere. After a few more platitudes, she seemed satisfied and called her dogs off. 'Rudi, Franz, come!' she commanded. My body relaxed, after what had seemed an interminable wait to get rid of her and the hounds. Poor Bob turned blue from holding his breath, almost fainted. Our heart-to-heart chat never took place. As soon as the coast was clear, I walked him quickly back up the corridor to the main part of the Mess, passing the harridan's room.

'Phew!' he exclaimed. 'That was a close thing!'

Good job the dogs only recognised my footfall!

As the subalterns were my brothers, two unaccompanied Majors became my uncles. Major Ian's wife remained in their Scottish home for the sake of their children's uninterrupted education. Major Rex's wife waited in England to join him as soon as a married quarter became available on the 'patch'. Separation wasn't ideal, but it was commonplace for a soldier and his family. Ian and Rex, both delightful men, decided to take me under their wing, although one night they plied me with whisky Macs, amused to see me stagger back to the Ladies' Royal.

'Don't phone Michael this week, Jackie, the phones are being tapped,' Major Ian informed me one evening.

Michael called twice a week. The free military phone in the foyer of the Mess, intended only for military business, was monitored from time to time to check on its proper use. There were restrictions on our private life; the dependence of being granted leave to visit each other, the distance between us preventing opportunities to be together for an evening. The telephone meant I could still speak to my boyfriend, but I had to request the call and pay a hefty charge. Apart from missing him, I had settled down reasonably well to life in E Mess. The members became accustomed to me, no longer a curiosity. At work, I gained the support of the Office, the clerks reminding me of appointments and bringing cups of NATO standard coffee. And a good bunch of girls in my platoon at Field Records. Yes, this was definitely a good posting despite the limitations on seeing Michael. Then, finally, I was given a week's leave to visit him.

I travelled up to Herford by train from Mönchengladbach filled with expectations. Our letters had fuelled inner thoughts and feelings. I longed to enjoy his company, to feel his arms around me, to be loved again. When I saw Michael waiting for me on the platform, I realised how much I'd missed him. We recaptured our relationship in Jan's spare room, melting together in the same large bed.

Martin stayed over with Jan and the two men planned another trip, this time along the Rhine Valley. Next day ready for more adventures, we piled into Michael's Fiat for the journey to Rüdesheim, our stop for the night. Michael and I shared a double room, signing in for the first time as a married couple. We could have been on honeymoon! The four of us got on very well, laughing and joking during the car journey. All went swimmingly until we arrived at Koblenz.

The men took it in turns to drive. Martin was at the wheel when we entered the beautiful city on the confluence of the Rhine and Moselle rivers, a point where the best of the Rhine

Valley commenced. Ahead in the main road, a motorcyclist had just come off his bike and was lying in the road. Martin braked and stopped the car well before the accident. I was in the back with Jan. A sudden impact shook the Fiat and we were thrown forward in our seats. The whiplash jerked my neck. I remember the pain, feeling mad at the careless driver. Martin, furious too, jumped out of the car to speak to the culprit, a young man, in charge of a large Volkswagen van, a pretty girl sitting beside him.

'Where are your eyes?' Martin shouted in German. The driver looked taken aback. Martin actually had said 'Wo sind deine eier?' 'Where are your balls?' instead of 'Wo sind deine augen?' Martin, realising his mistake, translated to us, laughed to break the mounting tension, following up with a remark of how apt his mistake had been. The girl was extremely attractive. Michael remained calm. He checked if Jan and I were all right, climbed out of his damaged car, resigned to the outcome of the accident. The Polizei arrived shortly afterwards to take statements from everyone and the motorcyclist was carted off to hospital by ambulance.

Our holiday ended there, the petrol tank ruptured. I'm sure it was dangerous for us to return by car to Herford, leaking petrol the whole way, but we did. The servicemen in BAOR were able to buy petrol coupons at reduced prices. These came in useful en route as we hopped from petrol station to petrol station to fill up the depleted tank. Overpowering fumes in the back of the car gave me a splitting headache. It was only by good fortune that the car didn't catch fire. We only stopped for fuel and quick dashes to the loo, arriving back at Jan's flat tired and hungry.

Despite the lack of wheels, Michael and I enjoyed our time together for the next few days until dejectedly, I caught the afternoon train on Saturday back to Mönchengladbach. Michael promised to visit. I remember feeling utterly wretched on the return journey, knowing it would be another long wait before he did. Driven by love and commitment, I had to accept our separation, no other man would do. He was the one who made my heart leap, my body sing. The man I trusted.

CHAPTER 29

MUTINY

The Company Office had been busy that morning, WRAC personnel coming and going to see the OC or Pam and me, the Platoon Commanders. I had the difficult task of interviewing one of my girls who was pregnant. The poor girl wasn't going to get any help from the father. She wouldn't reveal his name, and now would be sent back to Holding and Drafting Company at the Depot in Lingfield to be discharged. I hoped her family in Leeds would provide support when she arrived home. She was heartbroken leaving my office, and I too felt upset. It was at times like these when I disliked my job. It was my duty to tell Major Godin, who in turn would tell the Colonel. I began filling in the appropriate forms for the girl's discharge according to Queens Regulations. Definitely time for a coffee.

The telephone rang.

'Ma'am, it's Sergeant Major Halliday.' There was an urgent tone to her voice.

'Is everything ok?' I enquired.

'I think that you had better get over here. We've got a situation.'

That sounded ominous.

'What's happened, Sergeant Major?'

'The girls are refusing to go to work and Major Whelan is ranting. He's going to put the whole lot on a charge unless they turn up in the next hour.'

My heart sank. I'd not received training on how to deal with such a problem – a young officer's nightmare.

'What on earth is going on? Why have they done this?'

'I think that you should speak to them yourself, Ma'am.'

'I'll be over as soon as I can.' I concluded, replacing the

265

receiver.

Good heavens, a mutiny! I picked up the phone again.

'It's urgent, Sergeant Bryant. I need a car to take me to Field Records immediately. Make sure the message gets through to the transport office that I must be there in the next half an hour.'

I pulled on my beret, grabbed my handbag and hurried out of the building, mentally searching for answers to questions I didn't have. What had caused this state of affairs? What consequences would follow? I waited impatiently to meet my transport from the car pool. Anxious thoughts of how I could defuse the impending disaster continued to assault me. What was I going to find, and could I placate Major Whelan? Shortly, a Volkswagen pulled up and I wrenched open the passenger door to climb in beside the driver.

It was ten thirty-two precisely.

The journey seemed interminable to Mönchengladbach, minutes ticked by. At last, the car came to a halt and I saw, with some relief, that Sergeant Major Halliday was waiting for me outside the girls' lines. Her facial expression confirmed her concern, furrowed brow and lips clamped in a straight line. I jumped out of the car, returning her salute, and hurried over to find out the latest development.

'We've not got long, Ma'am, before Major Whelan sends in the RMPs.'

The Royal Military Police meant trouble. There had to be a reason for this drastic action. I still hadn't been given the pertinent details.

'Tell me what happened, Sergeant Major. When did this all start?'

'The girls are fed up that they have no recreational area of their own. They can't use the football and rugby pitches and they feel their requests are being ignored because they are women.'

Nobody had brought this subject up before and I wondered if that was the whole story.

'Where are they?' I asked, marching in step with her as we swiftly covered the ground to the girls' barrack rooms.

'In here,' she said, pointing. 'They've locked the door.'

There was no other option. The girls' reputations were on the line, and mine hung on my ability to resolve the situation. I took a deep breath and knocked loudly.

'It's Miss Skingley-Pearce, I need to speak to you.'

'We aren't coming out, Ma'am,' a muffled voice replied.

'Private Head, is that you? If you want me to help you I can't do it standing here.'

A couple of seconds went by and then, thankfully, I heard the sound of the key turning in the lock.

'Stay here, Sergeant Major, I'll speak to them.' I might have sounded confident, but I wasn't.

Inside the room I found a defiant looking group of girls. Removing my beret, I sat down on one of the beds to appear more approachable.

'Ok I'm listening. What's going on?'

'It's not fair,' said Private Head. 'We want to play netball and there's nowhere for us to go. We've asked the PTI but he's not interested.'

'Let me get this straight. You're jeopardising your jobs and careers because you haven't got a netball pitch?'

Some of the girls nodded. I sensed there was more to it than that. Rivalry with the men? Wanting to prove they were as good at sport?

'If I go and see your employment officer and tell him of your request, are you prepared to go back to work while I try and sort it out with him? If you stay here there are going to be serious consequences. I don't think you realise how serious.'

While the girls debated, I tried to keep calm, but I was getting more worried by the second, sure a catastrophe was inevitable.

'You have exactly seven minutes to make up your minds before the RMPs arrive to arrest you,' I blurted out.

That did the trick.

'Ok, Ma'am,' said Private Head. 'But we are serious too.'

'I can see that. Get yourselves to work straight away, there's no time to lose. Sergeant Major Halliday will go with you. And next time you have a problem, tell me first!' I ordered, opening the door to see Sergeant Major Halliday breathing a sigh of relief. Phew!

'Come along. I haven't got all day,' she barked. Subdued, they trooped out of their barrack room, not knowing what was in store for them.

I walked back to the Headquarters, dreading my interview with Major Whelan.

'Morning, Ma'am,' a burly sergeant greeted me with a grin, obviously aware of the situation.

'I'm here to speak to Major Whelan about the WRAC detachment.'

'Go straight up, Ma'am. He's expecting you.'

It was with some trepidation that I climbed the stairs to the OC's office. The girls had placed their trust in me to arrange sporting facilities and, somehow, I had to make sure the punishment for their actions would not be too severe.

'Well, Jackie, what have they got to say for themselves?' said the OC after I had knocked and entered.

'I know that they have committed a serious offence, disobeying your orders, Sir, but I have to say that they feel very strongly about not being given the same sporting opportunities as the men on camp, and I have to agree with that.'

'What do you mean?'

'They want a netball pitch. That's what has caused this whole incident.'

Major Whelan was a reasonable man and I had always found him even handed. I waited for his decision – to put them all on a charge, or worse – a court martial. Hopefully he'd just be giving them a 'bollocking.'

'Would you like a coffee?' he enquired.

It was nearly one o'clock by the time I returned to 14 Battalion. I knocked on Pam's door needing to share my news with her. We left the office and walked back to the Mess for lunch. On the way I told her of my experience.

'God, Jackie, what did he say then?'

'If it ever happened again they would be court martialled.'

'Blimey!'

'He told me that I had to give them a good talking to and then he would overlook the incident this once,' I confided. 'He's a really good chap and understands their need for recreational sport. He's going to arrange for them to have their netball pitch.'

'Result!' exclaimed Pam, a keen sportswoman. She was preparing to enter the four-day Nijmegen marches with some of her girls.

'I've just sent off our entry forms,' she said striding out ahead of me. 'We've got to practise so we'll do well against the men.'

'Do you know,' I said, 'I was so impressed by Private Head. She started the whole injustice campaign in the first place, then got the girls to return to work when she realised the consequences. I'm going to put in a request to promote her when the time is right.'

I valued Pam's opinion, the more experienced officer, but this time she listened. She hadn't encountered a mutiny and congratulated me on the peaceful outcome. I reflected on how I'd managed it! The Depot had taught me to empathise with the girls, to understand their needs. Tackling Major Whelan was different. My confidence dealing with the opposite sex had grown since living in a mixed Mess.

It had been quite a morning.

CHAPTER 30

CAPTAINS

Pam and I liked him from the first meeting, the new Intelligence Corps Captain who had arrived in E Mess that month. Bruce was short, chubby and extremely amusing. Later we learned that he had been on the EOKA hit list when he was posted to Cyprus during the troubles and he had to be pulled out in a hurry. EOKA was the party of Greek Nationalist guerrillas, active in the late 1950s. Bruce was mad about Amateur Dramatics. Not long after his arrival, I found myself involved in the productions, painting scenery for CATS, the Theatre Club in JHQ Rheindahlen. He knew that I liked art. Sometimes he roped Pam in too. He was to play an important role as close friend and confident in the coming months.

'Ah, Skinny,' he announced, using the nickname he had given me, 'I've just the thing for you. Need a talented artist to give a hand with the backdrop for our latest play. You should invite that young man of yours to come down for the first night and I will take you both out for dinner.'

There was something underlying his jolly exterior that I recognised – a loneliness, and a need for distraction.

One evening before dinner we were alone in the Mess Bar. He ordered an eccentric pink gin with cocktail onions and bought me a dry sherry. Our conversation was light and full of trivia at first. He asked when I would see Michael again.

'Not sure, it's difficult. He's on exercise up north. Haven't seen him for ages.'

'Why don't you invite him to stay here in the Mess when he gets back to camp? I'll book him in, then you can have some time together and come to the play.'

'Bruce, you're a brick. I haven't asked him before because I thought we would be put under too much scrutiny, but I'll see what he says.' Then I questioned, 'Do you have a girlfriend?'

His mood changed. 'No, my fiancée was killed in a car accident two years ago.'

'Oh, Bruce, I'm so sorry,' I said. My heart went out to him. 'There was someone I lost too before Michael. It was a parachuting accident and I was with him when it happened.'

'God, that's terrible!' he exclaimed. 'She was driving alone,' he revealed, sorrow etched on his face. 'A drunk driver hit the car head on, she didn't have a chance.'

A flicker of recognition, an acknowledgement of our shared experience of pain and loss, made its connection. Nothing was said as we privately revisited those moments of horror in the darkened recesses of our memory. I had always wondered if it had been my fault that Rudge had died. One of the witnesses had said that Rudge shouldn't have jumped because of the change in the weather. Surely, he had seen the Dropping Zone being rolled up before he left the aircraft the second time. Another witness thought Rudge had jumped out of a sense of honour. Would he have done so if I hadn't been with him? My guilt resurfaced.

Pam burst into the Bar with Bob and Nigel shouting her normal jovial greeting, breaking the emotional bridge between Bruce and me.

'Evening all! Jackie, we're playing snooker after dinner. You going to join us?'

'There you are, chaps,' Bruce said. 'I'm buying, what'll you all have?' he offered, grinning at the new arrivals.

'Sounds like we are going to have a party,' I said, forcing a smile, blocking out the indelible image of Rudge lying on the ground. Bruce and I replaced our self-protective masks.

* * *

Two weeks later, Michael sat with me at the Mess bar, sipping beer. Bruce, delighted to instigate our reunion, had driven me to collect him that Friday night from Mönchengladbach station. Reunited with him, I forgot all worries, only concerned how we would manage to sleep together in E Mess. It was not behaviour befitting officers and gentlemen/gentlewomen!

My brothers were curious about my mysterious boyfriend.

'We've heard a lot about you, Michael,' said Bob, lifting his glass of Pils in salute. 'We've had to put up with Jackie when you don't phone her.' The other subalterns pulled his leg and Michael took it all in good part. My 'Uncles' quizzed him too. Only Hamish was distant.

'You've found a little gem there,' Pam whispered.

After another round of drinks, Bruce offered to show Michael to his room in the male officers' quarters before dinner. We were subject to sidelong glances during the meal, especially from Major Marion Smith! Coffee followed in the anteroom, more sociable conversation and then I took my leave, making a point of publicly saying goodnight to Michael. With his discrete directions it wasn't long before I joined him, sneaking along the male wing to share his single bed. I was breaking the rules of the Mess, which added to the excitement, increasing our ardour. I left at dawn before anyone was up, unwinding my body from his, creeping back to the Ladies' Royal.

Our weekend flew past. Meeting at breakfast, we spent the morning discovering the sights of the Garrison. That evening we dined at the Officers' Club in the company of quick witted Bruce and amusing Pam and James, followed by the comedy at CATS. In a good mood, we gathered afterwards in the Mess for a nightcap before disappearing off to bed in our separate quarters. For the second time I slipped to his room, glad there were no dogs to alert a crusty old Major that a female was out of bounds.

An awkward moment happened the following morning whilst I was waiting for Michael in the foyer. I had returned early to my room to bathe and change before breakfast and had hurried down the empty corridors without being discovered, or so I thought. We had arranged to meet so we could go into the dining room together. One of the older majors walked past with a fellow officer heading in the same direction. He nodded towards me before remarking to his companion.

'Someone had a good time last night!'

I'm glad they didn't see my blushes. There was no chance of living in a Mess without someone knowing what went on.

I persuaded Michael to take me to the local restaurant for lunch, so we could be on our own for the last few hours of his visit. I remember walking arm in arm with him to 'Im Fuchsbau' restaurant in the woods where we shared a paprika chicken and chips. I didn't tell him of the remark made about us that morning and because of it, I never invited him to stay in E Mess again.

Meanwhile, Hamish continued sitting opposite me at meal times, watching me. He now made a point of joining the subalterns in the bar before dinner. He would catch me sometimes on my own and ask me if I would like to go out with him. He knew that I was 'spoken for' but that didn't stop him. I managed to find some excuse or another. There was no point in causing an atmosphere of hostility in the Mess. He persisted in his attentions and, in a way, I was flattered, but I also grew tired of being shadowed.

A couple of weekends after Michael returned to Herford, Hamish asked if I would like to accompany him to the pub in the woods. My friends were all busy or away and it was a bit boring without their repartee and jokes. I didn't see any harm in spending a couple of hours with him going for a drink that Saturday afternoon. We set off from the Mess, he with his walking stick and me in flat shoes. He asked me where I had grown up and told me about his childhood, hunting, shooting and fishing on his family's Scottish estate.

'When we're married, we're going on honeymoon to a little croft I know there,' he announced, looking at me for a reaction.

'Oh, come on, Hamish. Stop joking!'

'But I'm not.'

'You know that if I'm going to marry anyone, it'll be Michael.'

'No, it'll be me. We're going to have two children, Duncan and Fiona.'

'Are you mad?' I exclaimed.

'No, it's the sanest thing that I have ever said.'

'Sorry, Hamish, I'm in love with someone else.'

'We'll see.'

He is mad, I thought, as we arrived at the pub. I certainly needed a drink. What would he say on the way back? I hoped that he wouldn't try anything on! I found it difficult to deal with Hamish, who wouldn't take no for an answer. I valued my friendship with my other 'brother' officers, my relationship with Michael and I didn't want to lose my reputation by one false move with Hamish. The bush telegraph would hum, and Michael would hear some garbled account and come haring down to challenge him with, no doubt, serious repercussions. Michael had been the light heavyweight boxing champion at Sandhurst!

I sipped the lager Hamish had ordered, planning my escape by appealing to his better nature. I would have to rely on my developed sense of persuasion, practised on Frank at the hotel. Relationships with men remained complex.

CHAPTER 31

TROUBLE IN THE RANKS

Pam was back. She had been hiking with her girls in preparation for the Nijmegen marches, a four-day International event held in July, organised by the town of Nijmegen in Holland to promote exercise and sport. The girls had to be fit and mentally prepared for marching up to 40 kilometres daily.

'Hi, Crow,' she said, greeting me in her familiar way. 'What did you get up to this weekend?' Her door ajar, she sat alongside her record player with a pile of 78" and 45" vinyls. 'Come in, I've got the latest Everly Brothers. Want to hear it?'

'Sure,' I replied, glad to spend some time with her.

She took out the brand-new record and put it on the turntable. placing the stylus on the rim of the grooved vinyl. Out poured the harmonious voices of Don and Phil with their new song, 'Crying in the Rain'.

'Great one, don't you think?' she asked when the music had stopped.

'Love it, but a bit sad,' I replied. 'You asked me about my weekend. Pam, tell me, have you had much unwanted attention from Hamish. Is he a womaniser? He told me that we were going to get married!'

She threw back her head and laughed.

'Does Mike know?'

'You might think it's amusing, but it's damned embarrassing. He keeps following me around. If I told Michael he'd come down and sort him out. Not a good idea.'

'SAS guys are randy buggers,' Pam joked.

Sharing my experience with her had helped to put everything into perspective. Hamish had proved to be a gentleman and hadn't 'jumped me' on the way back and, according to her, didn't have a reputation either. I began to feel sorry for him.

'Oh, by the way,' I said, changing the subject. 'I'm Orderly Officer tomorrow. First time here, anything that I should know?'

'I'm not going to spoil Sunday by talking shop. You'll be fine, the Orderly Sergeant knows the drill.'

She closed the machine; we left her room and walked down the ladies' royal corridor to the anteroom.

'Lover boy isn't here,' she whispered.

'Reprieved!' I replied.

* * *

I reported to the Adjutant of 14 Battalion WRAC at nine o'clock on Monday morning. Orderly Officer duties at the Depot had prepared me for anything. Surely, this would be a doddle in comparison. Nothing of importance had to be recorded during the day; my rounds and inspections straightforward.

The duty driver arrived in a Volkswagen at eleven-thirty that night. I waited in the foyer of the Mess, wearing my full Number One dress uniform and greatcoat. We set off for Headquarter company office where the Orderly Sergeant held the fort.

'Evening, Ma'am, Sergeant Howell,' she announced. 'Your first time as Orderly Officer here?' she enquired. Sergeant Howell worked at the 'Big House' one of the NCOs in Pam's platoon.

'Evening, Sergeant. I've recently been posted here from the Depot,' I replied, hoping that she would realise that I didn't lack experience. 'Yes, this is my first duty at 14 Battalion.'

'You'll find it a bit different here, Ma'am.'

'Oh,' I said. 'Why's that?'

'It's the men.'

'What about them?'

'We have to lock them out of the girls' Barrack Rooms.'

I thought she was pulling my leg. The phone rang. Sergeant

Howell answered the call.

'There's been a disturbance at the Junior Ranks Club, Ma'am. Our girls aren't involved this time, for a change. But I've just had a tip off from one of the RMPs to keep an eye out here at the girls' lines, in case there's further trouble.'

She looked at the clock on the wall. Eleven-fifty. Great, just what we needed.

It was dark outside, but through the office window I could make out shadowy shapes on the patch of grass that hadn't been there before.

'I'll go first, Ma'am, and blow my whistle. You follow in a couple of minutes and tell the girls to go to their Barrack Rooms.'

This statement astounded me.

'Is that absolutely necessary, Sergeant?' I asked.

'You'll see, Ma'am,' she replied, putting on her greatcoat and going out into the cold night. I heard the long piercing sound of her whistle.

'Five minutes!' she shouted, coming back into the office, stamping her feet on the doormat.

'It's freezing!' she exclaimed. 'Doesn't put them off though, they are stuck together like clams. They'll take some prising apart. Your turn now, Ma'am.'

I had taken off my peaked cap and now replaced it.

'Good luck!' said Sergeant Howell.

Good luck! What did she mean? I stepped out of the door into the unknown. A lamp post let out a pale glow, casting ghostly shadows. In front of me was a sea of couples 'necking', their bodies writhed and twisted in grotesque embraces in some strange gothic ballet. I felt like an unwanted voyeur witnessing their performance.

'Time's up!' I called out.

Nothing happened. Kissing and cuddling continued, all oblivious to my command.

'Right,' I said. 'I'm not standing here all night. Get going!'

I tapped the man of the first entwined couple on his back and, reluctantly, they parted.

Sergeant Howell came back outside and together we cleared the mob, couple by couple. The girls signed in, then sloped off to their quarters.

'Give them a few minutes, Ma'am, and we'll follow them.'

This was a real eye opener. I had thought, naively, that I had seen it all! But Hobbs Barracks had lacked one important ingredient. Men. Who was I to judge? I had broken the rules with Michael and probably would do so again.

'How was it last night?' asked Pam the following morning.

'I'm glad that the Orderly Officer duty rota includes the Senior WRAC NCOs, so it won't come around that often,' I replied.

'Yes, it takes some getting used to,' she laughed. 'The long goodbyes, before the girls sign in. I know most of them, so it's easier for me in a way. Your girls are all at Mönchengladbach, except the handful of stewardesses in the accommodation here.'

'The bit that got me was checking that the girls were safely locked in their Barrack Block,' I remarked. 'I bet, despite the NCO living in, they could have found a way out after we left.' Mr. Profumo would have been pleased.

At least there were no rodents to deal with. But there were rats in the Garrison, of the two-legged variety, as I was to discover.

* * *

Pam, Bruce and I visited the Globe cinema on camp to see *West Side Story*, the best musical of 1961 – set in America and based on the star-crossed lovers, Romeo and Juliet.

'Got my hankie ready,' I whispered to Pam.

'Think we are going to need them,' she agreed.

The auditorium was packed. Down in the front stalls was a crowd of young male soldiers wreathed in clouds of cigarette smoke. We waited for the lights to go out and the film to start when a man turned around in the row in front of us and whispered something to Pam.

'What!' she retorted. 'Jackie, I've just been asked to pass a message for you,' she said, her eyebrows arching in surprise. 'There's a chap down there who says he knew you at the hotel and has slept with you.'

'Who would say such a thing?!' I exclaimed.

Looking down, I saw a whole row of goggling soldiers turned towards me. One waved.

'What a bloody cheek!' I exploded. 'It's Brian, the spotty assistant barman from Great Fosters. It's an insult. If I was a man, I'd go down and punch him.' I was astounded to see him there, the lanky youth who had made eyes at me when I was a receptionist at the hotel. He had no encouragement from me and now was getting his own back.

'Just ignore him, Jackie.'

'Who on earth would believe that I'd ever have anything to do with the likes of him?!'

'Anything wrong?' asked Bruce, overhearing the odd word.

'No, Bruce, it's fine, just mistaken identity.' I seethed with indignation. If there had been any confrontation, serious trouble would have followed. An officer assaulting another rank was a court martial offence. I kept quiet but internally fumed. Spotty Brian was destroying my reputation. I had no chance of exposing his gross lie. A lie to bolster his pathetic ego.

The lights went out. We became involved in the love story of Tony and Maria, enjoying the music and the drama. I managed to forget the spotted toad and enjoyed the evening. We went back to the Mess for a nightcap, humming the hit tune from the film, 'America'.

Alone later, I reviewed my recent encounters with Captain Hamish and Squaddie Brian. Though unpleasant, I wasn't going to give into their fantasies without protest. Perhaps I should have reported Brian. Then again, what good would that have done?

Pam, at least, was on my side and her advice of ignoring both men was perhaps the best solution for the present. Our solidarity and friendship came to the fore on such occasions. We lived in a male-dominated military world, and it would be decades before equality of duties and pay between sexes were realised.

* * *

A dinner night in the Mess fell on my twenty-first birthday. Michael couldn't get away mid-week and we were both disappointed.

Pam and I dressed in long gowns. Mine was pale pink brocade with embroidered flowers, empire line and low cut with short sleeves. I looked at my reflection in the mirror and silently congratulated my mother for sharing special moments with her beautiful creations. The gown complimented my chestnut hair and hazel eyes.

We joined the rest of the officers in the anteroom before dinner. Several new Majors accompanied their wives. A steward approached carrying a tray of filled glasses and a magnum bottle of champagne, he stopped in front of me.

'Champagne, Ma'am?'

'I didn't order any,' I replied.

'No,' said Pam. 'But we did.'

Everyone raised their glasses and wished me a happy birthday. Overcome, I blushed. The President of the Mess spoke about me reaching adulthood and everyone laughed. I felt true acceptance into their tight knit world. It was my coming of age, and I belonged.

After dinner in the anteroom, a wife I had not met came over and stood beside me.

'Make sure that you don't make a play for my husband,' she said, a spiteful look on her middle-aged face. I was affronted. What threat did I pose to her? I seemed to have been the target of deranged people in the last few weeks.

'I've no idea who your husband is. Besides, I'd have no interest in him; he'd be far too old for me. I've my own boyfriend, thank you.' Her crazy insinuations ruined my birthday. The steward came back into the anteroom with news of a phone call.

'Happy birthday, darling,' said Michael. He had the power to transform my mood and I felt valued again. Michael's support and love were all I cared about.

A few days later, I dressed for dinner, thinking about Michael. I hadn't seen him since the play. Jan and Martin had split up after he was posted to Krefeld and there would be no more weekend invitations. Michael, still without a car, was involved in the army rugby season, playing matches away most weekends.

'Hey, Crow,' said Pam, meeting me in the corridor. 'You look glum. What's wrong?'

'I'd just love to see Michael. It's been too long and I'm dying to find out what he has bought me for my twenty first.'

'I've an idea,' she said. 'Call him and see if you can go up this weekend. I'll see if I can get you a lift.'

Pam liked James from B Mess, good looking, unattached, and owner of a recently acquired Mercedes Benz 300 saloon.

'What are you up to, Pam?'

'Not for you to know, trust me. Go on call him.'

'This is unexpected,' Michael answered. We hadn't arranged to speak for a few days. 'Everything ok?'

'Are you free this weekend? Can I come and see you?'

There was no doubt he approved.

'Well?' queried Pam outside the phone booth after my call.

'He's phoning me back, sorting out where we can stay.'

Pam strode off on a mission, through the doors and into the dark night towards B Mess. I poured a cup of coffee from the pot on the side table in the anteroom, waiting for Michael's answer.

'It's all arranged,' he said half an hour later. 'One of my friends in the rugby team has offered to have us. He and his wife were married six months ago, and he remembers how difficult their courting days had been.'

Pam came into the anteroom. Her face lit up at the news the trip was on. She had fixed it with James to take me to Herford. She, a willing passenger, would accompany me.

The interior of the Mercedes smelt of new leather. I leaned back against the padded back seat, excited, anticipating my reunion with Michael. Pam sat alongside James. I hoped that something would blossom from this journey for her. There was definitely a chemistry between them.

The car roared up the autobahn, northwards in the dark night passing the Ruhr cities of Essen, Dortmund and Bielefeld bringing me closer with each kilometre to him. After two hours on the road, the Herford 'ausfahrt' shone in the light of the Merc's headlights. James turned the car off the autobahn, cutting the speed. Nearly there! Following signposts to the Signal Regiment, just after eight o'clock, we arrived at the barrier to the camp. My heart beat faster.

Michael, dressed in the requisite dark suit and tie, waited for us at the Officers' Mess. He shook James' hand, thanked him and admired his car. He grinned and gave me a hug. All my 'angst' disappeared in that embrace. I felt whole again.

James declined Michael's offer of refreshments.

'We'll head off and get a bite on the way back,' James suggested to Pam.

'Thanks for arranging the lift,' I whispered to her. 'I'm sure you're going to enjoy your drive back with James.' She gave me a knowing wink and beamed.

'Have a good time,' I murmured, watching the Merc's disappearing taillights.

It was a moonless night, dark and cold. Michael and I turned away from the Mess, walking arm in arm to the Married Officers' Quarters. We chatted, catching up after weeks apart, but I didn't tell him about Hamish or Spotty Brian, enjoying instead the masculine tone of his voice, the way he moved, the mounting desire rising between us. Michael rang the doorbell of an unremarkable semi-detached house. The door opened, light spilling onto the path. In the hallway stood a young man with a rugged face and twinkling blue eyes. He stretched out his hand to grasp mine.

'You're Jackie,' he said with a gentle Scottish accent. His wife, Mary, a petite blonde full of energy and sparkle, appeared. She gave Michael a kiss, welcomed me and insisted on showing us our room that she'd specially prepared. I blushed on seeing twin beds lashed together, a playground for love. Our relationship had obviously been discussed.

I couldn't be happier being with him now, watching as I unpacked my bag. Alone, safe with the man I trusted and soon to lie between those sheets with him.

'Ian and I are playing rugby tomorrow. Perhaps you'd like to come and watch?' he asked.

'Is it rough?' I queried tentatively. I had witnessed one dangerous sport and was not sure if I wanted to watch another.

'Sometimes,' he laughed. He promised to take me to the Mess afterwards for a drink and meet his friends, then on Sunday to the curry lunch. He dismissed my worries and, confident in his abilities, I looked forward to meeting the other team players and his fellow officers. The weekend was all mapped out.

'Supper's ready,' Mary called up from the stairwell, having prepared a delicious meal, stuffed tomatoes and apple crumble. A vegetarian, our hostess knew how to turn an ordinary vegetable dish into a triumph.

We retired to our room after coffee. Michael held out a gift wrapped present, uncertain and shy.

'Hope it fits,' he said.

Inside the coloured paper lay a set of sexy lingerie, red with black lace. I'd never received such a gift and was sure the bra and panties wouldn't fit. But I was wrong.

'Happy birthday,' he said, full of admiration, while I modelled his acquisitions. How clever of him to know my size I thought. And deliberately, slowly, I took them off, no longer needed.

The following afternoon at his regiment, I stood on the touchline with Mary. The early December wind blew arctic gusts across the sports field, spectators stamped their feet and I pulled my coat closer, pulling up the collar. I was introduced to the rhetoric of scrums, line-outs, tries and conversions. An army of testosterone-driven young men charged about the rugby pitch, throwing opposing players to the ground in an attempt to win the oval shaped ball.

'Get off him!' I heard myself cry as two burly players tackled Michael and pinned him to the damp earth, trying to wrestle the ball away. Others piled in. From under the mass of bodies the ball was seized by one of 'our' team and the chase continued towards the posts. Michael fought his way to his feet, his shirt ripped, blood oozing from the scratches on his face. He sprinted to join a line of 'forwards' passing the ball back and forth until one broke away and leapt for the line. Clutching the ball, he flew through the air and landed over it. The ball touched down. The whistle blew. It was a try. I clapped with the other spectators drawn in by the sheer energy and determination of the players.

Later in the Mess, Ian and Michael bought drinks to celebrate the triumph. A shower and a change of clothes had transformed them. They smelt of 'Old Spice', smart in sports jackets and cavalry twills. Gone was the aggression from the rugby pitch, instead replaced by the perfect manners of officers and gentlemen.

Next day at the curry lunch, I met the Colonel of the Regiment, the rest of the officers and their wives. Michael's Squadron Commander made a point of speaking to me while his wife enjoyed the company of the unattached subalterns – Michael being one of them. She gave me the cold shoulder. I didn't care. He was my boyfriend.

The moment we dreaded, time to say goodbye, came at Herford station.

'Ian and Mary have invited you to come up for Christmas. Can you get leave?'

'I'll have to ask. Pam will be away and I've extra duties. I'd love to come and have our first Christmas together.'

He kissed me and I climbed onto the waiting train. Through the window, I watched his figure disappearing as the engine gathered speed, taking me away from him. I sat down in the empty compartment, alone and contemplative. I could visualise him now with his friends at the regiment, playing the sport he loved, dining in his Mess. It had been a memorable weekend, one in which I had become his official girlfriend. We had been accepted as a couple in his Mess, as we had been in mine.

A week later, there was some astounding news. Michael told me of a rumour going around camp that he was having an affair with Mary. A wife on 'the patch' had seen him frequently coming and going from Ian and Mary's quarter and had assumed Ian was out. Unbeknown to the nosey wife, I'd been there. Michael was shocked by the vicious lie. Ian laughed it off, but Mary was furious. I was too. Michael and I had now both become victims of malicious gossip. I wanted to go away with him, far from prying eyes. But when would we have that chance?

CHAPTER 32

BETRAYAL AND TRUST

Someone had been in my room whilst I'd been away. On the table in front of the window a large brown paper cone sat with a dandelion flower inserted into the top. I lifted it up. A box lay underneath. Inside was a beautiful silver bracelet with Scandinavian designs, no card or suggestion from the person responsible. Whoever it was had dared to break into my room, risking the fury of the Harpy and her yappy dogs. The culprit had gone undetected; Major Smith had not reported any incident in the Ladies' Royal corridor.

Hamish was at breakfast on Monday, back from the exercise in Norway with the SAS. He smiled when I sat opposite him in the Mess dining room, waiting for me to say something, allowing his bacon and eggs to go cold while he gazed at me. I gave him a curt nod and began to eat my cereal. After breakfast, I caught up with him in the hallway.

'Thank you, Hamish, the bracelet is lovely, but I can't accept it.'

'Keep it. It's your twenty-first birthday present. I'm going to get a special marriage licence, so we can be married. I've been promoted and posted to the Far East and I want you to come with me.' I almost laughed, a nervous reaction. It was so absurd. But he was serious. Other officers were leaving the dining room, so I was saved from responding to his astonishing declaration.

'See you later,' I said, walking away quickly. I managed to avoid him at lunch, giving me time to think of a definitive answer to prevent his advances.

I was kept busy with my platoon in Mönchengladbach and administration at 14 Battalion. Pam was on leave and I covered for her. Corporal Lee came into my office with the mail and morning cup of coffee.

'There's someone here to see you,' she announced as she left the door open. A young woman wearing the uniform of a WRAC Lance Corporal put her head around the door announcing her name.

'Can I talk to you Ma'am?' she asked.

'Come in, aren't you one of Miss (here I gave Pam's full name) girls?'

'Yes, but I want to speak to you.'

She shut the door, sat down to face me, her hands twisting in her lap.

What followed was a revelation. I didn't realise then what drama would unfold.

'I'm being harassed by women drivers in 49 Company,' she blurted out.

'When does this happen?' I asked

'Mostly in the Junior Ranks Club.'

'Why have they picked on you?'

'They're lesbians, they know I've a girlfriend already and they are trying to get me away from her.'

She placed me in a difficult position. Homosexuality was illegal, not tolerated in the army for either sex at that time. It meant instant dismissal. The present government had been greatly embarrassed by a recent sex scandal – John Vassail, a British civil servant, had spied for the Soviet Union under the threat of homosexual blackmail. Posted to the staff of the Naval Attaché in Moscow in 1954, the KGB discovered his sexual orientation. A honey trap was set and compromising photographs had been taken at a party. Vassail's career continued in the Naval Intelligence Division at the Admiralty, followed by his post at the office of the Civil Lord of the Admiralty. Arrested in September 1962, Vassail had by then passed on thousands of classified documents to the Soviets. Guilty of spying, he was sent to prison for eighteen years. The Intelligence Services were on high alert.

'What do you want me to do about it?'

'Don't know, Ma'am. I'm scared, and just wanted to tell someone.'

'You realise that I should report this to the OC?'

'Please don't. I don't want to leave the army.'

She worked as a clerk in the Big House, not a department that would require high security clearance. I decided to wait a couple of days before acting on this information.

'Come and see me next week and we will talk again. I want to ensure you are safe and find out about these predatory women who are intimidating you. Monday at 16:00hrs?'

She agreed, and I noted the time in my diary. Would I have the experience to deal with this development? I needed to think about my approach and strategy to find out what really motivated her visit. But another problem popped up that afternoon.

The Annual Inspection was coming up in the New Year and WO2 Halliday was keen to have a blitz on the girls' uniforms and accommodation. A car had been ordered and I was about to go over to carry out a spot check. The OC called me into her office.

'I've something that you'll have to attend to when you go to Mönchengladbach. It has come to our attention that your platoon Sergeant is having an affair. You must tell her that she either ends the relationship with the married NCO or she'll be posted out immediately.'

'That's a tricky one, Ma'am,' I responded.

'Has to be done,' she insisted. 'I'm sure that you can talk to her and make her see sense.' She divulged the name of the man involved.

I mulled over what I was going to say to her in the car on the way to Field Records.

The girls were lined up in front of me for inspection.

'Platoon 'shun!' ordered the Sergeant Major.

I walked along the ranks checking their uniforms and came to Private Jenkins. Her uniform was filthy; her shoes hadn't seen polish for weeks and her beret dusty.

'What's this all about?' I asked, pointing to the stains on her skirt. 'It's disgusting. You look a complete mess. I'm putting you on a charge for damaging military property. Change this skirt and give it to Sergeant Major.' Visibly shaken, her eyes filled with tears.

'Perhaps you'll take better care of your expensive uniform in future. I will let Sergeant Major Halliday know the day and time to appear before the OC.' I took no pleasure from the reprimand, but she deserved it.

I wasn't in a good frame of mind to tackle Sergeant Forbes. We had spoken on the phone before I had left JHQ to arrange the meeting. I was dying for a cup of tea and wanted to get the interview over. I wouldn't be back at the Mess until well after six o'clock.

Looking relaxed and comfortable, Sergeant Forbes sat in a chair opposite me. In her thirties, not unattractive, although a little on the plump side, she was totally unaware of the reason I had asked to see her and therefore had no idea what was coming.

'I'm here to tell you that you must end your affair with Sergeant-,' I said in a quiet voice, mentioning his full name.

She looked alarmed, took a short intake of breath, covered her face with her hands and sobbed. *Poor woman*, I thought. I hadn't been able to connect with her before. She was a rather secretive person, didn't normally show her feelings and, therefore, I was taken aback by her reaction.

'I'm sorry,' I said, feeling her anguish. 'You know the consequences if you don't. You'll be posted straightaway.' I knew the pain of losing a lover. It would be like a bereavement for her, too. I waited for her to calm down. She looked up at me, distraught and pale.

'We thought that we were being discreet.'

'Too many eyes,' I replied. 'I hope you can deal with this.' She stood up as if to go. I put my hand on her shoulder.

'I know how it feels to lose someone. Good luck.'

Ten years older than me, she probably wondered if I had any experience of love. I wasn't patronising but sympathetic, and she accepted my sincerity.

'Thank you, Ma'am.' Downhearted, we both left the Sergeant Major's office.

* * *

Hamish cornered me before dinner.

'Jackie, I'll have shoes made for you every day if you come with me to the Far East. I'm leaving next week. Say that you'll marry me.'

'Hamish, I'm sorry, I don't love you.' I couldn't change the way I felt about him, although the promise of shoes could have been a tempting offer! I thought of Sergeant Forbes as well. How cruel love can be, taking its victims up to dazzling heights and then down dark and twisted paths, to dead ends, hopes dashed. He said nothing, just smiled and went into the dining room to sit opposite me.

James came over to our Mess after dinner. He knew that Pam was on leave, so I wondered why he was there. He joined the group of fellow Intelligence Officers, who laughed and joked with him. I was reading a newspaper, keeping a low profile.

'Hi, Jackie,' said James, standing in front of me. 'Can I ask you a favour?'

'Depends what it is.'

'Come out into the foyer and I'll tell you,' he said. It sounded intriguing and I followed him.

'I've an assignment tomorrow night. Can you come with me to Dusseldorf airport? I need you as a cover. Will you be my girlfriend for the evening?'

'What do I have to do?'

'Nothing. Just be there.'

'Ok,' I agreed, without any hesitation, ready for a new adventure.

'Thanks, pick you up at seven-thirty tomorrow night.'

I was excited about taking part in an intelligence gathering exercise. I just hoped Pam wouldn't think it was anything else, or Michael for that matter. The odd word in the wrong quarter could have dire results.

James left the Mess and I went back to the others, Hamish nowhere to be seen. Had I convinced him that I had no interest in his proposal? I felt guilty once again of hurting a suitor's feelings.

* * *

We stood in the crowded arrivals hall at Dusseldorf Airport. People milled about, looking at the Arrivals boards, buying coffee and magazines. Others waited at the barrier, for a loved one or a business associate.

'The person I'm to photograph is on the next plane,' whispered James.

'How are you going to take a photograph without this person noticing?' I queried.

'It's a concealed camera in the lock of my briefcase.'

'That's clever,' I responded, surprised.

'I'll see what shots I can get first. I might want you to put your arms around me, so I can lift up the briefcase when I put mine around you.'

'Roger,' I confirmed.

Passengers from the next plane came streaming out from the customs area.

'Ok,' said James. 'Keep looking at me and talking, here he comes. Arms round my neck,' he said in a low voice.

'Yes, sir,' I murmured, wanting to giggle. We held our 'clinch' for a couple of minutes.

'Thanks, Jackie, I think I got some good shots. Let's go.'

He had allowed me into his secret world and it had been exhilarating. A bond had grown between us and I felt at ease in his company. We chatted on the way back to Rheindahlen in his smart Mercedes Benz.

'Are you surprised by the number of lesbians in your battalion?' he casually asked. I found his statement astounding. I had only just encountered Lance Corporal D and become aware of the situation. What did he know about it? I had encountered lesbianism before at the hotel, and questions had arisen at the Depot about one of the officers who had come up through the ranks.

'Yes, I suppose I am,' I replied, not realising that repercussions were to follow.

He changed the subject, making small conversation of no consequence. He didn't once mention Pam, so I wondered if the spark of interest between them had died and kept quiet.

A few days later Major Godin ordered me to her office.

'I don't want my girls going out on assignments with Intelligence Officers,' she said. How had she heard of my adventure with James? 'Don't let this happen again,' she warned.

I had enjoyed the clandestine assignment and was disappointed that I could no longer take part. I had no option but to accept her decision. This was not, however, the last time I would be involved with the Intelligence Corps.

Returning to my office, somewhat deflated, I threw myself into the admin paperwork piling up. The desk phone rang, breaking my concentration.

'The car has arrived from Field Records, Ma'am,' Sergeant Bryant informed me. 'Sergeant Major Halliday is here with Private Jenkins. And the OC wants you in her office.'

Reprimands were to be the order of the day. Private Jenkins

was appearing in front of the OC charged with negligent damage to her uniform.

'Show them in,' Major Godin commanded Sergeant Bryant, holding the charge sheet in front of her. I stood beside her, ready for the military proceedings.

'By the left, quick march, left, right, left, right!' Dulcet tones of Sergeant Major Halliday pierced through the normal sounds of the company office. Private Jenkins marched in with the Sergeant Major

'Halt, about turn!' she ordered.

Private Jenkins faced us, saluted and stood to attention as the charge was read out.

'Where is the skirt?' asked the OC.

Sergeant Major Halliday handed it over. It was pristine, all the stains gone, no longer the filthy object I had seen. Clever Private Jenkins, she had duped us. I felt an idiot but kept silent. The OC, who was wiser, summed up the situation immediately.

'I see that the evidence has been removed. However, Private Jenkins, your officer has filed a charge against you. Both she and Sergeant Major Halliday witnessed the condition of your uniform on Tuesday 12th December at 16:15hrs. You are dismissed, but be warned you will be severely reprimanded and fined if this ever happens again.'

The girl's face softened almost into a smirk until Sergeant Major Halliday took over and marched her out of the office.

'Sorry, Ma'am,' I confessed to the OC. 'I should've confiscated her skirt at the time.'

'She has learnt her lesson, which is the main thing. Just be a bit more aware of how the girls help each other in a crisis. It's a good thing. It means that Jenkins has friends,' she said, letting me off lightly.

Sergeant Major had waited behind to see me. She apologised for the fiasco of the skirt, repeating to me what I had said to the OC.

'Don't worry, Sergeant Major, it was my fault, I should have done that. The girls will have to be on their toes from now on. I know that under your supervision we'll get an 'excellent' for the Annual Inspection in two months' time.'

We were back on a level footing. She saluted and left my office to escort Private Jenkins back to Field Records with, no doubt, a flea in her ear.

I filled out my application for the Christmas weekend leave, but left it for a couple of days before I approached the OC.

'I can't sign this, Jackie,' she said, looking at the dates, 22nd–26th December. 'You must be here to help serve the girls' Christmas lunch.' Officers continue this tradition of serving Christmas lunch to the troops in the modern army.

Disappointment must have shown on my face because she smiled and continued, 'I hear there is someone in Herford you'd like to visit. Well let's say that you can go away for that weekend but will be back by 12:00hrs on 25th.' She struck out the last day on my application and amended the date to 12:00hrs 25th December, 1962 and signed it. 'Thanks Ma'am,' I beamed, delighted that I was to be with Michael over the Christmas period.

Weekends in the Mess could be solitary ones if Pam, my 'brothers' and 'uncles' were away. I played squash occasionally with one of my 'uncles' and tested my skills on the .22 rifle range – but not on this particular Saturday afternoon.

'Will you come and say goodbye?' asked Hamish outside the dining room. 'I'm packing and leaving tomorrow. My room is number three along the first corridor.' I hesitated. The male quarters were out of bounds, but I felt honour-bound to go. After my rejection of his proposal, I wanted us to part as friends, not as I had ended my relationship with Charles, with anger.

'Ok,' I said, 'I'll come over in an hour.' He looked pleased as he strolled off to pack. I wished Pam had been there to give some advice. What would I do if he 'jumped' me?'

Nobody was about as I made my way down to his room. I

did feel nervous, not sure of how the goodbyes would play out. I found the right door, took a deep breath and knocked. It flew open and Hamish stood there with a welcoming grin.

'Come in,' he encouraged. I stepped through into his den. His room was dishevelled with MFO – Military Forwarding Organisation – boxes. A photograph album lay open on a table and bagpipes hung from a hook on the wall. To avoid any embarrassing conversations about marriage, I asked him about the pipes.

'Yes, love playing them. I learnt when I was a boy,' he said. 'It's a pity we didn't get together, I know that you'd have been a tigress.'

The conversation was definitely not going the way I'd hoped. I tried again.

'Interesting photos?' I queried, bending over the album.

They were black and white, taken in a foreign country, tropical vegetation, a jungle.

'Ah yes, Malaysia,' he said.

I looked again at the first picture and saw what looked like a body lying on the ground.

'My first guerrilla,' he informed me.

That did it; I wanted to get out of there as fast as I could. The guerrilla appeared to be a young woman.

'Just wanted to wish you all the best, Hamish,' I said, moving backwards to the door.

'Still won't change your mind?'

He stood in front of me, leaned forward and kissed my cheek.

'Bye Hamish,' I managed to blurt out as I turned the door handle and stepped back into the corridor. I left him standing there looking surprised and hurried back to the safety of my room.

On Monday morning there was a new officer sitting opposite me. An old major, who hated anyone speaking to him at breakfast – or at any other time, come to that.

* * *

My phone rang. An unknown male ordered my presence in his office immediately. James's boss. This unexpected summons from an Intelligence Corps Colonel filled me with apprehension. He continued to give precise instructions to his whereabouts at the 'Big House' and then hung up. Grabbing my beret and shoulder bag, I knocked on the OC's door to tell her of my plight, but she was out. Damn, what should I do? I had no option but to obey orders.

'I've to go to the Big House, Sergeant Bryant. Be back as soon as I can,' I said, leaving the Company Office, trying to keep my poise while fighting off negative thoughts. What had I done? It took a few minutes to walk across to the Joint Headquarters, every step taking me closer to an encounter I dreaded. Why had I been summoned? Were we in trouble about the Düsseldorf episode? I showed my identity card at the gate and followed the colonel's instructions to find his office.

James opened the door.

'So, Jackie,' said the colonel, after I had been introduced. 'You're surprised by the number of lesbians in your battalion.'

How did he know? I'd only spoken to James. I stared at James, who had betrayed me and set me up. He stood beside his boss, behind a wide desk, the pair of them intimidating, the male gang of two. I had been asked to sit on a low sofa in front of them and felt at a disadvantage, arranging my legs so they couldn't see up my skirt.

I was subjected to a tirade of questions. Never before had I felt so vulnerable, out of my depth. The seriousness of the situation hit me, cold and deadly. A memory of Reg cornering me when I was eleven returned. I fought for control and evaded the questions, but I was in the hands of a master. It was not long before the Intelligence Colonel with piercing eyes had found out I'd encountered one.

'Where does she work?' he barked.

And so, it went on.

'Her name?'

'I can't give you that, Sir, without speaking to my OC.'

'Jackie, I need to know where she works.'

I couldn't wait to leave the colonel's office and the third degree but not before he had gained the information he wanted, where my contact worked and that there were predatory lesbians in the MT Section. My orders were to find out their names and electronically record my interviews with the unnamed girl. I was furious with James.

'How could you do this to me?' I accused, when we were outside in the corridor. He gave a wry smile.

'Sorry, it's my job.'

'Well, I'm not using your recording equipment and that's that. I shall probably be in for a pasting now from my OC. You're a bastard.' I stormed off, angry with myself for having been drawn in to their conspiracy.

I had served two years in the WRAC. During that time, I had met some talented and inspiring women. The Corps played an important supportive and administrative role in the British army and I was proud to be part of it. Loyalty was high on my list of principles.

Major Godin called me to her office when I returned. Now I was for it and, sick to my stomach, I knocked on her door.

'What's all this cloak and dagger stuff I've just been hearing about from the Intelligence Colonel at JHQ?' she accused. 'Why didn't you come and see me?'

I confessed the whole story, the airport assignment, my ill-chosen reply to James' question about lesbians and the consequence of our conversation.

'You'll have to carry on interviewing Corporal D. and find out the names of the women involved. I'll inform the Colonel.' She showed her displeasure with abruptness, no doubt believing this reflected badly on us all. I was miserable.

Lance Corporal D. came that afternoon again, totally unaware of the morning's development. What could I do? I was under orders and she was the key witness. I was to learn more of the predatory women who frequented the Junior Ranks Club, and there were a number of them. Even more alarming was the statement that she believed I was a lesbian too. I was stunned by this incredulous assumption.

With Pam on leave, there was nobody else that I wanted talk to about the situation, not even my friend, Bruce. Depression set in. At the end of the week I'd planned to see Michael and hoped that he'd listen to my account after James deliberately led me into a trap.

Two days later, I received a Christmas card from Hamish, portraying a burning red candle surrounded by holly and ivy. Inside he had written 'The candle still burns for you, love, Hamish. P.S. Contact me at this address if you change your mind.' Bemused by his message but hoping he would soon forget me, I replaced the card in its envelope. He knew I'd never marry him.

CHAPTER 33

HERFORD, GERMANY – CHRISTMAS 1962

The Garrison came alive with seasonal decorations, days shortened, temperatures dropped. I focussed on packing for my weekend away; uniform, presents and party clothes. I needed a break from working with the Special Investigations Branch. On Friday, 21st December I made my getaway to Herford.

The train halted at the station where Michael waited for me on the platform, a welcome sight and, overjoyed at seeing him, I flung myself into his arms.

'Hello, Angel Face,' he whispered, hugging me.

Michael had borrowed Ian's car to collect me, and we chatted nonstop along the way. Christmas lights sparkled in the cold night, setting the scene for the festivities to come. We arrived at the married quarters, scrutinising the row of houses. No evidence of the nosey wife twitching curtains. Michael parked the car and, a moment later, Mary opened her front door with a glass of wine in her hand.

'Come in, you two, you'll have to catch us up,' she said, her animated face lit with Christmas cheer. The smell of glühwein permeated the house, hot red wine spiced with cinnamon and cloves.

'To love!' Mary shouted, lifting her glass. We laughed and repeated the toast.

'It's the Adjutant's duty on Christmas Day to be Orderly Officer,' Michael said later, watching me hang up my uniform in our room. 'But now I've been made Assistant 'Adj', I've volunteered to take his place so that he can be with his family. They've invited me for Christmas lunch. You'll be long gone by then, back to Rheindahlen. Don't worry, I'll get a driver to take you to the station in time for the train on Tuesday morning.'

I didn't want to think about work and the progressive interviews with Lance Corporal D. who slowly divulged the names of her tormentors. In the end I didn't mention it to Michael. I would forget the distasteful task that loomed ahead and concentrate instead on Christmas with him. We had four nights together.

Warm under the bedclothes, drowsy from glühwein and love, I lay in his arms.

'I've something to ask you,' he whispered.

'Umm. What is it?' I murmured.

He lifted his head, resting his elbow on the pillow, to study my face.

Then came the bombshell.

'My mother has returned from Canada and living in Manchester. I want to go and visit her next month and take you to meet her. Can you get some leave?' He paused. 'There's something else I want to ask you when we're in England. Can we stay with your parents? I need to speak to your stepfather first.'

'Do you mean?' I gasped

'Yes,' he grinned, waiting for my response. 'You know I'm crazy about you. I don't want to leave you in Germany after I'm posted to the Junior Leaders Regiment in Devon next May.'

My head reeled from his announcement and his news of being posted. I didn't give him a reply immediately, too stunned by his intentions. My first reaction was one of sheer joy. But did I want to be married? Did I want to give up my career? If I went with him, there would be no job for me in Devon. I wanted to continue in the WRAC, despite the recent developments, and I would miss the friendship and camaraderie of 'the girls'. Did I want to stay on in Germany without him? Would I get on with his mother? Thoughts of the future bombarded me. How sweet and old fashioned of him to want to ask my stepfather for my hand in marriage – not that I was Reg's to give away.

My jumbled thoughts began to clear. Florian and Wendy were already engaged, both to army officers. Matt and Florian were getting married in April, on the anniversary of meeting twenty months previously at Bordon camp. Wendy's fiancé was perfect for her too, older, kind and great fun. Michael too, was kind, generous and amusing, everything I could want for as a husband and best friend.

'Yes, I'll come with you!' I promised, certain of my decision. 'I'll put in my leave application after Christmas!

His kiss sealed our future.

'I'll have to ask the Colonel's permission to marry you,' Michael confessed.

'Good Heavens! Do you think that he'll approve of me?' I asked, snuggling up to him. 'He's already looked me over, when I came to stay last time. Will he give me marks out of ten?'

'I'll let you know,' he laughed, his arm around me.

'When shall we get married then?' I asked him.

'How about next summer?'

It was only a few months away, so much to organise. How was I going to do that from Germany? I would also have to resign my commission after the formal announcement of our engagement.

'There's a small problem. If I get permission to marry and I can't see why not, I won't get marriage allowance until I'm twenty-five and not be eligible for a married quarter. We'll have to find somewhere to rent.'

A few challenges lay ahead, but I had a solution for the first.

'New Barn Farm will be close by. You'll meet my lovely adopted family, Uncle Freddie and Aunt Bubbles. I'm sure they will help us find a place of our own. Frances is working in London but she'll be down from time to time. It'll be good to see her again.'

We talked of our plans, confident in our love that everything would fall into place.

On Christmas Eve, Mary made a special dinner and we

exchanged gifts around their tree, a beautiful, blue grey 'Edelbaum'. Michael and I knew that soon we would leave BAOR, but that evening we celebrated a German Christmas with the friends who had brought us together. In our room, Michael and I whispered goodnight and fell asleep in each other's arms, our last night together for a while. Snow fell heavily that night. A white Christmas! We looked out of the bedroom window to watch great snowflakes falling to the ground, joining others to make a white eiderdown below.

'Happy Christmas!' he wished.

'Hope so! I'm dreading the journey back,' I replied, fastening nylon stockings to my suspender belt. He was already dressed in his uniform.

'Got to go in a minute. Have to give the soldiers 'Gunfire'.'

'Gunfire?' I asked, puzzled.

'Yes, it's a concoction of black tea and rum which the officers traditionally serve to the soldiers on Christmas morning.' He gave me a hug.

'There's a driver coming for you in half an hour, at a quarter to nine. Have a safe journey,' he said – and, with a kiss, he was gone. Yes, the army would always have first call on him, I knew that, and as his wife I would have to accept our separation when duty came first.

Time to return to my responsibilities. I felt his absence but, buoyed up by our plans, I finished dressing, packed my case and carried it downstairs to the hall. Mary appeared from her bedroom in her dressing gown.

'Happy Christmas!' we announced at the same time.

'You look good in your uniform,' she remarked. 'Do you have time for breakfast?'

'Love some tea and toast,' I replied.

'I'll join you. I don't know when Ian will be back from the Barracks. He went with Mike.'

We had not long been sitting at the table when I heard a knock on the door. I jumped up, opened it to find a young soldier, the driver Michael had promised.

'Thanks for everything, Mary,' I said at the front door, 'I had a wonderful time with you. Back to work now,' I added, feeling rather sorry for myself.

The ground felt slippery under my court shoes. The driver took my case and I climbed into the army 'Champ', the open-sided Jeep, icy cold. My regulation green greatcoat helped keep out the arctic conditions as we set off for town.

Here I was again on Herford station. It looked desolate. The snow had stopped falling, the world silenced by the crisp white blanket. Nobody was about. The driver left my case and me at the entrance of the station. Wondering what to do next, I saw a man in the uniform of the 'Bahnhof'.

'Der zug nach Mönchengladbach?' I asked

'Der zug wird abgebrochen,' he replied.

'Wann is der nächste zug?'

'Elf uhr.'

I was in trouble. My train had been cancelled; the next one was at eleven o'clock. There was no way I would be back to serve the girls' lunch. The journey took nearly three hours. If I was lucky, maybe I could be there by quarter to three. I might only be given a couple of extra orderly officer's duties if I didn't make it. I sent up a silent prayer. Now what? I couldn't stay at the station, already feeling the cold. Resolved to find a lift back to the Barracks, I picked up my case and walked back out into the street. By some miracle, a taxi was parked outside. I waved at the driver and he wound down the window.

'Frohe Weinachten,' I greeted him. 'Kaserne Harewood bitte.'

The taxi driver looked me up and down in my uniform.

'Ok, it's Weinachten, I voz going home but I vill take you zere,' he said in broken English.

'Thank you so much, vielen dank.'

Saved, I climbed into the back seat of the taxi, relieved to be out of the cold. Too bad that I was late arriving at HQ BAOR, there was nothing I could do. I would miss my own Christmas lunch, too. I sat back and closed my eyes remembering other Christmases at Deramore Cottage, how subdued they had been with Reg sitting at the head of the table. A memory brushed my mind like a snowflake on my cheek, a memory of me as a small child during the war in that old Victorian house; my grannies, laughing in the kitchen, my mother big with Ross; the joy of seeing my father coming home and the strength of his arms around me. How I wished he had lived. Herford might well have been one of the towns in Germany he had bombed during the war, just as the Luftwaffe had bombed us near London. How ironic that I was posted to Germany, the little girl who was terrified of air raid sirens and the dark. But I had found my way. Losing Rudge had changed my life. He had shown me the meaning of love, its joy and pain, and I would never forget him. Michael had waited for me all these years and given me another chance to find that precious gift, to fall in love again. He had pieced me together and made me whole. I held the hope of our future happiness and adventures together.

The saloon tyres slewed on the road and I opened my eyes – we were nearly there. I would ask Michael if he could find someone to take me back to the station for the later train. In the meantime, I needed a hot cup of coffee in his Mess. The car skidded to a halt outside the guardroom of 7 Signal Regiment.

'Officers' Mess, bitte,' I said to the driver.

'Nein, ich halt hier.'

'How much do I owe you? '

'Nozing, it's Weinachten.'

'Danke schön,' I replied, appreciative of his goodwill and surprised by his gesture. Men continued to astonish me!

I opened the door and climbed out with my case. The taxi driver drove off, leaving me alone in the snow in front of the camp.

'Bloody hell!' I heard a gruff voice coming from the guardroom. ''Ere Sarge, come and 'ave a look at this, it's fucking Mother Christmas!'

EPILOGUE

Florian, Wendy and I were the first from our intake to resign our commissions prior to becoming military wives. We repaid a large proportion of the £114. 13s. 4d. clothing allowance as we had not completed three years' service.

Officer Cadet Wing moved to Bagshot Surrey in 1966 and became the Women's Officer Training College until 1984 when it moved to Sandhurst. In 1992 a new commissioning course finally unified the training of male and female cadets at RMA Sandhust. Huron Camp is no more; it has reverted to part of Bramshott Common, a haven for birds and butterflies. We, the band of sisters, flew the nest many years ago in December 1961.

My army career ended in the summer of 1963 when I joined forces with Michael. I followed him around the world to new postings, experiencing many adventures and continued to be amused and sustained by the wit and humour of that rare breed – the British soldier.

CHRONOS
BOOKS

HISTORY

Chronos Books is an historical non-fiction imprint. Chronos publishes real history for real people; bringing to life people, places and events in an imaginative, easy-to-digest and accessible way - histories that pass on their stories to a generation of new readers.
If you have enjoyed this book, why not tell other readers by posting a review on your preferred book site.

Recent bestsellers from Chronos Books are:

Lady Katherine Knollys
The Unacknowledged Daughter of King Henry VIII
Sarah-Beth Watkins
A comprehensive account of Katherine Knollys' questionable
paternity, her previously unexplored life in the Tudor court
and her intriguing relationship with Elizabeth I.
Paperback: 978-1-78279-585-8 ebook: 978-1-78279-584-1

Cromwell was Framed
Ireland 1649
Tom Reilly
Revealed: The definitive research that proves the Irish nation
owes Oliver Cromwell a huge posthumous apology for
wrongly convicting him of civilian atrocities in 1649.
Paperback: 978-1-78279-516-2 ebook: 978-1-78279-515-5

Why The CIA Killed JFK and Malcolm X
The Secret Drug Trade in Laos
John Koerner
A new groundbreaking work presenting evidence that the CIA
silenced JFK to protect its secret drug trade in Laos.
Paperback: 978-1-78279-701-2 ebook: 978-1-78279-700-5

The Disappearing Ninth Legion
A Popular History
Mark Olly
The Disappearing Ninth Legion examines hard evidence for
the foundation, development, mysterious disappearance, or
possible continuation of Rome's lost Legion.
Paperback: 978-1-84694-559-5 ebook: 978-1-84694-931-9

Readers of ebooks can buy or view any of these bestsellers by clicking on the live link in the title. Most titles are published in paperback and as an ebook. Paperbacks are available in traditional bookshops. Both print and ebook formats are available online.

Find more titles and sign up to our readers' newsletter at
http://www.johnhuntpublishing.com/history-home

Follow us on Facebook at
https://www.facebook.com/ChronosBooks

and Twitter at https://twitter.com/ChronosBooks